Critical Theory,
Cultural Politics,
and Latin American Narrative

Critical Theory, Cultural Politics, and Latin American Narrative

Edited by
STEVEN M. BELL,
ALBERT H. LE MAY,
AND LEONARD ORR

University of Notre Dame Press
Notre Dame and London

Library of Congress Cataloging-in-Publication Data

Critical theory, cultural politics, and Latin American narra-
    tive / edited by Steven M. Bell, Albert LeMay, and
    Leonard Orr.
        p.   cm.
    Includes bibliographical references and index.
    ISBN 0-268-00795-0
    1. Latin American fiction – History and criticism.
2. Criticism.   I. Bell, Steven M.   II. LeMay, Albert,
1936-   .   III. Orr, Leonard, 1953-   .
PQ7082.N7C685   1993
863 – dc20   92-53744
                                              CIP

∞ *The paper used in this publication meets the minimum requirements of
the American National Standard for Information Sciences – Permanence of Paper
for Printed Library Materials, ANSI Z39.48-1984.*

For
ROSARIO, MARCIA, and SARAH

Contents

III

IV

Preface

The eight essays collected for publication in this volume, some now in expanded or revised form, were originally presented at the First Biennial Conference of the Latin American Consortium, entitled "Narrative Practices and Cultural Discourse" and held at the University of Notre Dame in the spring of 1990. The first in an ongoing series whose site alternates between the University of Notre Dame and Indiana University, Bloomington, each conference is intended to promote intensive discussion and lively exchange on a special topic of moment in the field of Latin American Studies.

The original design of the first conference was to bring concepts and issues in critical theory, especially poststructuralist developments in such areas as cultural criticism and gender studies, to bear on Latin American narrative practices: their production, dissemination, and reception on regional, national, and international levels. In the prolegomenon that follows, Steven M. Bell discusses some of the critical interactions that the essays establish among themselves, as well as the rationale for the delimitation of our topic.

At the conference, four sessions of papers were organized around keynote presentations by Fredric Jameson, Mary Louise

Pratt, Roberto González Echevarría, and Luisa Valenzuela. The four topics were these: "(Neo)Colonialism and Cultural Syncretism: Latin American Narrative Responses"; "Engendering the Discourse of Latin American Fiction"; "Recoding Genre: Alternate Voices and Narrative Strategies in Latin America"; and "The Postmodern in Latin America: Cultural and Political Implications." The texts of the keynote addresses are accompanied here by one essay from each of the four sessions.

Funding for this project was achieved through the efforts of faculty and administrators at both the University of Notre Dame and Indiana University. The conference was cosponsored by the Kellogg Institute for International Studies, the AT&T Visiting Scholar Lecture Series of the Institute for Scholarship in the Liberal Arts, and the Departments of Romance Languages and Literatures and English, all at the University of Notre Dame; and by the Office of the Vice-president and the Office of International Programs of Indiana University, Bloomington.

The funding received from Indiana University was the product of efforts by Professor Russell Salmon, Director of the Center for Latin American and Caribbean Studies there. We are deeply indebted to him, and are thankful for their support to Kenneth Gros Louis of the Office of the Vice-president, and to Alexander Robinowitch of the Office for International Programs.

For their guidance and encouragement all along the way, we wish to express our gratitude at the University of Notre Dame to Ernest Bartell, Executive Director; Guillermo O'Donnell, Academic Director; and Fellows Roberto DaMatta, Scott Mainwaring, Samuel Valenzuela, Timothy Scully, and Leo Depres of the Kellogg Institute; to Joseph Buttigieg, Chairman of the Department of English, for his wise counsel and effective leadership; to JoAnn DellaNeva, Chairwoman of the Department of Romance Languages and Literatures; and to Nathan Hatch and Robert Burke at the Institute for Scholarship in the Liberal Arts.

Without the assistance of staff members from Notre Dame's Kellogg Institute and Indiana University's Center for Latin American and Caribbean Studies, the project would never have come to fruition. We would like to name, at Notre Dame, Caroline

Domingo, Daphne Shutts, Dolores Fairley, Rosario Bell, and Nancy Hall; and, at Indiana University, Susan Nystrom and Deborah Kvam. We are also grateful to Jeannette Morgenroth of the University of Notre Dame Press for a number of helpful suggestions and for her careful and professional attention to the manuscript.

The publication of a volume such as this one is not possible without the willingness of our colleagues at other universities throughout the country to submit papers and engage in the debate of significant scholarly issues. The contributors to this book are solely responsible for the intellectual quality and the directions in criticism that they establish. Our deepest gratitude goes out to all of the conference participants, to presenters as well as to students and teachers who came from many points of the compass to enliven our discussions. We hope the pages of this book may capture something of what we all experienced at the conference: a constructive exchange of ideas on a number of dynamic issues, argued upon by a special community of scholars who came together and worked to challenge, encourage, and stimulate their audience and one another.

                                                        The Editors

A Prolegomenon

STEVEN M. BELL

In Argentina there have been semantic displacements that constitute
an important ideological operation,
and that allow one to say, for example, that all Argentines are authoritarian. Now, between an authoritarian individual and the torturer Señor
Videla, let us say, there is an immea-
surable distance. . . . The use of one
common word to define two types
of discursive strategies – one on paper, the other acting on bodies, on
flesh – has to do with a current situation of theory, which I see linked
to the neoconservative wave, and
which, in brief, is the theory of the
total fictionalization of the world, the
theory that everything is discourse.
I see this as the theoretical realization of the political context in which
we move in these times, in which
there is no utopia and everybody is
a bit skeptical and nurtures a certain
conformist nihilism. That leads to a

> perception of reality as pure fiction:
> it is all discourse, it's all the same,
> what a writer says and what a mili-
> tary man says. . . .
>
> That has broad circulation today
> as a theoretical hypothesis. I think
> novelists and literary critics must
> take part in this discussion. . . . I be-
> lieve that Argentine history is criss-
> crossed by fictions but it is not a fic-
> tion. We Argentines know very well
> that . . . reality is discursive but not
> only discursive.
>
> *– An Interview with Ricardo Piglia.* [1]

The star of Latin American literature and the stock of critical (or literary) theory have risen sharply over the last thirty years. No one involved in literary studies today, or even simply abreast of issues in culture and education in the public domain, can fail to be aware of this. Literary theory and Latin American litera- ture continue to be the objects of increasing attention, intense scrutiny, and often the cause of invigorating or enervating po- lemic. The fortune of both literary theory and Latin American literature in the United States links indirectly to the growth of specialization in our academic domains, to ongoing realignments among disciplines, and to the marked transnational character of cultural stimuli and response today. One contributor to this volume, Fredric Jameson, has in this vein elsewhere called at- tention to the "internationalization of the national situations." Homi Bhabha adds further nuance, or complication, to this for- mulation when he speaks of "the *inter*national dimension both within the margins of the nation-space and in the boundaries *in-between* nations and peoples."[2] And Mary Louise Pratt here characterizes these developments summarily by remarking the new inflections taken on by the adjective "world," as opposed to those of the previous dominant, the "international." I view as a minimal common denominator and an essential point of departure for the work ahead the acknowledgment not only that the emergence into prominence of critical theory and Latin American literature has been strictly contemporaneous, but also that in their recent evolution the two domains have followed remarkably similar trajectories.

To suggest that the parallel evolution and simultaneous emergence into prominence of critical theory and Latin American literature is something more than coincidental might seem straightforward and unpolemical, given the obvious overlap between the two terrains. But if we move beyond generalities, the concrete interrelations of (First World) critical theory and (Third World) Latin American literature remain very much an open question, perhaps because to substantiate a direct causal connection proves as difficult as to sustain any categorical disconnection is untenable.[3] On the one hand, the independence with which developments in the two fields have been treated suggests a high degree of relative autonomy in their evolution. On the other hand, isolated arguments have been made for positive as well as negative correlations. From the Latin American side, the fiery volume *Literatura en la revolución y revolución en la literatura* stands as an early and now classic volume in this polemic.[4] This example confirms how, in this area and others, Latin American literature arguably has "always already" been at the game, as if to underscore the notion that theory can only be as developed as its object.[5] Yet as we see once again in the recent theoretical preoccupation with colonial discourse and postcolonial studies, in which examples from former French and English colonies in Asia and Africa have predominated, Latin America still risks being left out of serious critical study and scholarly discourse.[6] In any event, the fact remains that only recently, and for many on both sides still begrudgingly, have the potential complicities and concrete oppositions between literary theory and Latin American literature, between the (global) politics of theory and the (global) politics of literature, become a matter of explicit and sustained concern. This much, at least, recent debates within and around poststructuralist critical theory have brought to the fore.

We know that in a remarkably short time in our twentieth century, the dominant practice in critical theory and methodology has undergone a rapid and, in appearance, radical and unprecedented transformation. It has moved from traditional, historical scholarship, through the intrinsic analyses of formalism and structuralism, to the various poststructuralisms doing battle today. Twentieth-century Latin American narrative, for its part, has experienced a roughly analogous series of displacements, first of previously dominant forms of social realism by a modernist-based or structuralist-inspired "boom" of Spanish American fiction in the 1960s, which in turn has now given way to the current "postboom" climate.

Whether cause or effect, the terminological reduplication or redundancy of our present "postscript" age is a remarkable reflection of these convergencies: postmodern art and culture; poststructuralist critical theory; postcolonial societies in a postcolonial world order; and, of special interest here, a postboom Latin American literature.[7] In each area, the "post-" term appears as a dialectically synthetic one, signifying the partial rehabilitation of a sociohistorical approach that does not renounce the insights of so-called textualism but extends them beyond the limits of the properly literary to social and cultural intercourse more broadly conceived.[8] On the one hand, the "post-" prefix shared by the various critical-historical terms I have named points toward their potential identity and real complicity. Certainly, the consolidation of the postboom appears as only the most superficial sign of Latin American culture's direct responsiveness to and coparticipation in these developments. Yet at "root," as it were, the marks of difference among the various "post-" terms remain. As regards the case before us, for instance, many both inside and outside of Latin America have held that the formal or intrinsic analyses dominant in (First World) academic criticism during the apogee of structuralism stand at odds with the overt sociopolitical and historical bent (stereo)typical of Latin American literature (cf. *Literatura en la revolución y revolución en la literatura*).[9] Related polemics continue to wage today, now over the presence or absence of the Western postmodern in the Latin American postboom (and/or boom), an issue, not surprisingly, among those taken up in the essays here.[10] All of these polemics point to the political complexity of transnational and cross-disciplinary intervention. On the one hand, the emergence of such poststructuralist enterprises as cultural and gender studies, postcolonial scholarship and the new historicism, with their sociohistorical emphases, their transnational and multicultural awareness, have signified the promise of new opportunities for cooperation and reciprocal dialogue between Latin American writers and Western critical theorists.[11] Today, nonetheless, some ten years after Jean Franco somewhat precociously called attention to these new possibilities, reasons remain to doubt whether this potential can be realized.

Situated in this general context, this volume's modest proposal is essentially twofold. First, we sought to test an eclectic array of works in Latin American narrative literature against concepts and issues in poststructuralist critical theory, to explore further the fit between them in light of their many parallels, and to confront more directly their potential complicities and oppositions. The second, related aspect of our volume's structural design, perhaps more fundamental and ambitious, was to begin to address (and redress), against the grain of historical tensions and enduring resistance, the relative absence of reciprocal dialogue and direct interaction between First World (North American) criticism and theory and Third World (Latin American) culture and literature.[12] To this end, our contributors deliberately include a prominent First World critical theorist (Fredric Jameson) and a writer from Latin America (Luisa Valenzuela), as well as a diverse group of scholars of Latin American culture and literature. Our object was to bring the participants together to expose our common stake in the delimitation and evaluation of Latin American culture and literature, along lines echoed in the epigraph from Piglia. We sought thereby to encourage a more accurate assessment and realistic articulation of the significance of Latin American literature and of the cultural work its narratives perform on local, national, regional, and international levels. If (First World) critical theory stands on one side and (Third

World) Latin American literature on another, the title of this volume seeks to indicate that their intersection lies in the area of *cultural politics,* for whose construction we all bear responsibility, however diverse our spheres of (specialized) activity, our cultural identifications, our methodological premises and ideological presuppositions. John Beverley's essay here makes clear that this crucial understanding should emerge from critical contemplation of the very occasion and circumstances of our volume.

Of course, the essays in this volume make no pretense to any systematic exploration of this complex and controversial terrain, neither individually nor as collected. While sharing a common Latin American(ist) focus and a general poststructuralist theoretical orientation, the essays range widely in their particular objects of analysis and concern. Nonetheless, especially in the critical dialogues the essays here implicitly establish among themselves, the volume as a whole may give impetus to more conscientious mediations and productive negotiations.

Few doubt that real change has taken place in the academic study of literature and culture in recent years, even though many questions have been raised as to its substance and significance. Categorical distinctions among modes of discourse once considered discrete have eroded. The canons of Western art and culture have been challenged as previously silenced perspectives or marginalized voices are raised from within and beyond national, regional, racial, and gender boundaries. New disciplinary maps, new canonical structures, new affiliations, alliances, and oppositions are emerging in the "contact zones" among various subnational and transnational social and cultural groups, as well as between practicing artists and critical theorists, literary scholars, and critics. Particularly where discussions of the postmodern, the poststructuralist, the postcolonial – and, we might add, the Latin American postboom – converge, there has been a veritable barrage of new and ostensibly groundbreaking activity.[13]

The essays collected in this volume reflect and participate in these potential realignments; they intervene in the ongoing cultural conversation on such central issues in our postscript age as "discourse and power" and "culture and domination" as they pertain to the field of Latin American literature proper, to the more properly academic realm of critical theory, and to the space of their interaction.[14] At the same time, this volume's specific Latin American(ist) focus provides a concrete, alternative perspective that may serve effectively to challenge the underlying significance of recent developments in literature, criticism, and theory, and to question the degree of real change they may represent. For this and other purposes, the structural marginality or historical disadvantage from which a subaltern culture such as the Latin American must operate may turn, paradoxically, into a unique point of (ad)vantage.[15] Our "new" awareness of global interdependence, of the increasingly transnational character of cultural stimuli and response, in other words, is not nearly so new for the Latin American(ist). If the dominant Western cultures have long been able to leave the Latin American out of account, historically at least, this has not worked the other way around.[16]

One of this volume's original critical presuppositions holds that distinctions based on national, regional, cultural perspectives can no longer be categorically drawn, if ever they could be, though this recognition should not impede us from defining the site-specific implications of discursive enunciation and reception. Yet at the risk of forwarding just the sort of sweeping cultural or political generalization that runs against this grain, we may ask just how the recent changes in the academic study of literature and culture I have described are viewed by Hispanism. In response, I would dare state the illustrative hypothesis that from this viewpoint there remains considerable wisdom in the old adage that the more things change, the more they stay the same. With reference to literature "proper," for example, John Brushwood has poignantly asked whether the international boom that Latin American fiction has experienced since the 1960s has brought any real improvement in international relations or crosscultural understanding.[17] From quite different ideological presuppositions, Neil Larsen has also emphasized how the "indisputable cultural triumph" of the Latin American fiction boom "has not, as its earlier political visionaries imagined it would, been matched by a corresponding social and political emancipation from imperial bonds."[18] The point, among others, is that a superficial understanding of such notions as "magic realism" may perpetuate limiting and retrograde views of Latin America as an absolute other, as an exotic paradise or a primeval aberration. In this view, the current fashionableness of Latin American literature in the West may thus appear as the mirror image of the neglect Latin American cultural "products" have historically suffered, to the degree both entail a critical failure to see the work effected by Latin American cultural discourse in its broad historical resonance and sociocultural specificity.

Of course, one cannot but be pleased with the new international recognition that Latin American literature has received from many quarters. To have the writings of Jorge Luis Borges extolled, as they have been, say, in the work of French theorists Michel Foucault and Jacques Derrida, would appear to represent a significant advance, as would the praise and acknowledgment received from North American authors such as John Barth and William Gass.[19] Also encouraging has been to follow with interest the more systematic attention an American theorist, Fredric Jameson, from different critical presuppositions, has increasingly turned to Third World cultural products, including the Latin American.[20] Yet for some Latin Americans and Latin Americanists these interventions may involve dangerous simplifications and critical misrepresentations, not unlike those articulated in Aijaz Ahmad's friendly amendment to Jameson's widely read article, "Third World Literature in the Era of Multinational Capital."[21] There remains, in other words, a justifiable fear of seeing in this attention something like a repetition of that foundational gesture by which the New World was "invented" in the discourse of Europe as a precondition of its discovery, conquest, and colonization; a fear that at its worst this new critical, popular, and theoretical interest in Latin America is another appropriation that overlooks critical contexts – even while we must recognize that

the increasing transnationalization of cultural production is transforming the contexts right along with the texts, such that notions of inside and outside perspectives (in this case, on Latin
America) no longer hold (if they ever exactly did).

One of my central points here is that Latin American culture
does belong to us all, if differently. But as the peripheral and
the marginal move to the center, the questions become more
urgent of how they can, or whether they should, avoid cooptation; of how they can keep from losing their relative autonomy, their force of resistance, and their attraction as difference
(rather than as the exotic, purely rhetorical "other"). If Hispanics
have remained on the margins of the momentous contemporary developments in (First World) critical theory, perhaps this
represents a strategy of implicit resistance to the dangers of
cooptation.[22]

While clearly we are all implicated in this dilemma in ways
that are not readily articulated, we cannot establish categorical
distinctions on this score, say, between Latin American authors
and foreign scholars, theorists or critics. No one has been entirely guilty or innocent. We might point out, for example, how
many Latin American boom authors have themselves actively
postulated and promoted their direct descent from the "fantas-
tic" chronicles of conquest and discovery, on the basis of the
magic realism they purportedly share and the common exploration that this entails of myth and history, fantasy and reality. Yet
with what might be called insightful blindness, many of these
same boom novelists, along with some of their promoters and
critics, overlook another direct connection between contemporary narratives and the colonial chronicles: their continued appeal to, if not dependence on, "foreign" audiences in metropolitan centers. Indeed, while giving the impression of an overnight
discovery, a creation *ex nihilo* of unprecedented proportions,
attention to the boom may mask a long history of direct Anglo-
European impositions and Latin American dependence, as well
as an equally significant history of (usually nonreciprocal) intellectual contact, encompassing many of the most prominent writers in the Latin American tradition. For most of our metropolitan

centers and academic institutions one could trace a long and specific microhistory of this contact that should not be subject to blanket evaluation but should neither be too readily taken for granted.

If we turn from literature proper to the institutions of its criticism, it is remarkable that for all the notoriety Latin American literature has attained in recent years, Hispanism still often occupies a sort of basement below or ghetto within the various fields of literary scholarship, and so similar patterns reveal themselves. In spite of numerous advances, the direct, recognized contributions of Hispanic Studies to the development of concepts and issues in the area of critical theory remain few. This is not to say that the study of Latin American literature has lacked sophistication or failed to keep pace. Hispanists – and Hispanic writers – have been quite cognizant of developments in literary as well as social and political theory and have employed poststructuralist insights and premises to good advantage. But the camps of critical theory and Latin American literature have rarely had a truly reciprocal relationship or enjoyed true communication and interaction; with noted exceptions, the *active* relationship between critical theory and Latin American literature, their intersection in what Mary Louise Pratt calls the "contact zone" that at once unites and divides different cultures or practices of discourse has rarely been excavated or articulated critically.

My object is by no means to rail against Hispanism's structural disadvantage or historical marginality in anything akin to what Edward Said calls the "politics of blame."[23] Rather, I want to propose for consideration certain practical (and political) concerns that may deserve more detailed attention and reflection. The summary history I have sketched should suggest, minimally, that the struggle for recognition and the structures of prestige governing the various literatures and cultures are often reenacted in the interaction (or lack thereof) among the corresponding divisions of our academic institutions. As (selected) works of Latin American literature are "appropriated" in the metropolitan academies by departments of English and Comparative Literature (or interdisciplinary programs in Critical Theory, Gender Studies, or Cultural Studies), the Hispanist and the Hispanic author may find him/herself left observing the critical fireworks from the sidelines. In a pointed and telling comment on this general state of affairs, Jean Franco has observed that "anyone involved with Latin American studies knows what it is like to be placed last on the program, when everyone else has left the conference."[24]

At issue (in the intersection of Latin American literature and critical theory) is something closely related to, but at once more broad and immediate than, the marked theoretical awareness of literary artists throughout the world today, an inescapable fact of life for readers at least since the vogue of the French *nouveau roman* – and one reflected as well, incidentally, in the comments in the epigraph of my essay by Ricardo Piglia. At issue is also something more than the breakdown of barriers between critical theory and narrative practice articulated by Derridean deconstruction, by which every theoretical position implies a practical intervention, and vice versa. Indeed, what is in question even goes beyond the immediate, transnational character of cultural stimuli and response in our postscript age to arrive at the new and not-so-new but increasingly multiple and simultaneously available ways of drawing, erasing, and redrawing lines of identity and difference, alliance and confrontation, affiliation and complicity, within, across, and *between* geopolitical borders and disciplinary frontiers. If there is no way to theorize systematically or generalize categorically the historical relations between Latin American literature and critical theory, neither is there any escape from their – our – complicity.

To align the North American Hispanist with the Latin American "subaltern" is fundamentally misleading (though we must not overlook the large number of North American Hispanists who are themselves Latin American exiles and émigrés). Yet as Hispanists, we do structurally link our destiny to the fate of Hispanic literature, and little release from this complicity comes through recourse to academic objectivism or scholarly disinterestedness. If we should take care not to overestimate our importance as scholars, critics, and theorists, thereby falling backwards into the paternalistic trap, neither should we ignore the direct and indirect impact that our judgments and opinions have on the course of Latin American literature and culture. It can prove counterproductive to be so self-conscious of our positionality, the situation of our enunciation, that we fail to engage concrete issues.[25] An appropriate awareness of our direct and indirect involvement, nonetheless, should only heighten the pertinence, interest, and significance of our work (I take this to be a position argued differently in the essays here by Pratt and Beverley). Such awareness should keep us equally distant both from a self-conscious guilt that might paralyze us into inactivity and from an illusory objectivism or any idealistic notions of the possibility of absolute nonintervention.[26]

How difficult can it be to establish a theoretical basis for one's practical activity in the contact zone between cultures, discourses, and disciplines? The juxtaposition of positions recently articulated by Edward Said and Eric Cheyfitz establishes dramatically the range of possibilities and thereby underscores the difficulties at issue. The differences between their positions are all the more striking since one might otherwise attribute to them many similar ideological positions. While Said strategically deemphasizes the complications of crosscultural understanding and rejects categorical distinctions between an inside and an outside perspective, Cheyfitz approaches the espousal of an absolute concept of nonintervention and appears to doubt the usefulness, even the very possibility, of crosscultural understanding.[27] In the essays here, a similarly wide range of strategic positions is evident, with Roberto González Echevarría's essay perhaps best exemplifying Said's emphasis on common denominators as a basis for dialogue and shared responsibility, while Fredric Jameson might align himself more squarely with Cheyfitz's strategic insistence on nonintervention and difference.

All of the essays included here touch directly or implicitly upon these theoretical problems and practical dilemmas; in all of them a certain articulation of the intersection between critical theory and Latin American narrative is central. To view both narrative and criticism as forms of cultural discourse, as exercises of cultural politics, is one way to state unproblematically the general terrain that the essays occupy and dispute among themselves.[28] None of the essays treats works of Latin American narrative literature "in themselves," that is, independent of the historical, critical, and theoretical discourses that have built up around them. But within the bounds of their common Latin American(ist) focus and poststructuralist orientation, some of the essays strategically refuse to treat Latin American literature and culture "differently," while others highlight particularities and directly confront complicities. Similarly, one will find the Latin American reference point to be virtually incidental in some of the essays where theoretical propositions occupy the foreground. Others, in contrast, take a more practical approach to their Latin American narrative materials and the authors' theoretical positions remain implicit. Generally speaking, attention to contemporary Latin American boom, postboom, and testimonial texts predominates, though not to the exclusion of reference to letters and diaries, poems and essays, reaching back to the nineteenth century and beyond. Indeed, even the erstwhile unity provided by the essays' common poststructuralist orientation is eroded, under close scrutiny, by the diversity of concrete positions that have been reduplicated within this theoretical domain. Anyone conversant with current debates in the field of critical theory knows that the poststructuralist banner encompasses a whole gamut of critical and ideological practices with stops at many points in between the extremes of neoformalist deconstruction, which interprets poststructuralist premises to mean that everything is *textual,* and so-called left and post-Marxian criticism, whose preferred interpretation of poststructuralist premises holds that everything is *political.* Perhaps the essays here by Roberto González Echevarría and John Beverley best stake out the respective limits of this range and confirm the substantive differences among contributors here that cannot be explained away. The essays' coherence, then, is to be discovered not in methods employed, strategic positions adopted, or solutions proposed, but in a common set of questions and issues raised, beginning with the very delimitation of "Latin American" narrative and culture.

Any notion of a traditional sort of unity for the volume may quickly be put to rest by reference to the inclusion of Fredric Jameson's essay, "Americans Abroad, Exogamy and Letters in Late Capitalism," which focuses on Robert Stone's *A Flag for Sunrise,* a North American novel set in a fictional Latin American country. Clearly, Stone's novel falls outside the bounds of "Latin American narrative" as we conventionally conceive it, and the work would normally be discounted in a volume of this sort. But our inclusion of Jameson's essay is more than deliberately abrasive, in the terms I have just noted and more. For the Hispanist, Jameson's essay has an unexpected resonance that evokes long-standing and central problems in Latin American literary historiography, such as how we properly delimit "Latin American" narrative: by its language; by its author's cultural identity or national affiliation; by its subject matter, setting, themes, or ideology. That is, to contemplate a North American novel in a discussion of Latin American narrative recalls the difficulties of scholarship on the Latin American novel in the colonial period, where one may find arguments for the pertinence, say, of works by seventeenth-century French authors that dealt with Latin America and were written in Spanish and published in Paris.[29] If the paradoxical coherence of these essays lies in their interrogation of our conventional affiliations and delimitations (of what Latin American culture is), then it is perhaps appropriate that the volume's periphery and center appear inverted. Contributions that elsewhere would be considered questionable inclusions in the Latin American field, such as Jameson's, move curiously to the center of the volume. Indeed, references to Jameson's theoretical work traverse several of the essays and provide one of the volume's connective tissues. For this, our volume proves symptomatic of the very problem it raises and for which it would seek to instigate a cure (Hispanic criticism's deference to the authority of "non-Hispanic" theory). If my own introductory remarks seem overly concerned with justifying Jameson's intervention, in part this is an "objective" reflection of the volume's subliminal content, and particularly of what transpired at the conference where the essays were originally presented, i.e., an inordinate preoccupation with Jameson's presence, which he himself might be the first to decry.

On the other side of this same coin, one further reflection of the curious reversals and realignments of affiliation in which the volume participates is how the most "isolated" essays among those collected may be ones that by rights would be considered quintessentially Latin American(ist). Thus, in the context of the collection, the essays by Argentine novelist Luisa Valenzuela and by the renowned Hispanist González Echevarría may appear to be left as eloquent stalwarts of "minority" positions.[30] The juxtaposition of the essays by Jameson, Valenzuela, and González Echevarría also leads to other delicate questions, such as how or why "foreigners" are sometimes the most vociferous defenders of the inviolability of Latin American culture, while Latin Americans (say, Valenzuela and González Echevarría) often remain the most articulate (if not vehement) opponents of such categorical distinctions and demarcations.[31] My intention is not to derive grand conclusions from these circumstances here, but for the moment simply to point to their existence as itself a worthwhile issue.

As juxtaposed with Mary Louise Pratt's "Criticism in the Contact Zone," Jameson's essay exemplifies well the kind of implicit dialogues established among the essays in the volume. That is, for reasons already suggested, Jameson's essay serves dramatically to underscore and complement the question that Pratt's essay raises from the outset of what (Latin) American literature is, of how it may possibly be defined or delimited today, when so many cultural products are "aggressively transnational" and susceptible to diverse receptions in numerous local, regional, or transnational communities. Even if it was far from his original intention, in the context of the essays here Jameson's essay offers an intriguing challenge and effects the sort of radical interrogation of the delimitation of the "Latin American" sought by the volume as a whole. In presenting Stone's novel as a prototype of what he calls the "gringo novel," Jameson demonstrates how we all *use* our various concepts of "Latin America," how this postulated entity not only belongs (differently) to us all but indeed constitutes our very being. This is one form of the essential understanding of how the Third World is "always, already" implicated in the First World, whether through affirmation or negation.

If Jameson's essay may have the unwitting effect of reviving problems fundamental to Latin American literary historiography, particularly of the colonial novel, Pratt's essay raises similar issues for the nineteenth century, through her discussion of Latin American women authors of that period. While the first part of her essay challenges the (idealistic) homology between language, culture, and nation, her practical applications (in the essay's second half) reveal that there are at least two distinct, yet interrelated, types of contact zone at issue: the changing nature of historical contact between national and regional cultures (and their discourses); and the broader question of the fit between language (discourse) and lived experience (history), exposed in an exploration of the "nation" as the rhetorical construction of an "imagined community."[32]

Just as the Latin American "subaltern" may occupy a paradoxically "privileged" vantage point from which to observe the limitations of modern Western rhetoric, so, in Pratt's view, nationalism and its attendant baggage has always been a problematic and questionable notion, for women ("occupants but not full members of nations") more than for men, as evidenced by the particular resistance to it that women's writing has long posed. Gender studies such as Pratt's and Amy Kaminsky's are one way to break down "the homology of one person/one language/one community" and to affirm multiple alliances and affiliations, crossing national and regional frontiers, through which we construct identity.

Alternately, Pratt's essay may also be read in connection with Fernando Coronil's "Challenging Colonial Histories," since both touch on the inevitable contact and (im)possible fit between rhetorical constructs and lived reality – or, in Coronil's terms, between ideology and relations of production. Coronil argues that Fernando Ortiz's highly regarded work in Cuban sociocultural analysis, *Cuban Counterpoint,* playfully subverts the possible use of sugar and tobacco as metaphoric representations of the national character and the country's socioeconomic history. Even so, though Ortiz rejects any essentialist notion of the Cuban character as a simplifying and distorting construct that disguises real material relations and motivations, he cannot in the end resist founding hope in a certain utopian synthesis of his own. We glimpse a similar operation in Jameson's essay, in which he takes a largely critical view of the process of appropriation by which a North American novel makes its own use of (a certain representation of) Latin America. Yet in the end, Jameson values Stone's *A Flag for Sunrise* positively because as it unfolds it lays bare the very processes of appropriation that it employs. All of the contributors recognize the "inmixing" of difference and otherness as the precondition of identity. All, as well, follow the transposition of this recognition from the theoretical, individual, linguistic, or psychological realm onto a broader, sociohistorical plane. For each of the contributors, however, this gesture retains different practical and strategic implications.

There is a revealing interplay, perhaps not immediately apparent, between Jameson's position and that implied in Roberto González Echevarría's "Archival Fictions." Attention is drawn to the significant differences between their positions by the passing but telltale use of the notion of the "exogenous" that their essays share. For Jameson, exogamy has a primarily cultural or sociopolitical denotation. González Echevarría, in contrast, gives the concept a formal and more properly literary application: in the context of his essay it refers to the identity and difference between the novel as genre and other categories of discourse (the scientific or the anthropological, for example). From very different points of departure, both contributors present strong arguments against appropriations of the Latin American as "other." But González Echevarría implicitly refuses to see or accept essential differences (in Latin American literature, categorical or otherwise, of quality or originality, pertinence or centrality). Jameson, on the other hand, would adamantly reject our possibility of truly "understanding" or "comprehending" the Latin American. That is, though Jameson recognizes our construction and appropriation of (a certain image of) the Latin American as a "fiction" by which we represent ourselves to ourselves, he holds out that Latin America is also a very *real* other that we cannot understand and have no right to pretend to speak for or to "comprehend." This is a powerful, provocative, and polemic position, even among the contributors here. In this regard – not in the rather provincial one of not being a Latin Americanist – Jameson does represent an insistently alternative perspective.

Contemporary Latin American narrative, in González Echevarría's theory of the "archive," is simultaneously connected to, and disconnected from, the core of the Western literary tradition (to the origin, to the law, to power): he shows Latin American literature to be one with the Western canon and yet always other (much as Ricardo Gutiérrez Mouat's essay does with Latin American narrative's participation in the postmodern). For González Echevarría, there can be no facile, global vision of Latin America or its literature, not because of its uniqueness but because of its central Western character; its marginality, in González Echevarría's arguably deconstructive understanding, is the very source of its centrality. Like all the great works in the Western (novel) canon, it simultaneously constructs and undermines the archive of absolute knowledge and total mastery, affirms and denies the direct (and transparent) correspondence between myth and history, language and reality, the word and the thing.

How might we practice a critical consciousness of our direct involvement and complicity with Latin American narratives – as implied or potential addressees, for example? The essays here by John Beverley and Amy Kaminsky respond differently to this issue. Beverley makes our involvement as First World publishers, editors, and readers, of boom novels as well as of the testimonial texts more recently at the center of attention, a fully explicit consideration (though not one about which, as he clarifies, we need be so hyperconscious as to suffer from "guilt-tripping"). Kaminsky, in contrast, makes the work of selected contemporary women authors from Latin America (Luisa Valenzuela, Elena Garro and Rosario Ferré) "her own" more implicitly. She treats texts by these authors in all of their sociopolitical and historical specificity but does not make their Latin American origin as such a problematic issue. For Kaminsky, we all must deal with "residual authority." We all must cope, in other words, with the powers of discourse, its possibilities for critique and liberation as well as the limitations it may impose through its susceptibility to strategic manipulation. The contrasting approaches of Kaminsky and Beverley are revealed in the use they make of Gayatri Spivak's widely cited interrogative: "Can the subaltern speak?"[33] If Kaminsky's primary concern is to challenge us to listen to the subaltern, Beverley would also remind us how the "subaltern" as a conceptual category always retains a relative status and a relational character.

Any discussion today of new, transnational realignments of cultural and political affiliations, and of Latin America's participation in them, must deal with the politics and the culture of the postmodern. In the present collection, the extensive postscript to Beverley's essay, together with Ricardo Gutiérrez Mouat's "Postmodernity and Postmodernism in Latin America," explore this terrain. Both authors affirm Latin America's equal claims to the postmodern experience and their right both to participate in and to interrogate its discourse. However, some of the subtle differences in their approaches are marked by a minor transposition in critical-historical terminology, whereby Anglo-European modernism and postmodernism may become in the Latin American context boom and *testimonio* (for Beverley), or boom and post-boom (for Gutiérrez Mouat). A significant effect of both essays, and an explicit concern for Beverley, is to reject the bald affirmation of one class of texts as categorically "native" or "authentic" (for some, the boom; for some, the *testimonio*), over and against the other as unabashedly dependent or complicitous.[34]

Beverley and Gutiérrez Mouat insist equally on the importance of examining the postmodern's Latin American manifestations in their historical and contextual specificity. To some degree, they have followed Jameson's lead in recent work that revises earlier, predominantly pessimistic evaluations of postmodern potential.[35]

A "postmodern" or "postboom" Argentine author, Luisa Valenzuela brings to bear here a fiction writer's perspective on the issue of the fit between (poststructuralist) theory and (postmodern) practice. Her "So-Called Latin American Writing," provides an effective counterweight to the other essays. Though Valenzuela is not compelled to engage directly current issues in critical theory, she too emphasizes how writing is, after a fashion, "always, already" political. To write, to discover a voice, and to enunciate require a personal commitment to act and intervene just as much as other forms of political praxis. Thus, on the one hand, and in line with the comments made in my epigraph from Valenzuela's contemporary and compatriot, Ricardo Piglia, writing is patently *not* identical, say, to marching in the street or planting a bomb (acting on paper and acting on bodies and flesh are literally incommensurate). But, at another level, they are still something more than analogous, and the sometimes life-threatening prospects of oppositional discourse just happen to be most immediately apparent in the context of life under repressive political authority. The death threat recently imposed on Salman Rushdie, of course, only confirms what Latin American writers have long known, and these dangers, like so much else today, are not limited by national and cultural frontiers.

Valenzuela's emphasis on the personal commitment to action that writing involves links her essay indirectly to Pratt's and Beverley's arguments for a critical self-consciousness of the text's historical enunciation and reception, its addresses and uses. Her comments on a contemporary Brazilian novel, Clarice Lispector's *The Hour of the Star,* implicitly reject the sometimes narrow and often bitter polemics in Latin America that have divided the region's writers and intellectuals between the camps of "literature in the revolution" and "revolution in literature." In the context of a now almost universal disenchantment among Latin Americans and Latin Americanists with the (pernicious) effects of the concept of "magical realism," it is noteworthy that in the first part of her essay Valenzuela still insists on certain specific qualities possessed by Latin American reality and reflected in its literary representations. Yet at the same time, in a passing reference, she distances herself from simplistic or commercial glorifications of contemporary Latin American literature as it has been assimilated in the metropolitan centers.

It was perhaps inevitable that the high hopes for the "dialectical" syntheses to be achieved in their respective spheres of influence by poststructuralist critical theory and boom/postboom Latin American narrative would turn out to have been exaggerated or misplaced. In the field of critical theory, we have seen a whole gamut of competing critical strategies and ideological practices reduplicated under the poststructuralist banner. In the field of Latin American literature, the constant renewal of political differences that we witness belies comforting notions of the magical transcendence that literature was reputed to have achieved at various points in its historical trajectory, most recently and notably with the (in)famous boom of the 1960s. To a large degree, the "literature-in-the-revolution" and the "revolution-in-literature" positions have simply been rewritten today, in the space of the postboom, as what might be called, somewhat tongue-in-cheek, the "testimonio" and the "text-imonio" camps, another version of the differences reflected in the present collection of essays.

That real differences remain need not, however, be a necessary or sufficient cause for despair. Also apparent in the essays collected here is that from all sides there has been significant movement toward a rejection of bald distinctions, of strategic exaggeration and distortion of adversarial positions. Luisa Valenzuela insists that at the level of enunciation, writing itself (textuality) is a form of direct (political) activity. John Beverley lucidly illuminates the common denominators in the situation of enunciation of both boom novels and testimonial texts of resistance. And Beverley and Roberto González Echevarría come together at least in their refusal to reify the Latin American as categorical other; in very different ways, each sees Latin America's marginality as central to the problems facing the West today (its political realities, its problems of cultural identity and their representation in narrative). We may conclude, then, that the emergence of new dialogue, of new confrontations and mediations, is a more promising sign of the significance and vigor of Latin American literature than the rather unidimensional image made available with the promotion and diffusion of the boom novels, however considerable these works' merits. Their divergent literary and political premises notwithstanding, the boom novels and postboom testimonial texts share an essential common denominator: they are equally caught up in the multiplication, fragmentation, and transnationalization of cultural production and reception, and they must come to terms with their cohabitation of this critical space.[36]

If the "testimonio" and "text-imonio" camps have rewritten the previously paradigmatic positions of revolutionary literature and literary revolution, it is with a number of significant differences. One difference, it appears, is that the fervent debates on cultural politics long waged in Latin America are now more effectively "exported" to the United States – right along with the continuous flow of legal and extralegal immigrants that makes the distinction between domestic and foreign policy issues in our hemisphere increasingly problematic and tenuous. Indeed, "resistance" texts such as the *testimonio,* normally appearing under the imprint of small alternative presses, now effectively compete for the attention of the North American reader with the boom novels printed under the label of the major commercial publishing houses.[37]

In this general context, Jameson has remarked elsewhere on the "silence" that

> today is generated by the seeming perplexity in the West as to
> what politics – what *a* politics – might be in the first place: a
> perplexity no doubt meaningless in the rest of the world – very

emphatically including Cuba – where the political is a destiny, where human beings are from the outset condemned to politics, as a result of material want, and of life on the very edge of physical catastrophe, a life that almost always includes human violence as well.[38]

Whether or not recent developments may represent a viable response to this silence; whether or not, indeed, one even agrees with Jameson's evaluation of our circumstances – and this is one of the debates implicitly established among the essays here – there can be little question that in the United States many of the most incisive lessons that Latin American culture and narrative offer have not been understood.[39] Yet at the same time, today more than ever, Latin American culture and literature belong to us all, if differently, as a right, a privilege, and also a responsibility. It must go without saying that for writers, critics, and theorists all along the North–South frontier there is more to gain than to lose from a more active and reciprocal, creative and critical, dialogue.

Notes

1. Marina Kaplan, "Between Arlt and Borges: An Interview with Ricardo Piglia," *The New Orleans Review* 16.2 (1989): 72-73.

2. Fredric Jameson, "Forward," in R. Fernández Retamar, *Caliban and Other Essays,* trans. E. Baker (Minneapolis: University of Minnesota Press, 1989), xii; Homi K. Bhabha, "Introduction: Narrating the Nation," in H. K. Bhabha, ed., *Nation and Narration* (London: Routledge, 1990), 4.

3. Jean Franco is one of the few who have explored insistently and conscientiously the terrain covered in this prolegomenon. My arguments have many points of contact with positions she has developed. See, for example, her "Trends and Priorities for Research on Latin American Literature," *Ideologies and Literature* 4.16 (1983): 107-20; and "Criticism and Literature within the Context of a Dependent Culture," in A. P. Foulkes, ed., *The Uses of Criticism* (Bern: Lang, 1976), 269-87. Just recently, Barry Jordan has added a

welcome new title to the (scant) bibliography on the intersection of Hispanic Studies and Critical Theory: *Re-reading Hispanic Studies: British Hispanism and the Challenge of Literary Theory* (Warminster, England: Aris and Phillips, 1990). From the Latin American side of the equation, there is a substantial tradition of work on an "independent" theory of Latin American literature. It includes essays and books by Roberto Fernández Retamar, Carlos Rincón, Angel Rama, and Alejandro Losada, among others. Sources on the problems of a theory and history for Latin American literature include the twin volumes edited by Ana Pizarro: *Hacia una historia de la literatura latinoamericana* (Mexico: El Colegio de México/ Universidad Simón Bolívar, 1987); and *La literatura latinoamericana como proceso* (Buenos Aires: Centro Editor de América Latina, 1985). Conversely, Roberto González Echevarría and Gustavo Pérez Firmat are just two of the most noteworthy scholars who have adopted an alternate strategy and have worked to establish a tradition in English-language criticism of Hispanic literature that would make original adaptations and contributions to critical theory.

4. Oscar Collazos, et al., *Literatura en la revolución y revolución en la literatura* (Mexico: Siglo XXI, 1982). The extreme form of Collazos's "postboom" argument against his compatriots, the boom novelists, is that they have sold out to the imperialist/capitalist/ structuralist enterprise. Counterresponses are presented in Collazos's volume by Julio Cortázar and Mario Vargas Llosa. (The volume was originally published in 1970). For more on the differences between boom and postboom novelists in Latin American, two volumes edited by Angel Rama are invaluable: *Más allá del boom: literatura y mercado* (Mexico: Marcha, 1981); and *Novísimos narradores hispanoamericanos en marcha* (Mexico: Marcha, 1981). If the leftist critique of and aversion to (certain forms of) critical theory appears especially virulent in Latin America, this is perhaps because it is augmented by a more generalized disrespect for formal, academic criticism found among creative artists of very diverse ideological positions. Octavio Paz provides a recent expression of this attitude in *La otra voz: poesía y fin de siglo* (Barcelona: Seix Barral, 1990), 79: "El auge de la industria universitaria de la crítica ha convertido las modestas colinas de basura que dejaba la literatura en verdaderos Himalayas de desechos."

5. See Hal Foster, "Wild Signs: The Breakup of the Sign in

Seventies' Art," in A. Ross, ed., *Universal Abandon: The Politics of Postmodernism* (Minneapolis: University of Minnesota Press, 1988), 252.

6. With regard to the postcolonial, as with so many other critical/theoretical terms in current usage, the Latin American occupies an eccentric, a richly ambiguous, in-between position. These qualities, ironically, may make the Latin American case exemplary, even quintessentially postcolonial. The Latin American is not sufficiently white/European/imperial to be homogenized, nor sufficiently black/non-Western/colonial to be tokenized. It writes in Spanish, not in English – though this today is itself in question. Its formal independence came too long ago, and so it has not recently enough been "liberated," yet for this same reason, in many regards, it has always been "postcolonial," precocious rather than belated. Indeed, as it has emerged in usage, many restrictions on the scope of the postcolonial may be observed, for it has primarily been applied to English-language literature of former British colonies, sometimes, by extension, to the former colonies of other European powers, and seemingly always, in the last instance, to the former Spanish colonies. Yet even in these most restrictive terms, arguments for the exclusion or inclusion of the Latin American in the postcolonial cannot be made cut and dry. Today, for example, we increasingly find Latin American novelists turning to original composition in English – and many others who, just as significantly, are collaborating as equal partners in their works' translation. This factor further enables – or necessitates – their consideration in any discussion of "contemporary postcolonialism," however problematic the application of the term as an historical category to the Latin American.

7. Kwane Anthony Appiah discusses the possible homology between some of these terms in his article, "Is the Post- in Postmodernism the Post- in Postcolonial?" *Critical Inquiry* 17.2 (1991): 336–57. Other recent work appears to be moving toward a postulation of postmodernism and postcolonialism as strategically opposed and competing practices. See Neil Larson, "Forward," in D. E. Hicks, *Border Writing* (Minneapolis: University of Minnesota Press, 1991), xi–xxi; and Benita Parry, "Problems in Current Theories of Colonial Discourse," *Oxford Literary Review* 9.1–2 (1988): 27–58.

8. Danny J. Anderson articulates some of the parallels between poststructuralist critical theory and contemporary Mexican narrative in "Cultural Conversation and Constructions of Reality:

Mexican Narrative and Literary Theories after 1968," *Siglo XX/ 20th Century* 8.1-2 (1990-1991): 11-30.

9. Franco makes this point in "Trends and Priorities," 106-7.

10. Recent special issues of the journals *Latin American Literary Review* (1987), *Revista de Crítica Literaria Latinoamericana* (1989), and *Nuevo Texto Crítico* (1990), for example, have given particular attention to this issue.

11. See Franco, "Trends and Priorities," 106-8.

12. This aspect of our design is of course not entirely original either; it follows the "manifesto" to which I have just alluded, articulated by Franco in 1976 in the conclusion to "Criticism and Literature," 287. Obviously, then, change at the level of the deep structure of our practices is slow. In this vein, Stanley Fish has argued that to fall back into "conventional" practices is inevitable and not as "reactionary" as it might seem (see his "Commentary: The Young and the Restless," in H. Aram Veeser, ed., *The New Historicism* [New York: Routledge, 1990], 303-16). In the context of Franco's remarks, this volume may rededicate the road we have yet to travel.

13. Titles here include the recent *Nationalism, Colonialism, and Literature* (Minneapolis: University of Minnesota Press, 1990), with essays by Jameson, Said, and Terry Eagleton; *Do the Americas Have a Common Literature?* G. Pérez Firmat, ed. (Durham: Duke University Press, 1990); *Universal Abandon: The Politics of Postmodernism*, A. Ross, ed. (Minneapolis: University of Minnesota Press, 1988); *Out There: Marginalization and Contemporary Cultures*, R. Ferguson, et al., eds. (New York and Cambridge: New Museum of Contemporary Art/MIT, 1990); *Marxism and the Interpretation of Culture*, C. Nelson and L. Grossberg, eds. (Urbana: University of Illinois Press, 1987); *Consequences of Theory*, J. Arac and B. Johnson, eds. (Baltimore: Johns Hopkins University Press, 1991); and the previously cited *Nation and Narration* and *The New Historicism;* as well as slightly older volumes such as *Writing Culture*, Clifford and Marcus, eds. (Berkeley: University of California Press, 1986); *Criticism in the University*, G. Graff and R. Gibbons, eds. (Evanston: Northwestern University Press, 1985); and *Criticism without Boundaries*, J. Buttigieg, ed. (Notre Dame: University of Notre Dame Press, 1987). In the area of postcolonial scholarship, noteworthy texts by individual authors would include Mary Layoun, *Travels of a Genre* (Princeton: Princeton University Press, 1990); Timothy Brennan, *Salman Rushdie and the Third World:*

Myths of the Nation (New York: St. Martin, 1989); Eric Cheyfitz, *The Poetics of Imperialism* (New York: Oxford UP, 1991); Barbara Harlow, *Resistance Literature* (New York: Methuen, 1987); Ashcroft, Griffiths, and Tiffin, *The Empire Writes Back: Theory and Practice in Postcolonial Literature* (New York: Routledge, 1989); and Gayatri Chakravorty Spivak, *The Postcolonial Critic* (New York: Routledge, 1990).

14. "Discourse and power" is an allusion to work deriving from the writings of Michel Foucault. The term "cultural conversation" appears in Steven Mailloux's *Rhetorical Power* (Ithaca: Cornell University Press, 1989). "Culture and domination" invokes John Brenkman's book of the same title, *Culture and Domination* (Ithaca: Cornell University Press, 1987).

15. Octavio Paz's view of this paradoxical (ad)vantage is as follows: "The eccentricity of Latin America can be defined as a European eccentricity: I mean it is *another* way of being Western. A non-European way. Both inside and outside the European tradition, the Latin American can see the West as a totality and not with the fatally provincial vision of the French, the German, the English or the Italian" (quoted in John King, *Magical Reels: A History of Cinema in Latin America* [London: Verso, 1990], 4).

16. Said makes this point in "Intellectuals in a Post-Colonial World," *Salmagundi* 70–71 (1986): 44–64. H. Aram Veeser's call for a revision of the new historicism through the incorporation of insights and premises from postcolonial scholarship is another argument for the enrichment achieved through an inversion of vantage points. In "Re-Membering a Deformed Past: (New) New Historicism," *Journal of the Midwest Modern Language Association* 24.1 (1991): 3–13, Veeser speaks of moving toward a "more global, less nationalistic discipline of literary study" by more effectively "adopting the role of the subaltern." Reed Way Dasenbrock has also recently argued for a new approach to the study of literature that would transcend (make obsolete?) national or regional divisions in his "What to Teach When the Canon Closes Down: Toward a New Essentialism," in *Reorientations:* 63–76. Ross Chambers's recent book-length study, *Room for Maneuver: Reading (the) Oppositional (in) Narrative* (Chicago: University of Chicago Press, 1991), may exemplify some of the real practical benefits that can thus be achieved.

17. John Brushwood, "Two Views of the Boom: North and South," *Latin American Literary Review* 15.29 (1987): 13–31.

18. Neil Larsen, "Forward," in Hicks, *Border Writing*, xiv.

19. Apropos of the use made by Derrida and Foucault of Borges, González Echevarría might rejoin that there has long been a "criticism" (read: "theory") in Latin America comparable to First World critical theory, but that it has not been acknowledged as such because it is found in the "creative" writing of its literary artists. Here we find implied support for the argument with which I started, that the relationship of critical theory and Latin American literature has not been reciprocal (see his essay, "The Criticism of Latin American Literature Today," *Profession 87* [New York: MLA, 1987], 10-13.

20. See, for example, "On Magic Realism in Film," *Critical Inquiry* 12 (1986): 301-25; or the forward to Fernández Retamar's *Caliban and Other Essays*, cited above. Jameson may be indirectly responsible for the reinvigoration of this whole area of inquiry through the many critical debates that have been spawned by his provocative and controversial article, "Third-World Literature in the Era of Multinational Capitalism," *Social Text* 15 (Fall 1986): 65-88.

21. This is one of the central points made in Aijaz Ahmad's "Jameson's Rhetoric of Otherness and the 'National Allegory,'" *Social Text* 17 (1987): 3-25; and in Jameson's "A Brief Response": 26-27. See also Appiah, "Is the Post- in Postmodernism the Post-in Postcolonial?" and "Tolerable Falsehoods: Agency and the Interests of Theory," in *Consequences of Theory*, 63-90. Among Latin American critics, Carlos Rincón and Walter Mignolo have voiced similar concerns about First World critical appropriations. See Rincón, "Modernidad periférica y el desafío de lo postmoderno: perspectivas del arte narrativo latinoamericano," *Revista de Crítica Literaria Latinoamericana* 15.29 (1989): 61-104; and Mignolo, "Canons A(nd) Cross-Cultural Boundaries (Or, Whose Canon Are We Talking About?)," *Poetics Today* 12.1 (1991): 1-28.

22. Gayatri Chakravorty Spivak explores this dilemma as it applies to the realm of (academic) criticism and theory, as well as to that of literature proper, in "Theory in the Margin: Coetzee's *Foe* Reading Defoe's *Crusoe/Roxana*," in *Consequences of Theory*, 154-80.

23. On this question of "blame," two theorists prominent in cultural and political criticism, Jameson and Edward Said, appear to adopt very different positions that might merit further exploration. One of Said's particular strengths is that he withholds blame from

no one categorically, on any side of the divide, variously conceived (First World/Third World, dominant power/subordinate); see "Intellectuals in the Post-Colonial World." Jameson tends to adopt a stronger position that would minimize "blame" on the subordinate or dependent party. A compelled question is whether these differences may reflect the two theorists' own cultural backgrounds, one Palestinian, one American, though among my points is a rejection of such simple determinisms. A much more viable accounting may rest in the fact that Jameson, a more classical Marxist, insists on the priority of the system over the individual agent. Appiah discusses this issue of system versus agent in "Tolerable Falsehoods: Agency and the Interests of Theory," in *Consequences of Theory,* 63-90.

24. Jean Franco, "Beyond Ethnocentrism: Gender, Power, and the Third-World Intelligentsia," in *Marxism and the Interpretation of Culture,* 503-15. The design of this volume is an implicit response to just this kind of concern.

25. Stanley Fish levels this criticism, paradoxically, by arguing that to avoid positioning oneself on concrete issues is a practical impossibility. See, for example, "Commentary: The Young and the Restless," in *The New Historicism,* 303-16.

26. There is an extensive recent bibliography touching upon this vast terrain, encompassing the popular debate on "political correctness" in the university and the more specialized issue of the "political responsibility of the critic," the latter both in broadly theoretical and in more localized or site-specific terms. Much of this work would redraw disciplinary boundaries and promote revisionist pedagogy. But again, with such recent exceptions as Jordan's *Re-Reading Hispanic Studies,* most of this work applies to the revision of English and Comparative Literature Studies. Titles of note since James Merod's *The Political Responsibility of the Critic* (Ithaca: Cornell University Press, 1987) might include *Literature, Language, and Politics,* B. J. Craige, ed. (Athens: University of Georgia Press, 1988); Evan Watkins's highly original *Work Time: English Departments and the Circulation of Cultural Value* (Stanford: Stanford University Press, 1989); Nancy Fraser's "Introduction: Apologia for Academic Radicals," in *Unruly Practices* (Minneapolis: University of Minnesota Press, 1989); or the essays collected in *Reorientations: Critical Theories and Pedagogies,* B. Henricksen and T. E. Morgan, eds. (Urbana: University of Illinois Press, 1990).

27. The passages from Said and Cheyfitz to which I refer are as follows: Said, in "Intellectuals in a Post-Colonial World," states that "if you believe with Gramsci that an intellectual vocation is socially possible as well as desirable, it is an inadmissible contradiction at the same time to build analyses of historical experience around exclusions, exclusions that stipulate, for instance, only women can understand feminine expience, only Jews can understand Jewish suffering, only formerly colonial subjects can understand colonial experience. Nor does what I am talking about have to do with saying glibly that there are two sides to every question. For the difficulty with theories of exclusiveness or with barriers and sides is that once admitted these polarities absolve and forgive a great deal more ignorance and demagogy than they enable knowledge" (55). In contrast, Cheyfitz affirms in *The Poetics of Imperialism* that "in line with this politics, I have not tried to *understand* Native Americans or blacks in this book. I do not believe in philanthropy, which presumes an understanding of the position of the other, but in social justice, which presumes nothing, but grounds itself in the difficult politics of imagining kinship across the frontiers of race, gender, and class. This politics must begin and end with a critique of one's own place" (xiv).

28. The centrality of narrative to contemporary social, cultural, and literary theory is well known. It is reflected in Jean-François Lyotard's theory of "the postmodern condition." It also underlies the design of a volume such as *Narrative in Culture,* C. Nash, ed. (London: Routledge, 1990). John Brenkman has summed up well the general presuppositions of narrative as social and cultural discourse in *Culture and Domination,* 51. For the volume as a whole, though I would hesitate to speak for a very diverse group of contributors, our subscription to crucial points in Cary Nelson's reelaborated program for cultural studies would appear basic and unproblematical (see his "Always Already Cultural Studies: Two Conferences and a Manifesto," *Journal of the Midwest Modern Language Association* 24.1 [1991]: 24-38).

29. My reference is to *La tragicomedia de don Henrique de Castro,* by Francisco Loubayssin de la Marca. See José Anadón, *Historiografía literaria de America colonial* (Santiago: Ediciones Universidad Católica de Chile, 1988), 65-91.

30. Of course it should be objected that this is a function of the selection of contributions for the volume, not an objective reflection

of developments in the field. But I would argue that the spectrum covered here remains largely representative.

31. This state of affairs admits numerous and many fascinating explanations, including extreme arguments from dependence psychology (master/slave) that must be applied with great caution. See on this point Franco, "Criticism and Literature", 271. Also, on the vagaries of this general issue, see Ahmad, "Jameson's Rhetoric of Otherness."

32. The term comes from Benedict Anderson, *Imagined Communities: Reflections on the Origin and Spread of Nationalism* (London: Verso, 1983).

33. Gayatri Chakravorty Spivak, "Can the Subaltern Speak?" in *Marxism and the Interpretation of Culture*, 271–313.

34. Much of González Echevarría's *The Voice of the Masters: Writing and Authority in Modern Latin American Literature* (Austin: University of Texas Press, 1985) makes this point, particularly the chapter entitled "*Biografía de un cimarrón* and the Novel of the Cuban Revolution," 110–23.

35. See "Regarding Postmodernism – A Conversation with Fredric Jameson," in *Universal Abandon, 3–30*; and *Postmodernism, Or, The Cultural Logic of Late Capitalism* (Durham: Duke University Press, 1991). The question of the status of the postmodern is complicated but in some regards simplified in its application to the Latin American context. For example, the critique of the usefulness of the "monolithic category of 'the dominant'" in our postmodern age, undertaken by James Collins in *Uncommon Cultures: Popular Culture and Postmodernism* (London: Routledge, 1989), xiv, is facilitated in the "borderland" situation of the Hispanist, linked structurally both to the North American academy and to the products of Latin American culture. See also Hicks, *Border Writing*.

36. This is, in other words, one of the questions posed in our volume through the implicit dialogue established among our contributors. It is increasingly an object of explicit theorization by such critics as Larsen, Beverley, and George Yúdice. See, for example, the latter's "Puede hablarse de postmodernidad en América Latina?" *Revista de Crítica Literaria Latinoamericana* 15.29 (1989): 105–28.

37. Yúdice is one of the few to have addressed, if still in passing, Latin American participation in the politics of transnational literary marketplaces (see "Testimonio and Postmodernism," *Latin American Perspectives* 18.3 [1991]: 19).

38. "Forward," in *Caliban and Other Essays,* vii.

39. Others who have recently argued this point include Hicks and Larsen in *Border Writing,* and Patricia Seed in "Colonial and Postcolonial Discourse," *Latin American Research Review* 26.3 (1991): 181–200.

I

Americans Abroad:
Exogamy and Letters in Late Capitalism

FREDRIC JAMESON

> . . . But thou wouldst not think how
> ill all's here about my heart; but
> it is no matter . . .
>
> – *Hamlet*

I want to start with a proposition, namely, that the culture of late capitalism is not merely an empirically impoverished one, but one doomed structurally and tendentially to enfeeblement, whence its desperate need to revitalize itself with transfusions of the foreign and the exotic, the Other (this is then the "exogamy" of my title). It is a proposition I would actually be willing to argue for all three current centers of late capitalism, not merely the NorthAmerican superstate but also Japan and post-1992 Europe. The paradox is of course that very few societies have been quite so saturated with culture (in another sense) as this one, in which the effacement of the boundaries between culture and the noncultural (or superstructure and base, if you prefer) and the penetration of culture into the most remote crannies of social and individual life are well-known phenomena that have motivated the invention of new sociological conceptions, such

as those of image society, media society, the society of the spec-
tacle, and so forth. The cultural sterility I have in mind, however, in no way excludes the existence, in all three superpowers
but particularly in Europe and Japan, of spaces of extraordinary
elegance at their upper reaches while the lower ones are suf-
fused with commercial narratives and entertainment forms of
all kinds. But the vital source of language production is in them
sapped, as we shall see later; their older indigenous philosophical traditions have been colonized by Anglo-American analytic
philosophy to the point where very little of the critical or the
transcendent remains, and the content of their finest literary production can be shown, on closer inspection, to be borrowed from
what reality persists outside their own immediate national and
linguistic borders.

It is just such a closer inspection I propose to make here, of
one of the most remarkable novels of the decade that has just
ended, Robert Stone's *A Flag for Sunrise* (1981). I am going
to take this book as the exemplar for a genre I want to define
as the "gringo novel," which is to say, the novel written by gringos about Latin Americans, in this case an imaginary country
in Central America. I shall also have to keep reminding us that
this book (and some others I will mention) are not mediocre
products of the NorthAmerican imagination but, rather, are very
good writing indeed, and better than most fiction produced here:
for that is the strong form of my argument, that at its very best
and most intense the literature of late capitalism needs to borrow from its Others.

Otherwise, the literary production of the superstate would seem
essentially to boil down to two basic categories, leaving aside
that whole area of cultural production which is so-called para-
literature or the subgenres (such as detective stories, science fiction, harlequins, and the like), and leaving aside also the literatures written for the new publics of the so-called new social
movements or microgroups (such as gay literature or feminist
literature or ethnic literature or neo-ethnic literature). Thus, the
mainstream of white American cultural production would seem
to nourish two distinct areas and to articulate two distinct types

of raw material, which can also be characterized in generic terms as the soaps, on the one hand, and regionalism, on the other. The soaps, a category that today encompasses most NorthAmerican bestsellers and most "serious" NorthAmerican filmmaking, offer narratives organized around a fundamental category of NorthAmerican life, called, in media language, the "relationship." It would be wrong to think that this term designates private life alone, or the subjective or existential: rather, as a result of the effacement of the distinction between private and public, business realities and the public realm of the profession and of success are also now included within the objectified and depersonalized category of the "relationship," reified not least because it thus bears a peculiarly abstract name. The aesthetic point one wants to make here is that such commodified and pseudo-psychological categories have so deeply entered the very substance of NorthAmerican life that it is impossible to use the "relationship" as literary raw material without at the same time admitting the objectified trash of this language and its "concepts": we thus here witness the terminal stage of a process that began with Flaubert and his clichés and commonplaces, and it is a stage that no longer admits of internal innovation let alone of change – since the commodification and packaging of subjective goods have too great a functional stake in such pseudo-psychological categories for fresh subjective experience to emerge, on the one hand, while, on the other, the commercial colonization of the NorthAmerican psyche is too far advanced to permit any ironic distance or satiric perspective, save perhaps the Utopian wish to imagine a world utterly denuded of "relationships" in the first place.

As for regionalism, it was, with the Faulknerian narrative apparatus, one of the last great NorthAmerican literary technologies to have been successfully exported all over the world, and this second area of NorthAmerican literary production essentially consisted in the invention of a vertical regionalism that included history and the experience and memory of historical catastrophe within its local surveyor's map. It would not be fair to point out the obvious, that in a situation in which nature and the land have been abolished, these things can scarcely be revived in the imaginary as a form of national salvation or cultural therapy: after all, regionalism in its present form came into being precisely because of the postmodern abolition of nature and as a response to it. Indeed, if Faulkner is in any way the patron saint of the new regional literature, then, imperialism or not, we have to add that his new forms are our great gift to the rest of the world, and in particular to the Third World, whose extraordinary cultural production from García Márquez to the Chinese is inconceivable without Faulkner's invention of a vertical regionalism that includes history and the experience of historical catastrophe within its small local confines. But a regionalism after Faulkner not merely takes place in a South or a West that has superhighways and shopping malls just like everywhere else; it also governs regions from which obscure and ancient historical catastrophes have faded away, at least from the memory of white people. But the question of what a regionalism can possibly be worth that has no history left can also be reframed sociologically, and in a stronger way than in the opposition between country and city. For one would think that authentic and vibrant regionalism depends for its condition of possibility on the existence of a peasantry, something Faulkner had but which agribusiness has replaced by migrant workers (a substitution which at once raises the very constructional problem we will be confronting in the present study, that of the transcription of foreign speakers). So regionalism does not offer an authentic alternative to the inauthentic commodification of the soaps but, rather, confronts us in turn with its own internal contradictions.

A gringo novel like Stone's will now, outside the territorial limits of these two vast NorthAmerican generic entities, combine their mutual specialties in ways that modify both. The novel will go on dealing with "relationships," and very peculiar and historicized period relationships at that, 60s relationships, as distanced as specimens from the pathology lab, but will do so against the backdrop of regions that do not belong to us spiritually and culturally and thus are registered as exotic. But this is no longer tropical literature: Stone no longer has anything in common with

Under the Volcano or with Graham Greene, let alone with *The Plumed Serpent:* meanwhile, the replacement of Mexico by Central America is more than a mere change of scene, it is also a fundamental shift in time, as we shall see in a moment.

But it is also worth mentioning a few other possible generic categories for this unclassifiable book: the spy novel, for example, which is on my view an essentially theological genre that turns on the cosmic confrontation between Good and Evil in the universe, or the political novel itself – most problematical of all genres – which ought a priori never to be possible, so that when it rarely and miraculously comes into being it is its unexpected existence that needs to be explained and not, as with the other genres, its absence and its lack.

Meanwhile, even though the historical novel has become problematical in a different way – insofar as everything is history but yet the present is more historical than the past (and the future perhaps even more historical than the present) – it would be paradoxical but appropriate to advance the suggestion that *A Flag for Sunrise* is not only one of the rare great political novels of the period but is also one of the rare historical novels, even though situated in the present of its own writing. But this is so, for a reason that will situate it sharply in historical time and that will mark it fundamentally: it is a paradox one can only express by saying that despite but also on account of and through its Central American setting, this is a novel about Vietnam, a novel marked in all conceivable ways and scarred beyond any healing by the climactic encounter of the superstate with its Other. It is not only the fact that most of the characters of *A Flag for Sunrise* have lived through the Vietnam war itself; it is also the ominous and bewildering fact that Central America really is Vietnam, is still Vietnam; and not the least unnerving moments of this book are the ones when, like drugs repeating on you, unexpectedly and without warning everything turns back into Southeast Asia:

> As they passed the palace gatehouse the smells, the sight of the sentry box in its well of light under the jacaranda, the brown

sawed-off soldiers in MP's helmets brought Holliwell such a Vietnam flash that he was certain they must all be feeling it together
[i.e., the other post-Vietnam Americans in the car with him].
It awakened in him so potent a mixture of nostalgia and dread
that in spite of the morning booze-up which was still fouling his
blood, he began to feel like a drink.[1]

Here's the story: A small mission on the Atlantic coast of the
Central American dictatorship called Tecan houses the remains
of an order, an old alcoholic priest and a young middle-western
nun who are scheduled for repatriation back to the United States.
But the government and its NorthAmerican masters have the
feeling that these religious (Catholic missionaries being, as one
of the characters puts it, nothing but "a pack of reds" [FS 188])
are somehow involved in local politics, that is, have connections
with internal subversive groups. So the protagonist is set in motion, an alcoholic anthropologist and former "expert" in Vietnam,
who, invited to give a scholarly lecture in the neighboring "democracy" of Campostela, is encouraged in a variety of ways to
take the opportunity to visit Tecan as well and provide some
more reliable eyewitness evidence about the mission's activities.
Meanwhile, in the subplot, a young speedfreak who has deserted
from the Coast Guard gets himself involved in an arms-smuggling
venture that will also end up on the eastern coast of Tecan, near
the mission, in the middle of the predictable revolutionary explosion. He escapes along with the anthropologist Holliwell, and
not the least tactful and aesthetically expert feature of the novel
is the utter ignorance in which it leaves us about the fate of the
revolution itself (all we find out is that the president has fled to
Miami, something which could obviously have any number of
different sequels). The young nun, however, is tortured to death,
and Father Egan presides over the return to peace and quiet
in the jungle in a state of irreversible alcoholic decomposition.
    The novel's great formal triumph is that, unlike Stone's earlier
Dog Soldiers, it does not reduce in the mind or the memory
to a set of strings of individual destinies or plot-lines: out of the
two or three that can be coldly and analytically enumerated in

hindsight, the impression of a far greater multiplicity is disengaged, and this seems to me to be so for two fundamental reasons. The first is that these individual characters are themselves at distance from their own destinies, which therefore break down into a series of ungeneralizable experiences; while the second has to do with something like the doom of the historical process itself, transindividual if not collective, which rises above its individual participants or victims and grips them together in a cluster in its mighty convulsion.

What is it now that NorthAmericans are able to experience in this setting that they cannot find back home, in their own language? Violence, for one thing, of course: which is to say violence unmotivated by crime as such, or the familiar categories of criminal motivation. None of these characters, however technically illegal, is a criminal in the tradition of NorthAmerican television police procedurals. But even the great Sartrean theme of sadism and torture – impressively revived in this novel – becomes reduced to clinical and juridical banality when reimagined within the continental U.S. Our own cultural representations are thus forms that domesticate the scandal of violence and reduce it to the known quantities of already catalogued and named categories. The law-and-order shows in the U.S. service the cause of order in two different ways and on two different levels: they frighten the public and enlist its support for increasing funding and repressive legislation; but in some deeper well-nigh metaphysical way they reassure the public that the bewildering forms of violence with which it is sometimes confronted, or imagines itself to be confronted, are already under the control, as Foucault might put it, of the knowledge system itself, which has drawn up exhaustive tables of the acts in question and can explain them all to your satisfaction. The very act of *naming* a form of violence, as Stuart Hall and his colleagues have so dramatically shown for the category of "mugging" when it is deliberately imported from the United States into Britain,[2] is an act of social control and remastery, and the naming substitutes an ideological idea of the thing for the thing itself.

It is that name and ideological idea which Stone's non-

American restaging seeks to strip away, albeit at some cost, since one never manages to get outside of ideology in any absolute or ultimate sense. The price here, as I will try to show later, is the lurid reawakening of the old category of Otherness, along with the inevitable slippage from politics into ethics. Yet this is done in some sense in the name of politics itself: for the other great experience – linked, to be sure, to violence – that is unavailable within the NorthAmerican borders is the experience of classical revolutionary politics: this also has become an exotic, imported, when not to say tropical, product, that we have to get from abroad. We are told that nowadays (in late capitalism) the category of revolution or of total social transformation by way of the political level is irrelevant and philosophically incoherent, a view that sometimes strikes one as parochial First-World wishful thinking. As a form, however, Stone's novel itself must stand or fall with the validity of this category (however the practical chances of revolution are in it assessed). If revolution is henceforth meaningless in the postmodern sense, therefore, Stone's novel is as extinct as the dinosaur or as dead and mummified as the voluminous dissident and Gulag literature of the Eastern European countries, which must now also be consigned to the ashcan of History.

But we may begin this inquiry on a more formal level, which has to do with style and perception, landscape and the body. Clearly, when one raises the question of style today, one activates the problematic of postmodernism, for which a personal or individual style of the older modernist type is no longer possible. Stone's novels are of course representational or realistic in the classic NorthAmerican (if not bestseller) sense, a sense from which the most obvious earmarks of modernist experimentation, but also of postmodern textuality, have been repressed or effaced. Stylistically, however, the book is peculiarly thinned out, as though deliberately detoxified of the rich cholesterol of description and physical sensation; nor is this the ostentatious Hemingway-style silence and stoicism of omissions and renunciations: rather, it is something like a convalescent sensorium, about which then the other most important thing to say is the apparently contradictory, but obviously dialectically constitutive, appearance within this perceptual impoverishment of the "sublime" itself, rare enough at any moment of aesthetic history and here reinvented in the diving sequence, as we shall see in a moment.

What accounts for this peculiar combination of moments of great perceptual intensity and an otherwise seemingly constant indifference to the physical facts of life, to descriptions of the physical appearance of the characters for example? We find at least an emblematic key in Stone's next novel, the disappointing *Fields of Light,* about Hollywood and alcoholism, disappointing not least because, preceded by *Dog Soldiers,* with its motif of drugs and smuggling, the weight of the evidence thereby threatening to infect *A Flag for Sunrise* in its turn, rewriting it back into a drama of controlled substances, where the omnipresence of uppers and downers, rum, booze, dope, among all the main characters, now seem on the point of turning the political content of the novel into a mere excuse and pretext to deal with the now obsessive-seeming motif of addiction.

Yet it is important not to let this novel turn into yet another stereotypical rehearsal of the perils of the tropics for Northerners, yet another archetypal print-out of the well-known alcoholic disintegration of imperial bureaucrats in the heat of the Southern tier. As I have said, *A Flag for Sunrise* has in fact very little in common with Graham Greene or *Under the Volcano.* What saves *A Flag for Sunrise* (perhaps uniquely in Stone's work) from the specialized category of the novel of addiction is in fact the completion of what I began to say about Vietnam a moment ago: there comes a point in reading this book, indeed, when you realize that Vietnam is itself here an addiction, and perhaps the most powerful one of all – that searing experience of the outer limit which, no matter how horrible, empties the lesser experiences of peacetime of their savor and thus persists in the mind as an absent, obsessive fixed point. Once you realize that, however, all the other more local physical addictions in the book suddenly themselves become political, allegories of Vietnam, rather than the other way around.

And this can also account for the stylistic peculiarities just mentioned, which we can now see as incorporating the irritability of the exaddict, the withdrawal and privation of a disconnected sensorium. For that irritability and discomfort is itself the condition of possibility for the occasional electrifying stream of sensations, in a situation in which perception itself is little more than an exasperation of the sensory stimuli to which the external world condemns us in our vulnerable and hypersensitive, fragile condition. And that also accounts for the human relations here, and the dialogues in which people work up very close to each other, so close you can feel each remark inside the other's system. It probably has something to do with the relatively muted emphasis on description and the physical: very little of the heavy insistence on appearance and the body that most modern literature has found its satisfaction in; the rare sex scene is exceedingly disembodied, as is the climactic moment of torture (although you certainly do not remember it that way afterwards). But to this idiosyncratic synthesis of susceptibility and anaesthesia we also owe the great sensory breakthroughs, the momentary lifting of all of this, a suspension of all this, a suspension of irritability, and in particular the wondrous descent into the deep-sea, one of the great bravura pieces of modern contemporary writing and a new kind of opening onto the ontology of earthly space, such as we have not known since Lawrence: "It had been years since he had taken so much pleasure in the living world," the novel comments tersely, within a world full of excitements and intensity but virtually without pleasure.

But the diving sequence, in which alone the splendor of the created universe is retained, beneath a surface above which an atmosphere much more horrible than pollution reigns, is also the path towards some deeper, ultimate truth in this universe. That is a truth, not of the skin and of sensory perception, but rather of deep feeling tone and of something no longer even related to emotions in the older sense, and for which Heidegger's notion of *Stimmung* is now too weak; it is the ultimate bad trip or fear itself, "the Fear," as Burroughs's characters call it ("I've got the Fear!"), something very different from the energizing anxiety of the old existential period. Here it is, as without any physical embodiment (we never see the shark, or even learn whether there is one) it begins to resonate throughout this exotic tropical beauty:

> He was at a hundred and ten and his pressure gauge, which had pointed twenty-five hundred p.s.i at the jump-off, now read slightly under eight hundred. It was all right, he thought, the tank had no reserve and no J value; he would have enough to climb back as the pressure evened out. At a hundred and twenty, his exhilaration was still with him and he was unable to suppress the impulse to turn a somersault. He was at the borders of narcosis. It was time to start up.
>
> As soon as he began to climb, he saw shimmers of reflected light flashing below his feet. In a moment, the flashes were everywhere – above and below. Blue glitters, lightning quick. The bodies of fish in flight. He began pumping a bit, climbing faster, but by the book, not outstripping his own bubble trail.
>
> Some fifty feet away, he caught clear sight of a school of bonito racing toward the shallows over the reef. Wherever he looked, he saw what appeared to be a shower of blue-gray arrows. And then it was as if the ocean itself had begun to tremble. The angels and wrasse, the parrots and tangs which had been passing lazily around him suddenly hung in place, without forward motion, quivering like mobile sculpture. Turning full circle, he saw the same shudder pass over all the living things around him – a terror had struck the sea, an invisible shadow, a silence within a silence. On the edge of vision, he saw a school of redfish whirl left, then right, sound, then reverse, a red and white catherine wheel against the deep blue. It was a sight as mesmerizing as the wheeling of starlings over a spring pasture. Around him the fish held their places, fluttering, coiled for flight.
>
> Then Holliwell thought: It's out there. Fear overcame him; a chemical taste, a cold stone on the heart. (FS 226–227)

The condition of possibility of this splendor, but also its inner hollowness – which one might, in a postmodern age, designate as the scriptibility of the media image or the filmic travelogue –

shows what a displacement of region can afford in the gringo
novel; the displacement of relationship is much more complicated, because it involves the mimesis, not merely of an image,
but above all of a language, and of the language of the Other
at that. This is indeed the deeper topic of my present remarks,
and one of the fundamental problems posed by a world system to other national literatures, namely, whether it is possible
to transcribe the substance of one national life, with its specific
language, into the language of another one. Can the novel be
subtitled? Such is the dilemma in which cultural envy and translation meet, only to face the problem of pidgin as a stylistic dilemma; nor is this a problem of transcribing the English spoken
by foreigners, something born mimics can always bring off, but
rather that more critical one of inventing an English for what
people say in their own language – something that would seem
to present an absolute barrier and to stand as the fundamental
experience of otherness itself. This moment is also the crucial
place of the literary flaw, the point at which the stress on form
itself becomes virtually unbearable, and thereby releasing the
symptom and the clue for any thorough-going form-historical
analysis.

As for language, I would like to pose the principle that, in
late capitalism at least, its life is always the surest space or place
of contradiction. Living language – if I may revive so quaint an
expression – cannot be programmed or technologically organized and produced. The penetration of late capitalism into the
hitherto uncommodified area of language can be observed in
the elaborate computer technologies of language and composition teaching, whose necessary failure designates the seam between the commodified and the uncommodified more surely
than the media of yesteryear and that now-familiar and even
old-fashioned commercialization of the aesthetic (or reification
of fantasy). The businessmen's complaints – that help to know
how to write a letter is no longer available – are socially and historically a little more significant than mere organizational variants on the shortage-of-domestic-labor crisis: like the concept
of "mugging" and with equally racist overtones, these complaints

unerringly pinpoint the place at which machines cannot replace living labor in the production process, the place, I am tempted to say, where the labor theory of value is still alive and minimally capable of undermining the postindustrial hypothesis about the primacy of knowledge over production. We need to be very careful about reviving the old sixties' language-as-production theoreticism; careful also about awakening more spiritualistic doctrines of human creativity.

My hope is that both these misunderstandings can be contained as well as possible by a rigorous historicizing of the present in which what is here affirmed about language is understood to be applicable only to this system, which we call late capitalism, and even, if you like, only to this moment of that system. The thesis would therefore need to take a form like this, and to suggest that in a world of universal commodification and standardization such as our own, while stored human labor of unimaginably stacked varieties remains the basis of social appearance, human labor as such, labor nakedly visible to the living eyeball, can only be glimpsed in a few unique and privileged places, one of which is the production of real sentences. I put it that way to remind us that a great many unreal or false, imitation, sentences are also produced all around us, and that it is often a desperate matter, of more than tact and delicacy, to tell the difference any longer; maybe we should also add the qualifier that real sentences have a very short lifespan when exposed to the outer atmosphere and are at once subject to cooptation and reification.

In Stone's novel the moment of truth comes when he finds himself obliged to portray the Central American revolutionaries themselves, for whom no English equivalent can be found. For the comprador bourgeoisie, complicitous with the English-speaking power structure, are easier to do and more class-homogeneous, even though some nimble footwork is still required. We are never shown any of the ruling elites of Tecan, for example, only the sadistic Lieutenant Campos, about whose "evil" some ultimate questions must then be asked. But we are shown a sample of the neighboring bourgeoisie, in the nonrevolutionary client state of Campostela: Stone brings it off by a tactical displacement of a classic, indeed well-nigh archetypal, fashion – instead of showing us people, he shows us intellectuals. And indeed, it must be asked and wondered now whether the fact that one of Stone's two or three major protagonists and point-of-view figures is an intellectual and a professor may be thought to be a structural weakness or flaw, in a global situation in which all kinds of technicians and experts now have university connections (a situation sometimes, I believe, called "postindustrial society"): Holliwell was in any case himself just such an expert technician in Vietnam. So perhaps we are not yet in David Lodge after all, but in more suitable reproximity to the war novel (even though the latter's protagonist tends to be that ambiguous kind of intellectual called a journalist, rather than an academic).

But the urgency of this question is not only determined by the anti-intellectualism of a business society as well as by the transformation of that society into a technocracy in which the new functional space of the university is both an ivory tower from which reality and experience (sometimes also figured as manhood and virility) are absent, and also a place from which manipulative guilt and criminal complicity emanate: those new features are present, but it is easy to see how they also add up to a very old stereotype of the intellectual as well (who doesn't know real life but kills people anyway). I suspect that in the novel it is always the functional or structural distance of intellectuals from the constitutive social classes that is at stake and that renders precarious the use of an intellectual as a representational camera eye, no matter how keen his or her perceptions. So much stands or falls with the question of whether Holliwell is just a professor or is in fact a characteristically maimed product and veteran of Vietnam.

At any rate, the scene in which he makes contact (dead drunk) with the Campostelan bourgeoisie taps deep unconscious fantasies at the same time that it enables an expected and untimely kinship with Melville to find expression. Holliwell's drunken lecture, in which he explains the meaning of the United States, is a pendant to Father Egan's equally drunken sermon, in the jungle, among the Mayan stelae, in which he tells assorted lounging hippies about the meaning of the universe: the great interpolated text – the inserted pamphlet from another world of discourse – was not Melville's invention (in *Pierre*), even though through it he formally designated a profoundly modern impatience with the indirection of traditional narrative meanings and ripped his book apart in a way only healed by its ultimate replay in *The Magic Mountain,* where Mynheer Peeperkorn's prolix disclosure of the meaning of life is drowned out by a waterfall. On the other hand, at least in Holliwell's case, the lecture situation, vulnerable, unprepared, to a hostile public, is, as so often in Hitchcock films, the narrative equivalent of any number of archetypal nightmares of exposure and extreme social danger. The abortive lecture is thus also the antechamber to what I can no longer, owing to media debasement, call paranoia, but which is better characterized as sheer physical fear.

Here is now in any case Holliwell's lecture, which reveals the "secret culture" of the U.S. to an elite right-wing public in Campostela:

"Let me tell you now some of the things we believed: We believed we knew more about great unpeopled spaces than any other European nation. We considered spaces unoccupied by us as unpeopled. At the same time, we believed we knew more about guilt. We believed that no one wished and willed as hard as we, and that no one was so able to make wishes true. We believed we were more. More was our secret watchword.

"Now out of all this, in spite of it, because of it, we developed Uncle Sam, the celebrated chiseling factor. And Uncle Sam developed the first leisured, literature masses – to the horror of all civilized men. All civilized men – fascists and leftist intellectuals alike – recoiled and still recoil at Uncle Sam's bizarre creation, working masses with the money and the time to command the resources of their culture, who would not be instructed and who had no idea of their place. Because Uncle Sam thought of nothing but the almighty dollar he then created the machine-made popular culture to pander to them. To reinforce, if you like, their base instincts. He didn't think it was his job to improve them and neither did they. This debasement of polite society is what we are now selling you."

Again Holliwell paused. Voices were being raised but he was not being shouted down. He could make himself heard.

"I have the honor to bring you hope, ladies and gentlemen and esteemed colleagues. Here I speak particularly to the enemies of my country and their representatives present tonight. Underneath it all, our secret culture, the non-exportable one, is dying. It's going sour and we're going to die of it. We'll die of it quietly around our own hearths while our children laugh at us. So, no more Mickey Mouse, *amigos*. The world is free for Latinate ideologies and German ismusisms . . . temples of reason, the Dialectic, you name it. . . ." (FS 109-110)

This reproduces the now-familiar left diagnosis of imperialism in terms of consumerism, although the "lecture" certainly strikes out in a number of directions and seeks to satirize a certain left as well as a certain right (in any number of countries). I shall return to the ideological content of this view of the world system later on.

For the moment what interests us is how it negotiates the representation of the Latin American Other, for it is within the lecture situation that the collaborators are able to emerge, from spiteful academics all the way to a very interesting woman minister of culture, all speaking English to Holliwell in order to humiliate him and in general allowing the class resentment of a pro-American bourgeoisie to be, if not overdetermined, then at least redoubled and overlaid, by the more familiar gesturality of intellectual mediocrity associated with academic politics. Meanwhile, in Tecan, the only putative Hispanic or indigenous counterrevolutionary is a Cuban, whose psychology and ideological character structure is by now, since the Bay of Pigs and beyond (to 1898 itself), familiar to us and, as a former colony, virtually a part of NorthAmerican culture. (It would, however, be useful here to have a characterological equivalent for Bakhtin's conception of the chronotope, as an equivalent of some similar structural unity of ideology, historical experience, and character type in the actantial realm.) Thus, we must return to the left as virtually the only space in this novel in which a genuine approach to absolute otherness can and must be executed.

Stone's ideological position on the Christian left gives his still-ambiguous answer a certain representational coherence, and he does all this better than any other living writer I can think of, without, nonetheless, giving full satisfaction. The relationship between the various political figures is nicely salted or spiced by tacit personal appreciations: one is a dandy and a turncoat, another a cleric, another an Indio small businessman and activist, the new leader an art historian and painter trained at UCLA, and the returning leader of the older generation a man formed by the Spanish Civil War ("now we'll be off to Spain," thinks the younger leader sarcastically; "always Spain. Why not Algeria? Why not Angola, Vietnam, China?"). This silent subconversation of characterological tropisms is not altogether a concession to the aesthetics of the bourgeois novel and its commitment to individual character and personality as some ultimate intelligible unit of social life: for one thing we are shown how these distinctive individual personalities have all been forged in class situations and bear – or are even constituted by – scars of history that are not mere colorful accidents. This impression of narrative skill is then strengthened by the remarkable portraits of the "other side," of the American advisors, the mercenaries, the State Department and CIA people, as well as their local or indigenous collaborators: all of this is immeasurably superior to the demonology of Stone's previous novel (*Dog Soldiers*). The ideology of counterrevolution is persuasively analyzed, as we shall see in a moment, not least because it corresponds to a state in which the agents of that ideology are themselves conscious and self-conscious of it and ready and willing to express it themselves: nor is that any mere personal accident either (as was the case, for instance, of the Kurtz of *Apocalypse Now*, or the other maniacal figures as which alone the American "liberal imagination" has hitherto been able to represent the darker forces of domination within U.S. society). Stone is indeed very clear that the new foreign policy lucidity that gives his political figures their authenticity is itself profoundly historical and the result of a very special moment in American history, namely, the defeat in Vietnam (in this sense, also and again, *A Flag for Sunrise* is in the deepest sense a Vietnam novel).

And this is why it is sad and embarrassing, but not unexpected, to report that the revolutionary scene, with its pidgin Spanish, climaxes on all-too-familiar megalomaniac paroxysm on the part of the younger revolutionary leader, in which "power" is again affirmed as the ultimate drive in political praxis. Shades of Orwell, or of my favorite political villain, the evil genius of *Barbarella,* who murmurs, as at the end he disappears into the magma, "Earth, you have lost your last great dictator!" That the great dictator novel is a specific Latin-American genre with its laws, constraints, and internal traditions, does not entitle other national writers to go and do the same. Is anything more tiresome today – in full postmodernism and organizational standardization, after the well-known death of the subject (which seems to have different consequences than either the equally well-known death of God or the newly famous or infamous end of history) – than this demonology of power-lust, as though power were any more stimulating for jaded postmodern subjects than any other past time?

If language now marks the limits of political representation and understanding in *A Flag for Sunrise,* we need to turn to the other formal limits of this book, about which I have not yet said that, besides being a great political novel, it also has some claims to being a great religious novel, in ways I now want to explore. It may or may not come as a surprise, then, that the fundamental worldview of *A Flag for Sunrise* is what used to be called nihilism, but for which I now think we ought to find a better term. To be perfectly candid about it, and if we really want to be serious about ourselves, I think we have to admit that white America is characterized by two basic features: we are hypocritical as a people; and we are shallow (in the Russian sense of *nykulturny,* uncultured). This is an old tradition with us that probably goes back before capitalism proper to Weber's

"Protestant ethos." But it means that only one form of collective authenticity remains open to us, and that is cynicism, which constitutes at one and the same time the repudiation of our hypocrisy about ourselves and our motives, and the acknowledgment of what a world looks like that is reduced to only those things and forces that NorthAmericans can perceive and understand. Under these circumstances, cynicism is not some mere posture or momentary attitude: to become fulfilled, cynicism has to take on, as it does in this book, the proportions of an extraordinary gleaming nonhuman thing of tremendous purity and otherworldliness – a cynicism so absolute that it rejoins nihilism in the aesthetic museum of fundamental metaphysical worldviews.

Stone's achievement of this metaphysical resonance is, however, not unique in our recent period: it is indeed in one way or another shared by the other novels that would make up a little corpus of significant gringo novels, among them Joan Didion's *The Book of Common Prayer* (1977) and *Democracy* (1984), as well as a remarkable novel by Robert Roper that was published last year and has not yet received the kind of attention it deserves, entitled *Mexico Days*. In all these novels, the precondition for the achievement of an absolute and metaphysical cynicism is of course the Vietnam War. Their spiritual task, as it were, is the transcription of such a worldview, its notation and endowment with form; but the forms involved inflect the historical explanation of their subject matter in varying (and ideologically distinct) directions. Two (*The Book of Common Prayer* and *Mexico Days*) attribute the emergence of absolute cynicism to the sixties as a unique internal or domestic NorthAmerican condition in which youth and politics and, to a secondary extent, drugs are involved; the other two (*Democracy* and *A Flag for Sunrise*) more appropriately attribute it to the Vietnam War itself. There is a way in which Stone's preceding novel *Dog Soldiers* combines both explanations, but their value and consequences are in fact quite different and should be separated.

For the explanation by way of the sixties ends up attributing everything to the New Left, to political troublemakers who are in effect liberal bleeding hearts or worse. The narrator's sister, in *Mexico Days,* is mixed up with a group called No Pasarán, whose policy is to liberate all black prisoners from American prisons; her brother is a dope dealer: and it is important to understand how these two destinies or choices are identified and seen as being somehow equivalent. The originality of *Mexico Days* is to expand the time frame in which this diagnosis is effectuated and to blame both vices on the father, a wealthy mafia lawyer, whose allegorical significance thus now draws in the thirties and the forties and gives this work a kinship with Doctorow's wonderful *Billy Bathgate.* The relationship to Mexico here thus spans two historical periods, as it were from Dolores del Rio to the DEA, and has the merit of including the Mexican political sixties along with the NorthAmerican one, in the form of the massacre of Tlatelolco. In this one, then, our Other changes along with us and becomes in some sense our equal, even though the obligatory gringo scene of the "horror" of Mexican prisons is retained. In *The Book of Common Prayer,* a somewhat different Other is at stake, the now more familiar Central American Other, with its political terror and its death squads; indeed, the heroine ends her life in a round-up in one of those archetypal sports stadiums turned into a concentration camp. But the signifying equation here is again with the NorthAmerican political sixties, in the person of the absent daughter, who is a kind of fictionalization of Patty Hearst. Here too then, whatever the other messages, something is being said about the infantile leftism of the NorthAmerican sixties, and it is being said by way of a representation of a different, foreign, Latin American society in which evidently politics still exists or really exists.

In Stone these judgments are much harsher, and it is important to be clear about the essential and constitutive relationship between his "cynicism" (in our broader sense) and his repudiation of the left – in *Dog Soldiers,* both lefts, new and old, since hilarious portraits of old thirties' veterans are interlarded in the implacable indictment of the drug-smuggling journalist-protagonist, whose left-liberal lies about the one positive figure in this book (a dead soldier who seems to offer the glimpse of an "attitude in which people acted on coherent ethical apprehensions that

seemed real to them")[3] finally come to seem the sin for which
his troubles in this book are the atonement, even though he himself escapes safe and sound, leaving the Nietzschean Vietnam-
veteran "hero" dead behind him in a kind of martial apotheosis.
Ethics rather than politics: that is essentially the perspective against
which *A Flag for Sunrise* will attempt to confront politics itself.

What this will mean is essentially that sainthood is possible,
whereas socialism is not. "Do you really think the other guys
are going to resolve social contradictions and make everything
O.K.?" the CIA man asks the protagonist. "Worker in the morning, hunter in the afternoon, scholar in the evening – do you
really believe that's on, Frank?" "No," Holliwell said (FS 24-
25). And later on, in his infamous lecture on NorthAmerica's
manifest destiny, Holliwell tells us: "I regard Marxism as analogous to a cargo cult" (he's an anthropologist, remember), "it's
a naive invocation of a verbal machine" (FS 110). On the other
hand, the revolutionaries exist; and in the peculiar double standard of all these novels, what is inauthentic at home takes on
a very different resonance abroad, whether it is ultimately possible or not.

Sister Justin will now be in some sense the link between
these two opposite mirror images of sixties' politics: ethical at
home and political abroad (rather than the other way 'round).
"In her eyes, the hunger for absolutes. A woman incapable of
compromise who had taken on compromise like a hair shirt and
never forgiven herself or anyone else, and then rebelled. She
could, he thought, have no idea what that look would evoke
in the hearts of smaller weaker people, clinging to places of
power. She was Enemy, Nemesis, Cassandra. She was in real
trouble" (FS 343). But this, which motivates her final martyr-
dom in a nonpolitical way – the torturer, classically Sartrean, seeks
to destroy this image and this look – is in Stone imaginable only
in terms of sainthood, even though it might well apply to any
number of the other doomed heroines in these books, from the
Marin of *A Book of Common Prayer* to the Marta of *Mexico
Days*.

As for Sister Justin's own political commitment – the quality

of it, and its potential ambiguity as well, whether it can equally
well be read as something ethical that takes the place of politics –
besides her ill-considered involvement with the guerrillas (she
supplies them with medicines), we have only a few remarks, like
this one: "Am I ego-tripping?" Justin asked. "Isn't it supposed
to bother me that people starve so America can have Playboy
Clubs and bottomless dancing?" (FS 35).

This is at least interestingly ambiguous, in how it faintly raises
the question of puritanism or prudery behind the political passion (either in the character or in Stone himself). But it is more
important to underscore the consonance of the remark with
Stone's general analysis of imperialism in this novel, which is
politically intelligent and economically and socially up to date.
Indeed, the flaw in many otherwise admirable political novels
or films can often be located in the nonchalance and irrespon-
sibility with which the stage is set, the pretext for the narrative
is disclosed in passing, and the preconditions for political unrest
are dispatched, as though in the outside world revolutionary fer-
ment were a constant possibility that did not need precise ma-
terialist analysis. Stone is very lucid about the inadequacy of
simply endowing an imaginary Central American country with
a revolutionary movement a priori and without further justification. Its condition of possibility here is explained by the pres-
sures on the Atapa Indian population in the interior, whose farm-
lands are being destroyed by new government mining operations
on the one hand (the main chance of a poor supplier of valuable raw materials in the new world system) and the expansion
of multinational tourist industries and installations on the other:
base and superstructure: the combination of a 60s' economic
explanation of neo-imperialism with an 80s' and 90s' cultural
and media expansion version of that explanation.

As for Sister Justin, I am not qualified to make any sensitive
or reliable theological judgment on the quality of this sainthood,
reached at the other end of torture and physical agony. Certainly its theological framework depends very much on that conquest and appropriation of, commitment to, construction of,

conviction of, cynicism already evoked. Father Egan's sermon
at the stelae is a vision of cosmic horror; human, social, and
historical cynicism now projected through the cosmos; and ab-
sorbing elements of cultural and religious otherness such as the
cult of human sacrifice in the pre-Columbian era, a howling blood-
lust literally embodied in the homicidal maniac Weitling: "Oooh,
he is terrible," Weitling sang. . . . "He is more terrible than you
can know. His face is like Indian corn, of colors. Then sometimes invisible, the worst. The hair of him is blue. He is elec-
tricity. Arms and legs are made of worms. The power. And it
is like space beneath you, you are falling. I fall, I, poor myself,
I fall. He crushes me" (FS 365).

But as a cosmic principle human sacrifice turns out to be fun-
nier and more banal than that, not quite as American as apple
pie, but fully as mindless as the supermarket and the shopping
mall:

> A man came here once from the national museum. They took
> rubbings of those stones and they picked up everything that could
> be moved. They said it was for the museum's collection, but of
> course it was for the President's family to sell. They picked up
> bone carvings and shards with graffiti on them. The man said
> he thought the graffiti might tell him something about everyday
> life here long ago, about how people went about life. But it turned
> out that he was wrong, it turned out that every single stroke rep-
> resented human sacrifice – even the graffiti. It was as though there
> was no everyday life. Only sacrifice. (FS 368-369)

This is then alone the condition, I may even say the experimen-
tal condition, the laboratory precautions and arrangements, under
which Father Egan can posit the existence, under the tons of
garbage and dead meat, of a barely perceptible form of life: "a
glimmer? . . . who knows down in that mess? But maybe there
is something. A little shard of light" (FS 318). The two things
go together: the "living" can only be grasped "among the dead"
(FS 319); sainthood can only become momentarily imaginable
under the most extreme and inhuman, abominable suffering.

It is, as I've said, a plausible worldview, in a situation in which not many traditional ones are plausible any more.

But I want to make the other point, in our context, that the achievement of this particular worldview, its representability, the possibility of grasping it and entertaining it even momentarily, is altogether dependent on and inconceivable without a fundamental preliminary condition of possibility, which is the cultural iconography of the Aztec or pre-Columbian other – in short, a set of images and representations that does not belong to us gringos and that is henceforth illegal to export. I do not particularly care what Mexican artists and writers have excessively done with these materials, which are their own business (although Diego's great jaguar-clad resistance fighters haunt the mind as they desperately grapple with the conquistadors). My point is rather that, restricted to purely NorthAmerican materials, this vision could not be represented and would shrivel to the banal proportions of this or that serial murder (which is what the Weitling figure in reality amounts to); the great metaphysical *frisson*, the "scream of blood running through the cosmos" (as the Norwegian painter Edvard Munch once called it), would thereby be utterly missed. Manson offers a thrill certainly, but is much too American to afford you any satisfactory picture of absolute Evil, any more than – for our writers and novelists – the NorthAmerican political hippies and students of the 1960s seemed able to afford any satisfactory image of true politics and political praxis as such. But this can surely not only be the result of a collective national inferiority feeling in the superstate and its citizens and artists.

This does not prove that Stone is a bad artist; on the contrary, it is because he is a very great artist indeed that we can get a glimpse of these representational limits. Meanwhile, I think we have to be clear about the reason why this representation of Evil fails – it fails because all such representations fail, since in that sense Evil does not exist, it is a figment of the specifically ethical worldview and thus an optical illusion. What is more relevant for our present purposes is the nature of that illusion, which is fundamentally based on the category of absolute otherness. Evil is otherness, and only the Other is absolutely evil: that is the ultimate reason why we have to ransack exotic storerooms and foreign cultures for its representation, under conditions of increasing social standardization (I hesitate to call it democratization except in the very sociological sense of plebeianization, the universalization of wage labor), from which otherness has increasingly been excluded. (Don't get me wrong about this: Chacmool and the Hispanics are by no means the only source of "evil" in this novel: indeed the NorthAmerican CIA figures in *A Flag for Sunrise* are a good deal less scary than the Englishman who works for them; and I have already said that the NorthAmerican villains in *Dog Soldiers* do not make my flesh creep at all. Maybe we really are innocents abroad after all, as Henry James and so many others have thought! Only what we do abroad is rarely innocent.)

But evil brings us back to the matter of formal and narrative contradiction with which I began, and with which I conclude here. Briefly resumed, the point I have been trying to make is this: the imperial power cannot represent itself to itself, cannot come to any authentic form of representational self-knowledge, unless it is able to include within that representation the represented realities of its own colonies. This is something we have long since understood in individual terms, in terms of an individualizing psychology: if you are a jailer, for example, your truth cannot adequately be represented without your prisoners; if a tyrant, without your subjects; if a torturer, without your victims. It cannot be any different when we come to collectivities; and this is something we have gradually come to understand for the past, for the older or classical system of imperialism – whose central power was Great Britain – namely, that something peculiar happens structurally and formally to a literature that is forced by the nature of things to exclude those Others that in many respects constitutively define it. [4] The new world system is structurally very different from the old system of rival imperial powers; but the proposition that something similar holds culturally for it seems to me to be the formal lesson of the gringo novel as well.

Notes

1. Robert Stone, *A Flag for Sunrise* (New York: Knopf, 1981), p. 163. All further references to this work will be given within the body of the essay and the work designated as FS.

2. Stuart Hall, Chas Critcher, Tony Jefferson, John Clarke, and Brian Roberts, *Policing the Crisis: Mugging, the State, and Law and Order* (New York: Holmes and Meier, 1978).

3. Robert Stone, *Dog Soldiers* (Boston: Houghton Mifflin, 1973), p. 261.

4. See, for further reflections on this, my "Modernism and Imperialism," in Terry Eagleton et al., eds., *Nationalism, Colonialism, and Literature* (Minneapolis: University of Minnesota Press, 1990), pp. 43-66.

Challenging Colonial Histories: *Cuban Counterpoint* / Ortiz's Counterfetishism

FERNANDO CORONIL

NATION AND COMMODITY

By means of an analysis of Fernando Ortiz's *Cuban Counterpoint: Tobacco and Sugar,* I wish to explore issues related to the historical formation and cultural representation of collective identities as culturally represented in countries that form the periphery of the capitalist system – the so-called banana republics, oil nations, and, in this case, "the sugar islands," as Benjamin Franklin called the Caribbean sugar producers (Portell Vilá, in Ortiz 1947:xviii).[1] The history of these excolonies is frequently told as the history of their major export products. For many analysts, as Herminio Portell Vilá observed in his prologue to *Cuban Counterpoint,* "sugar and Cuba are synonymous" (in Ortiz 1947:xviii). Jean-Paul Sartre once referred to Cuba as a "diabetic monster – an island of sugar" (1974:40). This kind of identification between nation and commodity seems obvious, since production for external markets has profoundly affected the organization of these societies since colonial times.[2]

In *Cuban Counterpoint,* Ortiz offers an interpretation of the evolution of Cuban society narrated in terms of the actions of sugar and tobacco, products that he introduces at the outset as "the two most important personages in the history of Cuba" (1947:4). Throughout the book he describes their contrasting properties, as in this passage:

> Sugar cane lives for years, the tobacco plant only a few months. The former seeks the light, the latter shade; day and night, sun and moon. The former loves the rain that falls from the heavens; the latter the heat that comes from the earth. The sugar cane is ground for its juice; the tobacco leaves are dried to get rid of the sap. Sugar achieves its destiny through liquid, which melts it, turns it into syrup; tobacco through fire, which volatilizes it, converted into smoke. The one is white, the other dark. Sugar is sweet and odorless; tobacco bitter and aromatic. Always in contrast! Food and poison, waking and drowsing, energy and dream, delight of the flesh and delight of the spirit, sensuality and thought, the satisfaction of an appetite and the contemplation of a moment's illusion, calories of nourishment and puffs of fantasy, undifferentiated and commonplace anonymity from the cradle and aristocratic individuality recognized wherever it goes, medicine and magic, reality and deception, virtue and vice. Sugar is *she;* tobacco is *he.* Sugar cane was the gift of the gods, tobacco of the devils; she is the daughter of Apollo, he is the offspring of Persephone. (Ortiz 1947:6)

He also establishes their profound impact upon Cuban society and culture:

> In the economy of Cuba there are also striking contrasts in the cultivation, the processing, and the human connotations of the two products. Tobacco requires delicate care, sugar can look after itself; the one requires continual attention, the other involves seasonal work; intensive versus extensive cultivation; steady work on the part of a few, intermittent jobs for many; the immigration of whites on the one hand, the slave trade on the other; liberty and slavery; skilled and unskilled labor; hands versus arms; men versus machines; delicacy versus brute force. The cultivation of tobacco gave rise to the small holding; that of sugar brought about

the great land grants. In their industrial aspects tobacco belongs to the city, sugar to the country. Commercially the whole world is the market for our tobacco, while our sugar has only a single market. Centripetence and centrifugence. The native versus the foreigner. National sovereignty as against colonial status. The proud cigar band as against the lowly sack. (Ortiz 1947:6-7)

While at first sight it seems that Ortiz is producing yet another reductionist interpretation that privileges the role of the economy in the making of Cuban history, I suggest that this impression is deceptive. Instead, I wish to propose a reading of *Cuban Counterpoint* as an allegorical essay that explores uncharted possibilities of Cuban history by casting light upon the society whose imagination endows commodities with the extraordinary power of making history.

Many theoretical frameworks have been used to analyze the process by which material objects, plants, or animals come to stand for human communities or to represent social actors.[3] Of these, the Marxist analysis of commodity fetishism has thrown the greatest light on the meaningful misrepresentation that occurs when social relations appear encoded as the attribute not of people but of things. From this perspective, the appearance of commodities as independent entities – as potent agents in their own right – conceals their origins in conflictual relations of production and confirms a commonsense perception of these relations as natural and necessary. Marx viewed commodities as opaque hieroglyphs, whose mysterious power derives from their ability to misrepresent and conceal reality, and whose multiple meanings can only be deciphered through social analysis.

I am going to argue for a reading of *Cuban Counterpoint* as a text in which the fetishistic character of commodities is developed as a poetic means to understand the society that produces them. By treating tobacco and sugar not as things but as social actors, Ortiz in effect brings them back to the social world that creates them, resocializes them as it were, and in so doing illuminates the society that has given rise to them. The relationships concealed through the real appearance of commodities as independent forces become visible once commodities are treated as what they are, social things impersonating autonomous actors.

Ortiz did not want simply to unmask the fetish, but to use its power to explore an alternative image of Cuban society. In this respect Ortiz's work resonates with Benjamin's treatment of fetishism. Unlike Adorno or Horkheimer, who were primarily concerned with demystifying the fetish in the service of reality, Benjamin sought to apprehend how the fetish commands the imagination, at once revealing and appreciating its power of mystification. Moreover, by constructing this playful masquerade of tobacco and sugar, Ortiz used the poetic and transgressive possibilities of the carnivalesque, so insightfully analyzed by Bahktin, to seduce more than to convince his readers. In brief, I wish to suggest that Ortiz, while using the idiom of fetishized renderings of Cuban history, presented a counterfetishistic interpretation that challenged a prevailing essentialist understanding of Cuban society. Through this form of rhetorical jujitsu, *Cuban Counterpoint* counteracted those forms of political discourse – whether populist, oligarchic, communist, or fascist – which for the construction of their authoritative images of Cuba relied on fixed categories, be they of nature, people, class, gender, race, state, or nation.

In the spirit of Ortiz, I will look closely at this book not from the reifying perspective of what Jameson once called the "garden-variety semiotic practice today," which reduces social action or written works to isolated texts, "manageable written documents of one kind of another," but from a historical vantage point which "liberates us from the empirical object – whether institution, event or individual work – by displacing our attention to its *constitution* as an object and its *relationship* to the other objects thus constituted" (1981:297).

HISTORICAL CONTEXT

Cuban Counterpoint was published in 1940, when sixty-year-old Fernando Ortiz was at the height of his creative activity and

Cuba was at the close of a tumultuous decade that had brought a series of domestic upheavals ultimately arbitrated by the U.S., sharp swings in its U.S.-dominated economy, the collapse of a revolutionary civilian government, the consolidation of the power of the army under the command of Batista, and the growing power of fascism worldwide.

By the time Ortiz wrote this book he had established a reputation as a multifaceted and prolific anthropologist, man of letters, and nationalist. He had studied law in Spain and served as consular representative of newly independent Cuba in Italy and Spain. In 1906 he was appointed public prosecutor for Havana. He resigned from this position in 1916 when he was elected to a seven-year term in the Cuban House of Representatives. Throughout his life he combined academic pursuits with public service. He served several terms in Congress, where he sought to implement liberal political reforms, and in 1923 he headed the Committee of National Civic Restoration, created to fight against the rampant corruption of the period.

During the short-lived revolutionary government of 1933 headed by Ramón Grau San Martín, in the midst of the political crisis created by the U.S. government's unwillingness to recognize the regime, Ortiz was invited to participate in the cabinet and to offer a conciliatory formula. While he chose not to join the cabinet, he proposed a plan of national unity built around the participation of major groups in Grau's government.[4] The plan found general acceptance; even Sumner Welles, the U.S. Ambassador who strongly rejected Grau, found it a "reasonable compromise" (Aguilar 1972:189). But the formula failed "because of mutual suspicion and past resentment and the internal fragmentation of almost every group involved" (Aguilar 1972:189).

The failure of Ortiz's plan was soon followed by the end of the civilian revolution and the emergence of the power of Batista and the military (Aguilar 1972:190). Unable to rule without U.S. support, Grau went into exile in January 1934. Batista then ruled Cuba through puppet presidents until 1940, when he was elected president.

The defeat of domestic progressive forces and the consolidation of Batista's rule took place when the international situation was ominous. The Spanish Republic had been defeated, and Nazism was extending its hold over Europe. Concerned with the advance of fascism in Europe, Ortiz organized in 1941 La Alianza Cubana por un Mundo Libre (The Cuban Alliance for a Free World). It was in this context of domestic and international threats to liberal nationalism that Ortiz wrote *Cuban Counterpoint.*

Cuban Counterpoint was the mature expression of a diverse scholarly career guided by a concern to interpret Cuban society, analyze the sources of its "backwardness," and valorize its distinctive culture. His first major work, *Los Negros Brujos* (1906), was a treatise of criminal anthropology that focused on blacks, their "superstitions," and their deviance. Framed within an evolutionary positivist outlook influenced by the biological reductionism of Cesare Lombroso, who wrote the preface to the book, it sought to combat the conditions which promoted criminality and "backward" beliefs among practioners of "brujería" (sorcery).

By 1910, however, Ortiz had begun to elaborate a sociological understanding of race, placing emphasis on cultural rather than biological factors. Concerned as before with Cuba's backwardness, Ortiz felt that if Cuba was to advance, Cubans needed first to recognize their inferiority: "We are inferior, and our greatest inferiority consists, without doubt, in not acknowledging it, even though we frequently mention it" (1910:27). But he explained that this inferiority was not racial –"not our race . . . but our sense of life, our civilization is much inferior to the civilization of England, of America, of the countries that today rule the world" (1910:27). He argued that Cubans could be civilized or uncivilized, like all people, "like those who are victorious, like those more backward ones who still splash around in the mud of barbarism" (1910:28). His distance from biological essentialism was clear. All human beings were biologically alike: what Cubans needed, he argued, was "not a brain to fill the skull, but ideas to flood it and to wipe out its drowsiness. . . . We only lack one thing: civilization" (1910:28).[5] The "civilization" that

Cubans needed, however, was European. Ortiz in effect seemed to have transcoded biological signs into cultural signs.[6]

The cause of Cuba's backwardness, of the corruption of its politicians, of the precariousness of its institutions, was attributed to the influence of the sugar industry by historian Ramiro Guerra y Sánchez in his highly influential *Azúcar y población en las Antillas.* This book, published in 1927 when the rule of Gerardo Machado was becoming increasingly authoritarian, profoundly affected a generation of intellectuals who, like Ortiz, were involved in the civilizing struggle for political reform and public honesty. In this analysis, black Cubans appeared more as the victims of the growth of the giant sugar factories that had come to dominate the Cuban economy than as a source of Cuban culture.

For this reason, it is likely that a greater influence on Ortiz was Spengler's *The Decline of the West* (translated into Spanish in 1923) whose conception of multiple paths of historical development encouraged many Latin American intellectuals to view their societies as occupying, not a lower stage in the unilinear development of Western civilization, but a unique position in a different historical pattern – Latin America no longer had to be seen as an incomplete version of Europe, but as an alternative to it. González Echevarría has shown how the *Revista de Occidente,* founded by Ortega y Gasset in 1923, made German philosophy and historiography available to a generation of Cuban intellectuals for whom it provided intellectual means to redefine Cuban identity (1985:52-60). According to Alejo Carpentier, the journal became "our guiding light." It helped forge new links between Cuba and Spain, like the Spanish-Cuban Cultural Institute, over which Ortiz presided (1985:53). But Spain, perhaps because of its own marginality within Europe, became a conduit for German thought, especially Spengler's, which provided a compelling vision of historical diversity. As González Echevarría has suggested,

Spengler offers a view of Universal history in which there is no fixed center, and where Europe is simply one more culture. From

this arises a relativism in morals and values: no more acculturation of blacks, no need to absorb European civilization. Spengler provided the philosophical ground on which to stake the
autonomy of Latin American culture and deny its filial relation
to Europe. (1985:56)[7]

The shift in Ortiz's evaluation of the Afro-Cuban population and
his concern to establish the specific and "authentic" bases of Cuban nationhood can be better understood in the light of this
influence.

CUBAN COUNTERPOINT

Like Guerra y Sánchez's book, *Cuban Counterpoint* was
published in the midst of the consolidation in power of a strong-
man, Batista. But in contrast to *Azúcar y población en las Antillas,* Ortiz's book is a highly metaphorical interpretation of Cuban
history. Its framework is not positivist but literary; it is modeled
after the work, not of Lombroso, Guerra y Sánchez, or even
Spengler, but of the medieval poet Juan Ruiz, the archpriest of
Hita.

The core of the book is its first section (almost one hundred
pages). It creates a playful counterpoint between sugar and tobacco modeled after Juan Ruiz's allegorical poem, "Pelea que
tuvo Don Carnal con Doña Cuaresma" and was inspired by
Cuban popular traditions –"the antiphonal prayers of the litur-
gies of both whites and blacks, the erotic controversy in dance
measures of the rumba, and . . . the versified counterpoint of
the unlettered guajiros and the Afro-Cubans' curros" (Ortiz
1947:4). While Juan Ruiz made Carnival and Lent struggle
against each other, Ortiz engaged sugar and tobacco in a theatri-
cal interaction structured around their contrasting attributes.

The contrasts of tobacco and sugar, which are presented
throughout the book, can be briefly highlighted by means of a
set of binary oppositions:

indigenous – foreign
dark – light

wild – civilized
unique – generic
quality – quantity
masculine – feminine
individual craftsmanship – mass production
seasonal time – mechanical time
personal productive relations – corporate productive
relations
diversified independent – monopoly production
producers
generates middle classes – polarizes classes
represents the native liberators – stands for Spanish
absolutism
symbol of national – token of foreign
independence   intervention
the world is its market – the U.S. is its only market

This list could be extended considerably. But what seems to me most significant is that these contrasts, although originally described in Lombrosian fashion as the result of the "biological distinction" of tobacco and sugar (Ortiz 1947:4), unfold in the narrative as neither fixed nor absolute. For example, although tobacco is seen as male, tobacco's variety of types is attributed to its female characteristics. Tobacco is at once satanic, sacred, and magical. Although it expresses Cuba's unique identity, it also becomes a symbol of the power of foreign capital. Sugar is not only a civilizing but also an enslaving force; although sugar is identified with the foreign conqueror, it also stands for the energy of black Cubans. Their qualities are contradictory, they shift and evolve. In a typical baroque encompassment of diverse attributes, tobacco and sugar incorporate multiple meanings and transform their identities through time. As paradigmatic metaphors, they acquire new meanings by being placed within a syntagmatic structure through which they express an ever-changing historical flow.

Complex metaphorical constructs that condense multiple meanings, tobacco and sugar stand for themselves as well as for their changing conditions of production. Tobacco represents not only a native plant from which is made a product of extraordinary individuality and uniqueness, but also forms of production which are characterized by domestic control over the labor process, individual craftsmanship, and the flexible rhythms of seasonal time. Sugar, on the other hand, represents not only a generic product, but also stands for capitalist forms of production that reduce people to commodities, homogenize social relations and products, and subject labor to the impersonal discipline of machine production and to the fixed routines of mechanical time.

Symbols both of commodities and of productive relations, tobacco and sugar, as products, become defined reflexively by the conditions of production that they represent. This reciprocal interplay between products and their generative historical contexts constitutes a second counterpoint. As both products become increasingly affected by the same forces, they become less differentiated and their attributes converge. They represent not only distinctive qualities or identities but also their mutability under changing conditions.

Thus, the social identities of tobacco and sugar emerge from the interplay between their distinctive biological makeup and their specific productive relations. There is little that remains essential about them, for their biological attributes are always mediated by human activity and modified by evolving patterns of production and consumption. Thus, in the last pages of the first section of the book, just when Ortiz identifies sugar with Spanish absolutism and tobacco with Cuban independentism, he clarifies: "But today, unfortunately, this capitalism which is not Cuban by birth or by inclination, is reducing everything to the same common denominator" (1947:71). He returns to this idea in the conclusion of this section:

> We have seen the fundamental differences that existed between them [tobacco and sugar] from the beginning until machines and capitalism gradually ironed out these differences, dehumanized their economy, and made their problems more and more similar. (1947:93)

COUNTERFETISHISM

This book produces a strange effect on the reader. The more Ortiz tells us about tobacco and sugar, the more we feel we learn about Cubans, their culture, their rhythm, their musicality, their humor, their uprootedness, their baroque manner of refashioning their identities by integrating the fractured meanings of their multiple cultures. Imperceptibly, we also come to understand the social forces that have conditioned the ongoing construction of Cuban identities within the context of colonial and neocolonial relations. How is it that a book about two commodities produces this effect?

As the narrative unfolds, as tobacco and sugar indeed become historical personages – as they appear as full social actors, with political preferences, personal passions, philosophical orientations, and even sexual proclivities – it becomes clear that tobacco and sugar, far from being mere things, discrete objects with fixed essences, are constantly changing figures defined by their intercourse with surrounding social forces. By turning them into full-fledged social actors, Ortiz has shown that they can appear as autonomous agents only because they are in fact social creatures, that is, the products of human interaction within the context of capitalist relations of production. Like Marx, who in personifying Madame la Terre and Monsieur le Capital (vol. 3, 1981:969) highlighted as fetishistic their appearance as independent entities, Ortiz, in turning sugar and tobacco into social actors simultaneously presented them as consummate impersonators and unmasked their pretense.

This reading is supported by the second part of the book. This longer section (over two hundred pages) is preceded by an extraordinary introduction. In a two-paragraph statement titled "On Cuban Counterpoint," Ortiz explains that this second part is intended to give the preceding "schematic essay" supporting evidence. His first concern is to warn the reader against a simplistic reading of the first section:

> It [the first section] makes no attempt to exhaust the subject, nor does it claim that the economic, social, and historical contrasts

pointed out between the two great products of Cuban industry are all as absolute and clear-cut as they would sometimes appear. The historic evolution of economic-social phenomena is extremely complex, and the variety of factors that determine them cause them to vary greatly in the course of their development. . . . (1947:97)

This explanation is followed by a significant heading: "On the Social Phenomenon of 'Transculturation' and its importance in Cuba." Ortiz begs the reader's permission for introducing the term "transculturation," a neologism whose scientific validity Malinowski has approved in the preface. According to Ortiz, he has rejected the prevailing term "acculturation" and coined the word "transculturation" because it makes possible a general understanding of Cuban society. He argues that by means of this term we can understand

the highly varied phenomena that have come about in Cuba as a result of the extremely complex transmutations of culture that have taken place here, and without a knowledge of which it is impossible to understand the evolution of the Cuban folk, either in the economic or in the institutional, legal, ethical, religious, artistic, linguistic, psychological, sexual, or other aspects of its life. (1947:98)

Following this statement he makes the strongest claim of the book: "The real history of Cuba is the history of its intermeshed transculturations" (1947:98). But whose transculturations make up "the real history of Cuba"? Is he talking about the transculturation of tobacco and sugar, the actors whom he introduced at the outset as the most important personages of Cuban history? Ortiz makes no mention here of sugar and tobacco. Instead, in a packed paragraph, he summarizes the various human groups that have come to populate the island from the earliest times to the present, from paleolithic Indians to recent immigrants. He refers to the black migration as

the transculturation of a steady human stream of African Negroes coming from all the coastal regions of Africa along the

Atlantic, from Senegal, Guinea, the Congo, and Angola and as far away as Mozambique on the opposite shore of that continent. All of them snatched from their original social groups, their own cultures destroyed and crushed under the weight of the cultures in existence here, like sugar cane ground in the rollers of the mill. (1947:98)

He then tells us that after the African migration "began the influx of Jews, French, Anglo Saxons, Chinese, and the peoples from the four quarters of the globe. They were all coming to a new world, all on the way to a more or less rapid process of transculturation" (1947:102). According to Ortiz,

There was no more important human factor in the evolution of Cuba than these continuous, radical, contrasting geographic transmigrations, economic and social, of the first settlers, this perennial transitory nature of their objectives, and their unstable life in the land where they were living, in perpetual disharmony with the society from which they drew their living. Men, economies, cultures, ambitions were all foreigners here, provisional, changing, 'birds of passage' over the country at its cost, against its wishes, and without its approval." (1947:101)

While in the first section of *Cuban Counterpoint* we are told that "the most important personages of Cuban history" are sugar and tobacco, in the second section we learn that "the real history of Cuba" is made up of "the intermeshed transmigrations of people." The apparent contradiction between these two views is overcome by making tobacco and sugar highly complex metaphorical constructs that represent at once material things and human actors and that reveal their shifting character.

Moreover, by showing how these things/actors are defined by their social intercourse under specific conditions, Ortiz illuminates the forces shaping the lives of the real actors of Cuban history – of blacks "like sugar cane ground in the rollers of the mill," or of nationalists turned into interventionists, like the tobacco of the foreign-controlled cigarette industry.

The concluding statement of the book makes this clear. It

comes in the context of describing how Havana tobacco was accepted in Europe and its cigars "became the symbol of the triumphant capitalist bourgeoisie," and how the democratic cigarette eventually replaced the cigar. After indicating that these changes were affecting the way the commodities were produced, the book concludes as follows:

> But cigars and cigarettes are now being made by machines just as economy, politics, government, and ideas are being revised by machines. It may be that many peoples and nations now dominated by the owners of machines can find in tobacco their only temporary refuge for their oppressed personalities. (1947:309)

Tobacco, the symbol of Cuban independence, of exceptional human skills and unique natural factors, appears now as an increasingly homogenized mass product controlled by foreign interests, like sugar. But at this stage the issue is, not to dissolve once again the sharp contrasts established earlier between tobacco and sugar, but to unmask these pretentious actors as mere creatures of human activity. The point is not so much that they are products of machines, but of machines producing under specific social relations. At the end, the owners of the machines emerge, in effect, as the main actors, for they dominate the structure and aims of production.

As the counterpoint of tobacco and sugar unfolds, the pursuit of money and power surfaces as a major force structuring the pattern of Cuban transculturations ever since the conquest. Ortiz approvingly quotes Juan Ruiz's verses on the powers of money, the fetish that stands for all commodities:

> Throughout the world Sir Money is a most seditious man
> Who makes a courtesan a slave, a slave a courtesan
> And for his love all crimes are done
>   since this old earth began.
>
> (1947:81)

For Cubans, however, the chase after money and power had helped fashion a social world that trapped them in subordinate relation to external conditions beyond their control. As Portell Vilá explained:

A difference of half a cent in the tariff on the sugar we export
to the United States represents the difference between a national
tragedy in which everything is cut, from the nation's budget to
the most modest salary, even the alms handed to a beggar, and
a so-called state of prosperity, whose benefits never reach the
people as a whole or profit Cuba as a nation. (in Ortiz 1947:xix)

Cubans, with no control over the winds of history, appear as
"birds of passage," transient creatures with fluid identities.

Just as money made a courtesan a slave, it made tobacco
a mass product like sugar. I would like to suggest that without
referring to parties, groups, or personalities, in *Cuban Counterpoint* Ortiz was describing Cuban society, its changeability, the
shifting loyalties and identities of its major actors, the provisional
character of its arrangements and institutions. Ortiz had wit-
nessed turbulent years of political strife, when political loyalties
and personal identities shifted violently. Nothing seemed per-
manent: noninterventionists asked U.S. Ambassador Sumner
Welles to intervene, pro-civilians allied themselves with the military, advocates of honesty became paragons of corruption. Since
1934 Batista ruled behind a civilian facade, speaking the language of populism while helping consolidate the hold of U.S.
capital over the Cuban economy. No names needed to be mentioned, for tobacco and sugar became a mirror in which one
could glimpse social identities. Perhaps this explains why Ortiz
wrote a book about tobacco and sugar at the close of such a
turbulent decade.

The timing of the book's appearance could not have been
more significant. Just when Cubans elected Batista president
in 1940, Ortiz published *Cuban Counterpoint*. While Batista
employed a populist discourse that addressed Cubans as an undifferentiated mass, Ortiz depicted the Cuban people through
their multifaceted creativity.[8] This contrast between populist and
popular representations of Cuban culture is vividly captured in
their writings. While a book of Batista's speeches brought forth
a flat image of Cubans, graphically illustrated by means of stereotypical fascist images borrowed from Europe by way of Hollywood (Batista 1944), *Cuban Counterpoint* vividly depicted the

diversity and validity of Cuban culture through its playful interpretation of Cuban history.

In the 1934 preface to the second edition of his classic *Azúcar y población en las Antillas,* Guerra y Sánchez praised his own book for predicting the sugar crisis of 1930 as an unavoidable event determined by the "historical laws" that govern this industry, and for demonstrating how these events followed "with mathematical precision" from his account of Cuban history. In contrast, while also recognizing the growing grip of foreign capital on Cuba, Ortiz's *Cuban Counterpoint* sought no predictions, no premature closure.

The playful construction of contrasts between tobacco and sugar is certainly countered by a sobering view of the growing domination of capital over Cuban society. As Ortiz states in the conclusion of the book, in response to this domination "many peoples and nations may find in tobacco their own temporary refuge for their oppressed personalities" (1947:309). Yet the first section concludes, in the form of a fairy tale, with a utopian critique of ideological closure. Asserting that "there was never any enmity between sugar and tobacco," Ortiz constructs a historical option which is premised on the alliance of the main actors of Cuban society (just as he had proposed during the political crisis of 1933):

> Therefore it would be impossible for the rhymesters of Cuba to write a "Controversy between Don Tobacco and Doña Sugar," as the roguish archpriest would have liked. Just a bit of friendly bickering, which should end, like the fairy tales, in marrying and living happily ever after. The marriage of tobacco and sugar, and the birth of alcohol, conceived of the unholy ghost, the devil, who is the father of tobacco, in the sweet womb of wanton sugar. The Cuban Trinity: tobacco, sugar and alcohol. It may be that one day the bards of Cuba will sing of how alcohol inherited its virtues from sugar and its mischievous qualities from tobacco; how from sugar, which is mass, it received its force, and from tobacco, which is distinction, its power of inspiration; and how alcohol, the offspring of such parents, is fire, force, spirit, intoxication, thought, and action. (1947:93)

This poetic solution entailed a recognition of the open-ended character of history, of its uncharted possibilities. It is poetic justice that at the end, tobacco and sugar, these impersonators who had taken the license to borrow so many human attributes, would reciprocate by becoming models of the generative powers of the Cuban people. Perhaps *Cuban Counterpoint,* too, is a model of an alternative vision of Cuba, offered to counter those abstract images of its history and its people constructed by procrustean narratives of reified essences.[9]

This utopian allegory, however, bears the marks of its intellectual origins within Cuban reformist nationalism. It conjures up the "unity of a collectivity" (Jameson 1981:291) by means of a typical trope of the liberal imagination: a fruitful marriage-compromise and fusion, rather than conflict or rupture. Ortiz sought national unity through the celebration of the positive and authentic bases of Cuban culture. Yet alcohol, like tobacco and sugar, could not escape from the growing grip of monopoly capital or stimulate more than a transient illusion of commodity within a fractured nation. Ortiz's utopia was imagined within the confines of a neocolonial landscape, revealing, once again, how utopia and ideology constitute each other in the battle over history. As as intervention in this battle, Ortiz's counterpoint stands as an extraordinarily innovative account of Cuban history that challenges colonial histories and prefigures contemporary concerns with the politics and poetics of representation.

Notes

1. An earlier version of this article was presented at the 1988 Latin American Studies Association meetings in New Orleans. I am grateful to John Comaroff, Roberto Da Matta, Paul Friedrich, Roger Rouse, Rafael Sánchez, David Scobey, Rebecca Scott, and Julie Skurski for their comments and valuable suggestions.

2. The difficult task of analyzing capitalist societies' using modes of conceptualization inexorably conditioned by commodity culture is highlighted in important books written by Wolf (1982) and Mintz

(1985). The acrimonious polemic spurred by Taussig's caustic review of these books (Taussig 1989; Wolf and Mintz, 1989) reveals interesting facets of this intellectual difficulty, even as its own variety of academic fetishism mimics the commodity fetishism of the capitalist culture it criticizes. Ironically, despite a nod or two towards Ortiz's work, in this heated exchange occurring at the center about people denied history or voice, Ortiz is left on the periphery.

3. The literature on this subject is vast. Most contemporary thinkers build upon the insights of Marx and Durkheim. For a discussion of anthropological perspectives on totemism and fetishism, see Terence Turner (1985). Also useful is *The Social Life of Things*, edited by Arjun Appadurai (1986); for a perceptive review of this book, see Ferguson (1988).

4. His solution was to "keep Grau as provisional president while changing the structure of the government so as to include representatives of all important political groups, thus working toward a genuine 'national' government" (Aguilar 1972:189). See also Pérez (1986).

5. "No cerebro que llene el cráneo, sino ideas que lo inunden y limpien su modorra. . . . Sólo nos falta una cosa: civilización" (my translation).

6. I am indebted to Julie Skurski for this formulation.

7. Ironically, this denial of a "filial relation to Europe" took place through filial links to Europe, making these enduring ties shape the intellectual landscape in which Afro-Cubans were imagined as a source of culture, not an obstacle to it. This irony reminds me of a cartoon by Quino, the Argentinian humorist, who in a dialogue between Mafalda and Libertad (two young girls who often discuss political affairs) had one of them say: "The problem with Latin Americans is that we always imitate others. We should be like North Americans, who do not imitate anyone."

8. Most of Ortiz's work can be seen as an attempt to represent the richness and complexity of Cuban popular culture. Two significant examples are *La Africanía de la música folklórica de Cuba* (1950) and *Los bailes y el teatro de los negros en el folklore de Cuba* (1951). Because his work made Cubans recognize and appreciate their complex culture, Juan Marinello regarded Ortiz as "the third discoverer of America" (after Columbus and Humboldt) in a tribute to Ortiz published by Casa de las Américas when he died (1969:4).

9. Antonio Benítez Rojo discusses *Cuban Counterpoint* as a

postmodern or proto-postmodern text on the basis of its formal properties and its distance from positivism, in an interesting discussion that parallels my argument concerning the value of this book as a demystifying work and as a model for understanding Caribbean culture (1989:152-57). Because Ortiz's book promiscuously mixes what Benítez Rojo considers to be "premodern" with "modern" and "postmodern" modalities of knowledge, he concludes by defining it as a "dialogic" and "acentric" account (1989:160). While sympathizing with Benítez Rojo's attempt to characterize the originality of this text, I think we would be more faithful to Ortiz's legacy if we spared his book from the tendency to cast Latin American culture in procrustean categories derived from imperial centers. Just as Ortiz uses his familiarity with European culture to supersede modernist perspectives that obstruct the understanding of Cuban history, we may view Ortiz's *Cuban Counterpoint* as a model that challenges rather than instantiates postmodern schemas that blind us to the forces shaping contemporary societies worldwide. Ortiz's book illuminates the dynamic and complex articulation of stabilizing and disruptive historical forces throughout Cuban history and both questions metropolitan assumptions about the existence of separate "premodern" and "modern" domains and demystifies modernity itself. In this light, the representation of the fluid microstories of postmodernity as epistemologically superior to the stable master narrativities of modernity may be seen as an ethnocentric imperial conceit blind to its own condition of possibility. I thank Ricardo Gutiérrez Mouat for making me aware of Antonio Benítez Rojo's work on Ortiz after I presented this paper at the 1990 conference at Notre Dame.

Works Cited

Aguilar, Luis. *Cuba 1933: Prologue to Revolution.* Ithaca: Cornell University Press, 1972.

Appadurai, Arjun, ed. *The Social Life of Things: Commodities in Cultural Perspective.* Cambridge: Cambridge University Press, 1986.

Batista, Fulgeno. *Revolución social o política reformista (once aniversarios)* La Habana: Prensa Indoamericana, 1944.

Benítez Rojo, Antonio. *La isla que se repite.* N.H.: Ediciones del

Norte, 1989. In *The Repeating Island: The Caribbean and the Postmodern Perspective*. Durham, N.C.: Duke University Press, 1992.

Ferguson, James. "Cultural Exchange: New Developments in the Anthropology of Commodities." *Cultural Anthropology* 3, no. 4, November 1988.

González Echevarría, Roberto. *The Voice of the Masters: Writing and Authority in Modern Latin American Literature*. Austin: University of Texas Press, 1985.

Guerra, Ramiro. *Azúcar y población en las Antillas*. La Habana: Cultural S. A., 1927.

Jameson, Fredric. *The Political Unconscious*. Ithaca: Cornell University Press, 1981.

Marinello, Juan. [Untitled.] *Casa de las Américas* 10, no. 55, July–August 1969.

Marx, Karl. *Capital*. Vol. 3. New York: Vintage Books, 1981.

Mintz, Sidney. *Sweetness and Power: The Place of Sugar in Modern History*. New York: Penguin Books, 1985.

Mintz, Sidney, and Eric Wolf. "Reply to Michael Taussig." *Critique of Anthropology* 9, no. 1, Spring 1989, 25–31.

Ortiz, Fernando. *La reconquista de Américas: Reflexiones sobre el Panhispanismo*. Paris: Sociedad de Ediciones Literarias y Artísticas, 1910.

———. *Cuban Counterpoint: Tobacco and Sugar*. New York: A. A. Knopf, 1947.

Pérez, Louis A. *Cuba under the Platt Amendment, 1902–1934*. Pittsburgh: University of Pittsburgh Press, 1986.

———. *Cuba: Between Reform and Revolution*. New York: Oxford University Press, 1988.

Sartre, Jean Paul. *Sartre on Cuba*. Westport, Conn.: Greenwood Press, 1974.

Taussig, Michael. "History as Commodity in Some Recent American (Anthropological) Literature." *Critique of Anthropology* 9, no. 1, Spring 1989, 7–23.

Turner, Terence. "Animal Symbolism, Totemism, and the Structure of Myth." In *Animal Myths and Metaphors in South America*, ed. by Gary Urton. Salt Lake City: University of Utah Press, 1985.

Wolf, Eric. *Europe and the People without History*. Berkeley: University of California Press, 1982.

II

Criticism
in the Contact Zone:
Decentering Community and Nation

MARY LOUISE PRATT

In the spring of 1986 two books appeared within about a week of each other on the United States literary scene, both issued by the large commercial publisher, Random House. One was *Shallow Graves,* an autobiographical work by two women, Wendy Wilder Larsen and Tran Thi Nga. The two authors had met in Vietnam during the war, where Larsen was a reporter and Tran an office worker. Years later, they renewed their relationship in the United States and collaborated to produce this two-part work. It was unusual in form: a verse narrative in English, but following a Vietnamese literary form called the *truyen.*

The second book was a sentimental comic novel called *The Golden Gate* by Vikram Seth.[1] Seth, an East Indian by birth, had trained at Oxford as an economist, studied for several years in China, and wound up in the 1980s working as a book editor in California. His novel, which prominently figures a gay love story, is set in San Francisco. Surprisingly, this book, too, was written as a verse narrative, inspired, according to the author, by his reading of Charles Johnston's English translation of Pushkin's *Eugene Onegin.* Were these books, I wondered as I read the reviews in the Sunday literary supplements, works of American literature? How would one decide? On the basis of the authors' nationalities? (Did they have their green cards?) On the basis of the works' forms? – This certainly not. It would be hard to imagine any more unAmerican activity in 1986 than writing verse narrative. (Indeed, given the Russian and Vietnamese traditions these books drew on, it is perhaps fortunate they were not declared communist footholds in this hemisphere!)

But if *Shallow Graves* and *The Golden Gate* were not works of American literature, whose works were they works of? Who would claim them? In the case of Seth's book I got two answers to that question, both of which could have applied to *Shallow Graves* as well. One colleague said *The Golden Gate* was an example of world literature. Another said, "Oh yeah, you know what that is, it's a California book." Both answers, one invoking a global and the other a regional category, sidestepped altogether the question of the national. And rightly so. These two books, and many others that received notice in the late 1980s, were aggressively *transnational* in character, and readers were called on to receive them as such. Not simply did they challenge the traditional homology of the cultural and national, but, rather, they worked as if no such homology existed or applied. In a course about such texts, my colleague Beverley Allen used the term "postnational."

Among the many global shifts experienced in the momentous and catastrophic 1980s, one of the less catastrophic (or so it has seemed) was the emergence in the domain of culture and the entertainment industry of a "postnational" organizing principle denoted by the label "world." By 1988 the concept was sufficiently established to give rise to a huge "world music" tour in which music groups from a half-dozen countries banded together and played in major cities in every continent. In New York City one of the large-scale artistic experiments that same year was a festival of "world film." Meanwhile, a group of U.S. academics put the finishing touches on a *Norton Anthology of World Literature*. In all these instances, the label "world" was understood, among other things, to signify the laying down of lines of solidarity and intercommunication between first and third worlds. A world film festival meant you could count on seeing cinema from Africa, Asia, and Latin America, as well as from Europe and the United States; the world music tour included groups from at least four continents and visited as many; the anthology of world literature, unlike Norton's other anthologies would be proposing an international canon that included writers from Latin America, Asia, Africa, India, the Caribbean, and the Middle East alongside authors from Europe and North America.[2]

"World" signaled an attempt to heal the wounds of Euro-Imperialism, an often naive effort to dissolve white ethnocentrism and break up the hegemony of first world (Euro-American) cultural norms. The label has a utopian panhumanist flavor in the domain of culture, connoting an integration beyond the pushes and pulls of geopolitics. The latter continue to be denoted by the label "international," as in the international studies programs that began to burgeon in U.S. universities in the 1980s (and whose agenda exclude the arts). Indeed, in the United States at least, a division of labor seemed to emerge between the "international" (read conflict-based) spheres of political and economic interaction and the "world" (read integrated, harmonious) spheres of artistic expression and intercultural understanding. A critique of this utopian dimension may have been what lay behind Fela Kuti's announcement at a June 1990 concert in San Francisco that what he was about to play was not world music, but African music.[3] Or perhaps he was declaring the new hegemony of the non-European – signaling as well he might in California, his autonomy from white metropolitan culture. "World" or otherwise, Kuti's performance remained thoroughly trans- and postnational. There he was in San Francisco, on a bill with Jamaican reggae star Jimmy Cliff, with an audience more diverse than the U.N. General Assembly. In the 1980s both categories, the "world" and the "international," were determined by the unprecedented acceleration of two global-scale phenomena: immigration and communication – flows of people, flows of messages, flows of money.

The transnationalization of culture at the global level has co-incided with the dissolution of correspondence between culture and the national *within* the metropolitan nation-states. Internal social groups with histories and lifeways different from the official ones began insisting in the 1980s on asserting those histories and lifeways *as part of their citizenship,* as the very mode of their membership in the national community. In their dialogues with dominant institutions, many groups began asserting a rhetoric of belonging that made demands beyond representation and civil rights. National institutions responded with, among other things, rhetorics of diversity and multiculturalism whose import at this moment is up for grabs. As an organizing principle for culture, the national has simultaneously exploded and imploded. In the days this paper was written, Canada was facing a crisis produced by its attempt to formulate a constitution that met the demands of French Canadians for recognition as a distinct society and for special powers to go with it. The final blow to the accord came from representatives of Canada's native peoples who rightly claimed they were no less distinct from English Canada than the Québecois.[4] In the era of multiculturalism, constitutions cannot be written as they have been in the past, and perhaps they cannot be written at all. On the other hand, it was unclear what Canada could be if it were to be neither an appendage to Britain nor a nation with a constitution. In the postnational period, new situations develop, yet nationalism, nationhood, and the nation-state remain overarching historical determinants. As this paper was drafted in March of 1990 the new nation of Namibia was "born," as they say (Who, one asks, was its mother?), out of processes of decolonization begun in the 1950s, while the breakup of the Soviet Union was being swept along by an over-powering reassertion of nationhoods, nationalisms, and national boundaries.

In what follows I propose to speak further about shifts in cultural understanding in relation to the implosion/explosion of the national. I shall first address some questions of theoretical and political perspective. Specifically, in connection with the trans/ postnational era, I want to consider ways to decenter the communal and fraternal modes of understanding that have organized discussion of nationalisms and subnationalisms. I shall then read some of my proposals back into literary history, examining a tradition of critical reflection on the national in nineteenth-century writings by Latin American women.

As Benedict Anderson has argued, in prevailing conceptions the nation represents itself to itself as a community, an "imagined community" whose members, without knowing each other face to face or even by name, imagine themselves as linked to each other by horizontal, fraternal bonds.[5] The nation as a whole is imagined as discrete and autonomous. The power of these imaginings, Anderson argues, is most starkly embodied in the figure of the citizen-soldier, who is willing "not so much to kill as to die" for them (Anderson, 15).

This fraternal, communal conception of the social bond has permeated the self-understanding of modern societies, shaping the ways they represent themselves to themselves, as well as the ways they represent others to themselves. Elsewhere I have examined how the identification of nation and citizenhood with language has marked modern linguistic thinking, producing what I called a "linguistics of community."[6] Sociolinguistic scholarship has typically defined as its object of study the "speech community," construed as a largely unified and homogeneous social world. Behind, or within, the concept of the speech community stands the idealized model of the nation-state, a unified totality with a discrete, fraternally shared national language. Assumptions of community have often meant that linguistic hierarchy, social differentiation, and conflict have tended to get bleached out of the picture or to be assigned the status of aberrations and deviations from the code. Social hierarchies get explicitly horizontalized and implicitly reproduced by such analyses, even when resistance to hierarchy is discussed. In community models, internal social differentiation is commonly represented in terms of identity, of people being members of different (sub)communities (class, ethnic, gender). In language, this means that people are identified as speakers of different discrete language varieties (such as Black English Vernacular or women's speech).

I want to suggest adding an optic that decenters community (and its corollary, identity) to focus on how social bonds operate across lines of difference, hierarchy, and unshared or conflicting assumptions. Such an approach would consider how differences and hierarchies are produced *in and through contact* across such lines. Class, ethnic, and gender differences would be analyzed not in terms of people's memberships in particular communities but in terms of the production and reproduction of those differences in the socially structured *contact* between groups bound together in their separateness. Such a "contact perspective" would assume the heterogeneity of a social group and would place in the foreground the relationality of meaning. A contact perspective would see a phenomenon like segregation as consisting not just of separateness or mutual isolation, which is how segregation defines itself, but as a form of togetherness that assumes the socially and historically structured copresence of groups within a space – a contact zone. In such a perspective, the "invisibility" of colonized and subaltern groups to the consciousness of a dominant group would be understood not as what it declares itself to be, that is, invisibility (*B* does not exist for *A*), but as a form of copresence (*B* is there to *A* in the form of the denial of *B*'s presence; *B* can only be "not seen" if *B* is first there and known to be there). Invisibility names the subaltern's presence for the dominant party.

In a contact perspective, borders are placed in effect at the center of concern while homogeneous centers move to the margins. Interestingly, that is pretty much how the world looks from "minority" or subaltern perspective: economic and civic life is likely to be conducted in contact zones, ongoingly comprising struggles to operate in institutions made by others. Fraternity and homogeneity are found, if at all, in safe spaces at the margins to those alien institutions.

To sum up, then, a contact perspective decenters community to look at how signification works across and through lines of difference and hierarchy. Rather than circumscribing the object of study, those lines are within it. The idea is to capture the relationality of meaning not as a structural phenomenon, as in Saussurian *langue,* but in social historical dimensions. In a shorthand way, one could say that a perspective of community can give you race, sex, class, or national identity, but you need a perspective of contact to give you the dynamics of race-ism, sexism, class-ism, or national-ism. With respect to language, for instance, a linguistics of contact would set aside the homology of one person/one language/one community and take up the fact that many, probably most, people in the world are native speakers of more than one language; the fact that nobody's world is linguistically or socially homogeneous; the fact that dominant and nondominant knowledges and lifeways are copresent in the communal (or national) social spaces; and the fact that everybody can understand many more varieties of language than they can produce.

These issues of community and contact have obvious consequences for approaching the dynamics of literature and the national. Ethnic literatures, for example, at least in the U.S., are often conceptualized as expressions of particular communities or identities. But within ethnic (especially Chicano) studies, this perspective is being complemented by another point of view that regards ethnic cultures not in terms of their autonomy and discreteness but as something quite different: as borderlands, sites of ongoing critical and inventive interaction with the dominant culture, as permeable contact zones across which significations move in many directions. This proposition was dramatically explored by Gloria Anzaldúa in her influential book *Borderlands/ La Frontera: The New Mestiza.*[7] Writing as a Chicana lesbian working-class philosopher, Anzaldúa refused to locate herself within any single identity or community. She adopted a mestiza perspective from which she advances agenda for the whole society. This permeable, borderlands perspective is not expected to replace the constructs of autonomy, authenticity, and community which often legitimate minority discourses. It rather adds a relational optic, specifically a way of making claims for the inventiveness and ongoing criticalness of ethnic cultures and

minority perspectives. It brings into relief their engagement with
other occupants of the contact zone, and their *availability to* reception outside the subnational community. That this perspective
has been developed by Chicano/a cultural critics and theorists
for whom the border exists not as a line but as an absolutely
distinctive cultural space is no accident.

A borderlands or "contact" perspective assigns ethnic cultural
practices and intellectual production a particular kind of authority in the contact zone. Obviously it must be possible for ethnic
intellectuals, without renouncing their ethnicity, to make claims
as intellectuals and leaders of everybody; otherwise "minority"
is always going to mean subaltern, and ethnic artists and intellectuals will face only the choice either to assimilate or to be contained as the incarnation of a circumscribed culture.[8]

A related point can be made with respect to what must be
a paradigmatic art of the contact zone, the testimonio. Here is
a genre, treated brilliantly in this volume, in which a hierarchical relationship between a metropolitan intellectual and a proletarian activist produces a collaboration aimed at intervening in
metropolitan and elite consciousness. Such texts raise the possibility, and necessity, of reading habits and critical practices
tailored for the arts of the contact zone. The authority that testimonios claim for themselves is anchored mainly in community
and authenticity. Those of us who wish to transmit the works'
authority and political force often find ourselves with nothing
to say as critics, for the critic's task is to understand works in
ways other than the ways they understand themselves; our work
is to seek, as papers in this volume do, critical frameworks not
coterminous with the authority structures of the text. It involves,
for instance, theorizing both parties in the text-producing collaboration of testimonio, and theorizing the political force of that
collaboration.

Another context where contact perspectives have been shaping critical thought is the colonial discourse movement. Unfold-
ing over the ten years following the appearance of Edward Said's
Orientalism in 1978, this movement has striven for forms of textual and political understanding that decenter an autonomous

authentic Europe and center the histories of contact between Europe and other parts of the world, especially Africa and Asia. This work has reshaped many people's understanding of the global orders of meaning that have underwritten capitalism and imperialism. Focusing initially on the ways Europe (and Euro-America) has represented others to itself, colonial discourse studies have undertaken to see the west *in its relations* with other parts of the world. It has countered the orthodox diffusionist view of the west which sees the west as rising *sui generis* the diffusing outwards as capital, as empire, as civilization. The colonial discourse movement itself is a contact zone. Its challenge to Eurocentrism has been possible only through the impact on the western academy of African, Asian, and Latin American intellectuals.[9] Diffusionist logic is uncontradictable from within.

In showing how Europe has sought to make the rest of the world, the colonial discourse movement has also demonstrated the ways in which the west is made by, and makes itself out of, the rest of the world. When the west is seen as constructed from the outside in, expansionism and the history of global contact no longer appear incidental to its "identity"; Europe becomes unthinkable apart from these activities.[10]

Long before the colonial discourse movement, Venezuelan novelist and essayist Teresa de la Parra made just this point in her novel *Memorias de Mama Blanca* (1929). Her memorable character, the elderly aristocrat Mama Blanca, argues that romanticism was born in the Americas, not Europe. Its emblem is the empress Josephine, a *criolla* from the Caribbean. "I believe," says Mama Blanca,

> that like tobacco, pineapple, and sugar cane, Romanticism was an indigenous [i.e., American] fruit that grew up sweet, spontaneous and hidden among colonial languors and tropical indolence until the end of the eighteenth century. Around that time, Josefina Tascher [later the empress Josephine], unsuspectingly, as if she were an ideal microbe, carried it off [to Europe] tangled up in the lace of one of her headdresses, gave the germ to Napoleon in that acute form which we all know, and little by

little, the troops of the First Empire, assisted by Chateaubriand, spread the epidemic everywhere.[11]

It is a richly transculturated set of images. The reference to head-dresses recalls the iconography of America as an Amazon with a huge feather headdress carrying the head of a Spaniard by the hair; the image of the microbe recalls the history of syphilis as the disease of empire, blamed by Europeans on America and by Americans on Europe.

It is of course no accident that this contestatory, anti-eurocentric figure of romanticism is articulated by a woman character (Mama Blanca) about a woman agent (Josephine) in a text by a woman writer (de la Parra). The role of cultural mediatrix here is a direct corollary of woman's status as the object of exchange between men. She is seen as both conqueror and infiltrator of France's fraternal communal edifice. One is struck that de la Parra's character identifies the site of the transcultural "infection" as the army, the institution Benedict Anderson marks as the quintes-sential embodiment of nationalism and citizenhood. The army as guarantor of the integrity of the nation contrasts with Mama Blanca's equally true-to-life image of the army as a contact zone which on the borders and peripheries of the national terrain becomes the point of entry for external "infection": transcultural contact imaged as sexual and venereal. With respect to the inher-ently male national and imperial subject, the transcultural Other is a woman.

So, in fact, have women writers often defined themselves in their dialogues with the national. Not as venereal infectors, to be sure, but as outsiders and mediators whose authority is con-structed out of the very ambiguity of their citizenship. From the moment they were denied equal political and legal rights, the relation of women to ideologies of the nation and to the imag-ined fraternal community was sharply differentiated from that of men. However inevitable it may seem, this was a tragic turn in the history of society, for it created within all nations a struc-ture of exclusion involving fully half the membership of all classes, including elites.[12] Despite its neoclassical vocabulary, José María

Heredia's poem "Plan de estudios," which appeared in Cuba in 1822, fairly laid out the prescription for containing and disenfranchising women that accompanied nineteenth-century nation building. "A Minerva te consagras?" the poem begins ("To Minerva you devote yourself?"):

> Perdone Amor tu imprudencia:
> Advierte que tanta ciencia
> No es propia de la beldad.[13]

Conquest and empire figure in particular among the knowledges the woman subject should avoid:

> En el mapa nunca busques
> Los climas tristes, lejanos,
> Que de griegos y romanos
> Vieron el bélico ardor
> (Heredia, 11.25-28)

"La política historia" should also be avoided: "En la cansada lectura/Crimen, furor y locura//Tus ojos fatigarán" (Heredia, 11.42-44). As might be expected, the poet's final recommendation is the sweet oblivion of romantic love: "Yo te amo . . . Sabiendo amarme? No quieras aprender más" (Heredia, 11.55-56).

Structurally speaking, the disenfranchisement of women from the fraternal national community produces within the space of the nation a radical instability that is held in check only by intense degrees of coercion, much of it exercised directly at the level of the body. As *occupants* but not full members of nations, women who have had access to the public sphere have engaged critically with the habits of mind of national imaginaries. In politics, autonomous women's movements have most commonly been internationalist and antimilitary, for example. In letters, at least in Latin America, women intellectuals over the past hundred-fifty years have operated in terms not of national patrimonies (which have typically excluded their own work) but of eclectic, transnational canons. As commentators, journal editors, translators, anthologizers, and mentors, they have often made transnational cultural mediation the focus of their cultural work.[14] As creative writers, they have often played in fascinating ways with the cultural imaginary of the nation, in texts that the nation-culture homology made unreadable or often invisible. Once that homology is decentered, such texts come into view and become intelligible. I propose to end with some remarks on two such texts by Spanish American women, written during the mid-nineteenth century, when nation building, autonomy, and self-identity were overarching preoccupations of the creole elites.[15] In both, I argue, the women establish a subject position on the borderlands of nationalist ideology, with one foot in and one foot out.

The first text is the opening of a novella by the Argentine writer Juana Manuela Gorriti, composed in the 1850s during her exile from the dictatorship of Juan Manuel Rosas. Titled "Una ojeada a la patria" ("A Look at the Fatherland"), the text opens with the narrator-protagonist traveling on foot through a dense forest from which she emerges to contemplate the landscape of her youth. An "infortunio inaúdito" had obliged her and her "brillante familia" to abandon their homeland, and only she has survived to return:

> Mis ojos se fijaron con una mirada profunda de indecible gozo, de indecible dolor, en aquel encantado panorama, que presente incesantemente a mi memoria, se desarrollaba en ese momento ante mi.
>
> En ese mi pequeño universo de otro tiempo, yo sola había cambiado: todo estaba como en el día, como en el instante en que lo dejé.[16]

> My eyes rested, with a gaze of deep, unspeakable joy, on that enchanted vista which, eternally present to my memory, now displayed itself before me. In this my little universe of yester-year, only I had changed; everything else remained as it was the day, the instant that I left it.

Green hills, flowered meadows, a sparkling river spread out before her, along with the ruins of a Jesuit mission, a cemetery, and her family's hacienda (now owned, interestingly enough, by a Spaniard). The narrator-protagonist, we find out, is a woman traveling disguised as a man. She also suffers, she tells us, from a mysterious and dreaded sickness. On her arrival at her former ancestral home, the new owner, ignorant of her identity, offers her the rural hospitality so many travelers have written about. She is shown to her old bedroom where childhood drawings by her and her sister still hang on the walls. Even nature is not primal, but saturated with history and memory:

> Cada árbol, cada hoja, cada recodo del camino despertaba en mí alma un mundo de dolorosos recuerdos. . . . Aquel llano interminable a la vista conduce a Ortega . . . y en esa verde esplanada hacíamos correr, carcolear y dar saltos a nuestros caballos. (Gorriti, 111)

This narrative of return furnishes the frame story for a longer tale of a local outlaw figure name Gubi Amaya.

Despite its dreamlike atmosphere, Gorriti's title, "Una ojeada a la patria," invites a reading within the discourse of the national. As soon as one attempts such a reading, this landscape of ruins and memory enters into relation with another one common to creole literature of this period: the empty, primal landscape of America invoked by so many of the reinventors of America in the period of independence and its aftermath. Readers of canonical Latin American literature will remember how many of the foundational texts of the independence period open with a panorama of the vast and empty American wilderness, the future national territory onto which the writer goes on to inscribe the march of human history. Andrés Bello's "Silva a la agricultura en la zona tórrida" follows this pattern, as do other *independentista* classics: Heredia's "En el teocalli de Cholula," Echeverría's "La cautiva", and of course Sarmiento's *Facundo*. This foundational trope couples the question of the national with issues of territory and mastery.[17] The potential master is the creole speaking subject, the new American citizen who is the seer in these panoramas and who himself remains unseen. His actual historical agency as yet remains unspecified; his hegemony is imagined but remains to be established. The primal empty landscape is staked out as the point of departure for a new beginning of history and a new hegemony. This landscape, as I have argued elsewhere, is transculturated (not simply copied) by creole nation-builders from European discourses on America, especially that founded at the turn of the century by Alexander von Humboldt.[18]

Gorriti's narrator, though disguised as a man, does not mimic this discourse of territory and mastery when she looks out on the *patria*. The homeland she depicts is neither primal nor empty, but is saturated with a history *whose continuity she is trying to restore*. She depicts herself not as an invisible and static observer but as an agent already in motion (she is running, in fact, in the opening scene). What is implied, I would suggest, is a very different national project and a different foundation for citizenship in the nation-building period. Gorriti's narrator-protagonist is a survivor of the old order whose task is to recover the shreds of it left following revolutionary upheaval. Her project is weak and vulnerable – the woman is solitary, sick, forced to conceal her gender in order to enter the fatherland at all. (One recalls Gabriela Mistral in the *Poema de Chile* descending into the national landscape as a returning ghost.)[19] Fragility is not the only gendered feature of this role Gorriti's protagonist defines for herself. Survivorship and continuity constitute women's work, and their national duty in times of crisis and war; they are the essential, omnipresent complements of the work of the solider-citizen, the condition of possibility for his fraternal heroics. This complementarity of soldiering and survivorship has, not surprisingly, been overlooked both by ideologies and by theories of nationalism. In Gorriti's story, written by a woman of intense political engagement, survivorship and continuity appear as historical mandates, albeit fragile, sick, and in disguise.

About the same time as Gorriti wrote her story, the Cuban writer Gertrudis Gómez de Avellaneda, living in Spain, wrote a poem that likewise revises the foundational Americanist landscape. The poem is titled "El viajero americano" ("The American Traveler"). It was written, Avellaneda says in a footnote, in response to an ambitious young writer who had written a poem congratulating her on her work and expressing his opinion that "sólo la gloria es un bien grande, capaz de llenar el alma y de satisfacer los deseos del corazón humano" ("only glory is a great good able to fulfill the soul and satisfy the desires of the human heart").[20] We are in the realm of romantic *poesía cívica*.

Avellaneda's response opens with a traveler's vision of the canonical Americanist panorama, reminiscent both of Humboldt and of Avellaneda's compatriot and mentor José María Heredia:

> Del Anahuac vastísimo y hermoso
> En una de las fértiles comarcas,
> De las que tienen por custodios fieles
> Al Pinahuizapan y al Orizaba;
> Que unidos por cadena inmensurable
> De montañas agrestes y escarpadas,
> Con nieve eterna ornadas sus cabezas,
> Se alzan a ser de una región de encantos
> Inmutables y enormes atalayas
>   (Avellaneda, 11.1-9)

There on the edge of a "great savannah" the "spellbound traveler" sees "a new paradise" ("un nuevo paraíso") of "jardines bellos de abundantes galas, / Con cenadores, parques, grutas, bosques, / y lagos mil de cristalinas aguas" (Avellaneda, 11.20-22). Without hesitation the traveler flings himself toward the vision and arrives exhausted to find only "un gran desierto que tapizan lavas" (Avellaneda, 1.41). The moral of the story, of course, is laid out in the final stanza:

> Pues esa gloria – que tu afán exista –
> Tan deslumbrante y bella en lontananza,
> Y esa ventura que en su goce finges,
> Son ilusiones ópticas del alma!
>   (Avellaneda, 11.44-47)

In what one might call its preferred reading, this text presents a moral and spiritual rather than a national allegory: ambition leads to illusions and disappointments. Yet beginning with its

title, the poem is firmly engaged with the foundational Americanist rhetoric of its time, whose utopian aspirations it reduces
to mirages of ambition in a great desert of lava. The culminating
image of a field of congealed lava is telling. In the early nineteenth century, America's volcanos became a widespread metonymy for America's untapped and untamed energies. They
were cast both as objects of scientific fascination (beginning with
Humboldt's classic essay in *Views of Nature* [1806]) and as social metaphors ("A great volcano lies at our feet," wrote Simón
Bolívar in 1826. "Who shall restrain the oppressed classes?")[21]
The desert of lava where Avellaneda's mid-century American
traveler ends up is a particularly Spanish American, postindependence version of desiccated hopes and stagnated dreams.
While Gorriti in "Una ojeada a la patria" sketched an alternative set of significations, Avellaneda takes up the civic rhetoric
of her immediate forbears (including the poet Heredia, her some-
time tutor) and hangs it out to dry. Interestingly, the authority
of the speaker in this poem is generational, but not, so it seems,
maternal.

By the first decades of the twentieth century, both nationalism and feminism were firmly and self-consciously established
in Spanish America, and subjects of widespread public discussion. In this context, a gendered critique of nationalist ideologies surfaced more explicitly than before. I would like to end
with a text in which two woman intellectuals of this period collaborate to explode the categories of the national in ways designed to produce a genuine culture shock. The text is an interview between Chileans Amanda Labarca Hubertson and Inés
Echeverría Bello which appeared in the magazine *Familia* in 1915,
and which has been brought to light by the Chilean scholar Marcela Prado.[22] Labarca was one of the founders of socialist feminism in Latin America; Inés Echeverría, who often published
under the pseudonym IRIS, was an absolutely noncanonical
Chilean writer of aristocratic background who had run one of the
most liberal literary salons in Chile, and had published several

volumes of essays and reminiscences. She went on to write a thousand-page trilogy of historical novels following the trajectory of Chile since independence. This fact will seem entirely at odds with what follows. The interview reads like a vehemently perverse playing-out of the categories of Heredia's "Plan de estudios" (AL=Amanda Labarca, IE=Inés Echeverría):

> AL: ¿Por qué ha escrito Ud. en francés su último libro *Entre deux mondes?*
>
> IE: Porque es el idioma de mi arte; porque yo pienso y siento en francés.
>
> AL: ¿A usted no le gusta el castellano?
>
> IE: ¡No! ¡mil veces no! El castellano es para mí la lengua de la cocinera, del proveedor, de las cuentas de la casa . . . Si alguna vez me riñeron fue en castellano . . . ¿Y usted quiere que lo ame?

Echeverría presents herself as having fully and uncritically acquired the (impoverished) identity that the nation assigned to her. Her national consciousness is constituted by ignorance, infantility, and domesticity. She goes on to apply the same deconstructive maneuver to the race and class dimensions of her nationality, identifying them as fraternal associations which she likewise was never taught to feel:

> Los que estuvieron cerca de mí en los años dúctiles de la infancia y en los años milagrosos de la juventud, no hicieron nada por desarrollar en mí esa solidaridad racial. Hasta los treinta años yo fui una cosa, algo que habría podido llamarse sin desmedro un ser esclavo y hasta inconsciente. ¡Y pensar que aquí hay mujeres que no pasan nunca de los treinta!

Patriarchal categories are inverted and laid bare. In nationalist ideologies women's social and civic value is defined exclusively in terms of her reproductive and nurturing functions, her role as mother of citizens rather than as citizen herself. Here Inés Echeverría depicts herself in her reproductive years ("hasta los treinta años") as "a thing, an enslaved, even unconscious creature"– a feminist version of the masculinist ideal. Labarca goes on to raise the question of patriotism, eliciting a response that explicitly questions both the image of horizontal brotherhood and the image of America as land of freedom and promise:

AL: ¿Y la patria tampoco habla a su conciencia de artista ni a su alma de chilena?

IE: Menos todavía. ¿Qué es la patria? ¿Quién la puede definir? ¿Por qué han de ser más hermanos míos los que ven ocultarse el sol tras de los mares que los que lo vieron esconderse detrás de las montañas? A mí no me educaron en el amor a la patria ni yo lo he aprendido a sentir después. Amo la Europa mucho más que la America, porque a pesar de que aquí hay solamente repúblicas y suele haber allá monarquías, puede vivirse en ellas una vida más libre, más consciente, menos llena de enredos, de chismes, de pequeñeces; más amplia.

I suggested earlier that this interview could be read as a feminist response to Heredia's "Plan de estudios," especially given its emphasis on education, that is, national subject-formation. In Echeverría's self-description, Heredia's "plan de estudios" indeed succeeded in producing the unlettered "ser esclavo" his poem called for – "hasta los treinta años." After that, however, the unconscious "thing" has somehow become something else: a cosmopolitan woman of letters with no feeling for her nation or her race. A dangerous being.

In the space Labarca offers through her highly strategic questions, Echeverría constructs a highly strategic self-representation that blows the whistle on the bankruptcy of the official national interpellation of women. She does so not by refuting that interpellation, but by presenting herself as a full-fledged product of its workings. One can read Echeverría's discourse through an optic of identity and community, seeing it as an expression of her eccentricity and her aristocratic class. This is the way her work has tended to be read, when it has been read at all.[23] From a perspective of contact, however, Echeverría and Labarca look more like the coproducers of a testimonio. Sitting down together, a renegade aristocrat and a socialist feminist politician, they create a contact zone; in the guise of personal history, their collaboration produces a transgressive, interruptive engagement with the official categories of nationhood and community.

Notes

1. Wendy Wilder Larsen and Tran Thi Nga, *Shallow Graves;* Vikram Seth, *The Golden Gate* (both New York: Random House, 1986).

2. As this language suggests, countries have been replaced in the "world" discourse by continental labels.

3. I am indebted to Mike Soto for sharing this anecdote with me.

4. The claim to Québecois distinctness was anchored, of course, in culture. See Richard Handler, *Nationalism and the Politics of Culture in Quebec* (Madison: University of Wisconsin Press, 1988).

5. Benedict Anderson, *Imagined Communities: Reflections on the Origin and Spread of Nationalism* (London: Verso, 1983).

6. For this discussion see Mary Louise Pratt, "Linguistic Utopias," in Fabb et al., eds., *The Linguistics of Writing* (Manchester: University Press, 1987).

7. Gloria Anzaldúa, *Borderlands/La Frontera* (San Francisco: Spinsters/Aunt Lute, 1988).

8. These issues came into play recently in the U.S. in the national controversy that broke out when a Florida judge banned a rap album released by the group 2 Live Crew, for its obscene and violent lyrics. Attempts to vindicate the album from within black culture as an expression of parodic, carnivalesque vernacular culture were refuted by other black commentators who found such an argument paralyzingly acritical. The question arose as to whether and how in a multiethnic public, values could be formulated that would apply in a genuinely equal fashion.

9. A partial list of such figures includes, for example, Edward Said, Talal Asad, Gayatri Chakravorty Spivak, Homi Bhabha, Abdul Jan Mohamed, V. Y. Mudimbe.

10. For a fuller discussion, see Mary Louise Pratt, *Imperial Eyes* (London: Routledge, 1992), chapter 6.

11. Teresa de la Parra, *Memorias de Mama Blanca,* in *Obra* (Caracas: Biblioteca Ayacucho, 1982), p. 329.

12. It is also true that groups other than women were disenfranchised on grounds of race, property ownership, and other factors. However, gender was the broadest of such exclusions.

13. José María Heredia, "Plan de estudios," in *Poesías líricas* (Paris: G. Hermanos, 1893), pp. 70-71.

14. One thinks, for instance, of such women as Victoria Ocampo in Argentina, Nélida Vientós in Puerto Rico, Gabriela Mistral in Chile and Mexico, Clorinda Matto de Turner in Peru.

15. See the essays in *Women, Culture, and Politics in Latin America,* The Seminar on Feminism and Culture (Berkeley: University of California Press, 1990).

16. Juana Manuela Gorriti, "Una ojeada a la patria," in *Gubi Amaya o la historia de un salteador,* collected in *Sueños y realidads* (Buenos Aires, 1865), pp. 109-120.

17. One cannot help remarking what the new rulers of Namibia said in the spring of 1990; Namibian independence was celebrated with the words: "Now we are masters of this pastoral land of our ancestors. . . . The destiny of this country is now in our own hands" (*New York Times,* 21 March 1990, p. 1).

18. I draw here on the fuller discussion of these dynamics in Pratt, *Imperial Eyes,* chapters 7-8.

19. Gabriela Mistral, *Poema de Chile,* ed. Doris Dana, 1954. The volume was not completed during Mistral's lifetime and was published posthumously.

20. Gertrúdis Gómez de Avellaneda, "El viajero americano," in *Obra completa, Obras literarias* (Madrid: Imprenta Rivadeneyra, 1869), pp. 213-214.

21. Simón Bolívar, Letter to General Paez, 8 August 1626, in Michael Bierck, ed., *Selected Writings of Simon Bolivar* (New York: Colonial Press, 1951), vol. 2, p. 628.

22. Marcela Prado Traverso, "Novelistas chilenas, inicios y transición de siglo xix a xx," Ph.D. dissertation, Stanford University, 1991. I am indebted to Prado for her sharing her findings with me. Her dissertation is the first serious study on the work of Echeverría Bello.

23. For a comprehensive review of critical reception of Echeverría Bello's work, see Prado, op. cit. 1991, especially chapter 2.

Residual Authority
and Gendered Resistance

AMY KAMINSKY

"Can the subaltern speak?"
– Gayatri Spivak (1988)

"Yes, you just haven't been listening."
– Myra Santos (1990)

Soy Isabel Moncada, nacida de Martín Moncada y de Ana Cué-
tara de Moncada, en el pueblo de Ixtepec el primero de diciem-
bre de 1907. En piedra me convertí el cinco de octubre de 1927
delante de los ojos espantados de Gregoria Juárez. Causé la
desdicha de mis padres y la muerte de mis hermanos Juan y
Nicolás. Cuando venía a pedirle a la Virgen que me curara del
amor que tengo por el general Francisco Rosas que mató a mis
hermanos, me arrepentí y preferí el amor del hombre que me
perdió y perdió a mi familia. Aquí estaré con mi amor a solas
como recuerdo del porvenir por los siglos de los siglos. (Garro,
295)

Elena Garro's novel, *Los recuerdos del porvenir,* ends with
these words engraved in a rock, words ascribed to a woman who,
according to them, betrayed her brother and her family because
she was helplessly in love with her enemy. Written in stone, un-

alterable, this is the compelling story of woman's fickle nature, the danger of her unbridled passion, the catastrophe of her sexuality unleashed on an entire community. Though Garro gives ample evidence in the text that the stone's inscription is of questionable validity, even feminist readers have failed to challenge it. This willingness to give credence to a narrative that reinforces traditional power relationships and retells a familiar story about women's lives is attributable to residual authority.

By "residual authority" I refer to that authority which is still brought to bear on the production and reception of texts, despite oppositional feminist literary acts such as writing, narrating, and reading that call into question the authoritative discourses of male domination, as well as those of, for example, class hierarchy and European rationalism. Residual authority is not a quality of any particular text, author, or reader but, rather, is an effect that floats among them in the literary process. It may occur as a culturally conditioned reading effect, as in *Los recuerdos del porvenir;* or in relation to the kind of critical strategy evident in the class-based reading of Rosario Ferré's *Maldito amor;* or as a deliberate narrative strategy, as in Luisa Valenzuela's *Aquí pasan cosas raras.*[1]

As readers of *Los recuerdos del porvenir* we are called on to accept, and do, that the town itself, looking down on itself, narrates its own story. We are asked to believe, and do, that the town is frozen as if in a movie still, while the beautiful Julia Alvarado makes her escape with a mysterious stranger who was, perhaps, her lover in an earlier time. Our socialization as readers of fiction encourages us to suspend rational disbelief over and over in reading this story. When it comes to the reading of the Isabel-stone, on the other hand, our socialization into the culture's gender mythology induces us to accept its familiar validity. Yet a close reading of Isabel's lapidary confession calls into serious question the truth of its claim. Though the text engraved in the stone is written in the first person and attributed to Isabel, she did not put it there; the curandera, Gregoria, carved Isabel's "confession" into the rock.

Whenever she appears, Gregoria misinterprets what she sees,

relying on clichés born of traditional gender ideology to make sense of events. Called on to heal Julia after her lover, General Rosas, beats her, Gregoria mistakenly assumes that Julia – who at every moment displays nothing but passive, indifferent acquiescence toward the general – seduced Rosas with a love potion, not that Rosas kidnapped Julia as war booty. Ever interested in enlarging her knowledge of herbal remedies and potions, Gregoria asks Julia, "–Y dígame, perdonando la curiosidad, ¿qué hierba le dio usted allá en su tierra para ponerlo así? . . .

> – Ninguna, Gregoria.
> ¿A poco él solito se engrió tanto?
> – Sí Gregoria, él solito. (Garro, 125)

Later, summoned to accompany Isabel to the cemetery when the young woman is urged to beg Rosas to spare her brother's life, she classifies Isabel first as self-sacrificing sister and then as unrepentant whore. Gregoria thinks Isabel needs to pray to the Virgin to release her from her sexual frenzy, and when Isabel dashes away to confront her traitorous lover, Gregoria can interpret that only as the weakness of the flesh. It is Gregoria who wants Isabel to confess, and when Isabel refuses, Gregoria manufactures the confession herself. She has no capacity for comprehending the subtlety of the three-way relationship among Isabel, her brother Nicolás, and Rosas. She is unaware that Isabel has no concern for propriety and cannot understand that Isabel's passionate chase after Rosas is not an act of sexual desire. At the moment Isabel realizes that Rosas has betrayed her and shot her brother, Gregoria's weeping prevents her from seeing Isabel's dry-eyed reaction:

> Gregoria se acomodó junto a Isabel y lloró con la dulzura de los que conocen la desdicha y la aceptan. Se ensimismó en sus lágrimas, sin mirar a Isabel, perdida en una soledad sin llanto. (Garro, 290–291)

Gregoria does not question misfortune; unlike Isabel, who has tried to interrupt history by participating in the Cristero rebellion, Gregoria is a fatalist. Which means that the story, for her, is already written. The words she inscribes on the stone as Isabel's omit Isabel's apparent betrayal of both a political cause and her community's struggle, a further indication that Gregoria is unable to see women outside the prescribed familial/sexual sphere.

In the final scene between Isabel and Gregoria, the old woman, steeped in traditional lore, continues to invoke the tragic story of sin and lust, and with her questions and observations about love, banishment, and repentance. Isabel's silence in response to Gregoria suggests that these terms are meaningless to her, and her declaration that she must see the general again after he has executed her brother has less to do with the desire to return to a lover's bed than it does with a desire to confront a murderer. If Gregoria misunderstands, Rosas certainly does not. After ordering the execution of Nicolás, Rosas flees, fearful of having to look Isabel in the eye and of seeing himself accused once more. Gregoria, however, caught in clichés about love and sexual desire, interprets Isabel's words in the manner of soap opera. The narrator, whose knowledge is the collective wisdom of the town and so, in a circular manner, depends on Gregoria's own report of the incident, tells how Isabel disappeared from Gregoria's view, to be found much later, transformed into stone:

> – ¡Aunque Dios me condene quiero ver a Francisco Rosas otra vez!
>
> Su voz sacudió la colina y llegó hasta las puertas de Ixtepec. De sus ojos salieron rayos y una tempestad de rizos negros le cubrió y se levantó un remolino de polvo que volvió invisible la mata de pelo. En su carrera para encontrar a su amante, Isabel Moncada se perdió. Después de mucho buscarla, Gregoria la halló tirada muy abajo, convertida en una piedra, y aterrada se santiguó. Algo le decia que la niña Isabel no quería salvarse: estaba muy sembrada en el general Francisco Rosas. (Garro, 293–294)

The "something" that told Gregoria that Isabel did not want to be saved, that she was too infatuated with Rosas to accept Christian forgiveness, is nothing more than the consecrated story

of women's unbridled passion. Gregoria is a believer in authority, and the story she tells is not an intentional lie but rather the
best explanation she can find for Isabel's disappearance. Ixtepec
believes it too. What is remarkable is that contemporary readers
also believe Gregoria's version of the events. Not even sophisticated feminist analyses of this text have questioned the reliability of Gregoria's story.[2]

This "misreading" of Garro's text is attributable to the extratextual common knowledge deriving from dominant modes of
discourse that find their way into the production and reception
of literary texts that I am calling "residual authority." Nancy K.
Miller deals with this problem from another angle, when she discusses the ways in which women-authored texts are discredited:

> The critical reaction to any given text is hermeneutically bound
> to another and preexistent text: the *doxa* of socialities. Plausi-
> bility, then, is an effect of reading through a grid of concor-
> dance. . . . If no maxim is available to account for a particular
> piece of behavior, that behavior is read as unmotivated and un-
> convincing. . . . A heroine without a maxim, like a rebel with-
> out a cause, is destined to be misunderstood. (Miller, 36)

If women's writing is "unconvincing" when it achieves a new
plot, as Miller argues, then to find ways to read it as conforming
to the old plot is a strategy for making sense of it. Gregoria's
"reading" of Isabel follows this model. This is neither Gregoria's
conscious decision nor the novel's reader's but rather residual
authority operating to make sense of a text that might otherwise
be discredited on account of its transgressive nature.

Manuel Alcide Jofré's neat taxonomy of literary communication is useful in describing the way residual authority functions.
Looking at the communicative process, he shows how the "emitter" and the "receiver" of the text are both affected by the multiple and often contradictory codes that determine discourse. He
offers hope that textual analysis can help disentangle the way
that elements of different discourses affect the production and
reception of texts, for our purposes, to unmask residual authority: "el análisis textual o análisis de discurso podría servir para

mostrar cómo los textos toman elementos provenientes de diferentes discursos" (Alcide Jofré, 210).

Alcide Jofré echoes Joanna Russ's classic argument that the stranglehold of the How-She-Fell-in-Love and the How-She-Went-Mad stories cannot be broken using traditional narrative patterns.[3] For his part, Alcide Jofré claims that the processes of both emission and reception take place in a field populated by multiple codes that predetermine patterns of literary processes:

> En el proceso de recepción acontece lo más complejo del proceso comunicativo, el que consiste en el uso simultáneo de una multiplicidad de códigos en la re-creación de un mensaje cultural o artístico.
>
> Para el acto de emisión literaria misma, la presencia de una determinada tradición u horizonte literario es determinante. . . .
>
> La literatura y la teoría literaria están pues muy remitidas a los horizontes de expectativas, al sistema de posibilidades vigentes en un cierto momento y lugar de un determinado ejercicio literario. (Alcide Jofré, 202)

Oppositional writing is produced within a context or a series of shifting contexts that make its reception especially problematic, since it is always in danger of being reincorporated by the dominant mode:

> Tal vez no haya un contexto sino que varios contextos, con cuyo trasfondo exafórico, es decir extratextual, los textos pueden ser leídos de diferentes maneras. Obviamente, el contexto no puede ser visto como una estructura solidificada y estática, sino como un sistema dinámico y en constante rearticulación. (Alcide Jofré, 204)

What Alcide Jofré leaves out here is the differing levels of credibility afforded to these competing contexts. Yet his own notion of a multiplicity of contexts raises the question of just which version to believe when one of them is telling the authorized story and the other allows it to be known that the first is unreliable.

Alcide Jofré suggests that neither emitters nor receivers can escape the contexts that inform the literary processes they are engaged in. The more human terms, "writer" and "reader" make these participants in the literary process sound less like radio components and more like embodied, sentient beings, in and with their own history, and suggest that they possess a measure of free will in the acts of writing and reading. In part, writers choose to include the stories that derive their power from residual authority.

Why *are* the old stories there at all? For one thing, they serve as mooring, so that readers can see where they are departing from and perceive the movement from there to a new plot. By deliberately including it, writers take charge of the authoritative version, whose presence is, in any case, inevitable. Garro's alternative to the version of Isabel's fate etched in stone, however, is ambiguous and ultimately pessimistic. She undermines the old plot but puts nothing but silence in its place. The old plot's traces still remain inscribed in the stone, and no other voice surfaces to refute it. Garro provides information that exposes Gregoria's unreliability, but neither the collective voice of Ixtepec nor any individual character intercedes to provide an alternative. Speech and silence conspire; both are lethal in this text.

In "Feminist Criticism in the Wilderness," Elaine Showalter presents the notion of women's double-voiced discourse – a narrative strategy that makes it possible for women to tell one, subversive story while appearing to tell another, conventional one. Sandra Gilbert and Susan Gubar offer a similar analysis in *The Madwoman in the Attic*, where they demonstrate how nineteenth-century British women writers inscribe in the text a repressed Other who embodies women's fury and refuses the constraints of femininity, including the injunction to keep silent that the author herself is contesting. Though all three critics acknowledge the dominant discourse in which these oppositional strategies are embedded, they assume in their accounts that the narrative strategy will be successful, that the madwoman will emerge, that the muted discourse will escape from the shadow of the dominant.

In *Recuerdos del porvenir* the danger of speech is that it all gets swallowed by the master narrative. Julia magically escapes from the text, but even so the townspeople try to re-incorporate her into it, repeating tales of her having been seen in other places. Isabel's unconventional relationship with her brother, in which they were, as soulmates and playmates, equals, is reduced to a case of betrayal when she seduces the enemy, General Rosas. No one refutes the final words of the novel. The "madwoman in the attic" in this text, the character who should emerge to spill the beans, is, in fact, a madman who hoards words instead of spewing them.[4] It is not, finally, surprising that readers have over-whelmingly accepted Gregoria's story. Offering nothing in its place, Garro all but silences the muted voice of resistance.

The assumption of success made by Showalter and Gilbert and Gubar is not only optimistic; it is also belied by the fact that it took heroic acts of analysis to reveal them. We have been learning to read women's writing, finding in it the resistance and opposition that so satisfies us as feminist readers. Women's texts, and our feminist readings of them, are, as Adrienne Rich has pointed out, not just aesthetic pleasures, but a matter of women's survival in a hostile world, and a matter of considerable labor, and not always guaranteed of success.

The critical texts by Showalter and Gilbert and Gubar be-long to the first of two moments of feminist criticism. This first moment claims woman's difference from man and relies on a sameness within the category "woman." It represents a unifying gesture in which all women, by virtue of gender, are oppressed, and in which most women writers, as a result, have been dis-regarded by literary history or disdained by literary criticism. The task of the feminist critic in this first moment is to locate resis-tance to authority in texts, and these pieces of criticism focus on the repressed voice struggling to be heard. The second mo-ment of feminist literary analysis, the one in which we currently operate, recognizes the diversity among women that often re-sults in intragender oppression. Marked by the realization of the differences within the category "woman" and the subsequent pluralization of the noun to reflect the multiplicity of women's experience, reality, history, and representations, the second mo-ment openly acknowledges certain attachments that women have to systems of power by reason of class or race, nationality or age, sexuality or religion. These two moments are not in fundamental contradiction to each other: the first recognizes the pull of dominant discourse on women; the second focuses on the ways that that pull divides us.

Residual authority manifests itself differently in response to these two moments. The manifestation of residual authority in the reception of Isabel's story in Garro's novel is a function of the sisterly and inclusive analysis of the first moment of feminist criticism. Here is the residual authority that acts on all women, the dominant codes all of us have internalized despite the damage they do to us. This form of residual authority emerges in women as writers and readers; it is the authority that urges us to incorporate as well as to read as normative, and therefore natural, the punishment of the transgressive woman. It has been called internalized sexism, the power of hegemonic discourse.

The second manifestation of residual authority has become definable within the second moment of feminist criticism. It is that authority which functions, at least to some extent, to benefit some women at the expense of others. Residual authority here is imputed to the writer who we assume has some allegiance to systems of dominance by virtue of her class, perhaps, or her race, or nationality. Reading for residual authority in this mode is a critical strategy designed to get at what Elizabeth Meese and Alice Parker call "the difference within."

Rosario Ferré, for example, was born into the Puerto Rican ruling class. She is island rather than mainland Puerto Rican (even though she has lived in the continental United States for many years), and she is, increasingly, read as a speaker for her class.[5] Such readings, which come out of an impulse to pay attention to the differences that divide women, can be a welcome corrective to the assimilation of all women into a white, middle-class representation. They can also result, however, in the misrepresentation of the work of writers who come from a position of relative privilege.

Misreading attributable to residual authority, then, is not al-

ways a matter of our being in thrall to hegemonic discourse but
may also be a result of an attempt at oppositional reading. Aurora Levins Morales, for example, misreads Rosario Ferré when,
in a review essay on recent Puerto Rican women's fiction, Levins
Morales quotes a passage from *Maldito amor,* citing the words
of Don Hermenegildo, the notary who is writing the town's history. His is the official version, and it represents the most retrogressive element of the novel. Levins Morales accepts the validity
of this residually authoritative voice, conflating it with Ferré's own.
As Diana Vélez has pointed out, this could not be further from
the critique of the oligarchy from within that Ferré wrote; but
it fits Levins Morales's theory about the nature of Puerto Rican
island writing and its containment in an upper-class system, written by people nostalgic for the good old days.[6] As far as Levins
Morales is concerned, the only authentic critique of dominant
values can come from the working class itself. She writes in her
interchange with Vélez:

> Vélez claims for the current literature, a "subversion of dominant
> social values," and certainly some exists. But individual excep-
> tions notwithstanding, we have yet to see a strong working-class
> literature emerge from the island. Puerto Rican writers in the U.S.
> have clearly taken the lead in producing such a literature, some-
> thing that should come as no surprise, given the class make-up
> of the diaspora. (Levins Morales, 5)

Carmen Vega-Carney, too, looks for working-class authenticity, though she implicitly disagrees with Levins Morales, insofar as she identifies a strong working-class voice in an island
writer, Ana Lydia Vega, whom she contrasts to Ferré. Vega-
Carney focuses not an island-mainland split but, rather, on competing class interests in what she calls the writing of Puerto Rican
national biography. Like Levins Morales, Vega-Carney reads
Ferré as an upper-class writer who reinscribes a nostalgic class-
bound story. There are, I think inevitably, traces of nostalgia,
particularly in Ferré's early works. Yet despite them Ferré is above
all writing her way out of an embedded class position, having
chosen, like her protagonist in "El regalo," to drop the glittering

prizes, as well as the rotten mango-cum-sacred-heart, into the lap of the sterile guardians of the upper class, and good riddance.

Ironically, Ferré shares her critics' belief that a truer truth comes from the oppressed classes. In *Maldito amor* she relies on the putative innocence of the oppressed to contest Don Hermenegildo's version of the story of the de la Valle family. She attributes absolute honesty to the servant, Titina, whose naively subversive testimony to Don Hermenegildo is a gesture to the emerging genre of testimonial literature. Critics on the left, including feminist critics, have looked to testimonio as a genre that derives its authority from the epistemologically privileged standpoint of the oppressed. One reason that Titina is a more reliable (if more gullible) narrator than Don Hermenegildo is that she tells him the facts, and he maliciously utilizes the raw materials of her testimony to fashion, both discursively and materially, the textual outcome he desires.

More wary than Titina is the working-class woman, Gloria, who reproaches the loyal servant for relinquishing ownership of the testimonial text to her class enemy. Through Gloria, Ferré rejects the authority that resides in the privilege of class and race that will, it is assumed, necessarily falsify the truth of the information garnered from the underclass, as the oral story is transformed into the written one.[7] What is taken for granted here, as in most accounts of testimonio, is that the informant is simpler, and therefore guileless; closer to truth, she speaks with the authority of innocence. This is a somewhat romanticized, not to say patronizing, version of the subjects of testimonio, but it is a convention of the genre. So when Ferré's Titina gives her testimony to the untrustworthy Hermenegildo, Ferré is signaling the reader that what Titina says is truth, as opposed to what Hermenegildo writes, which is false: Hermenegildo is writing his romantic, novelized version of the past; Titina is speaking out of the immediacy of her knowledge and needs.[8]

Since Ferré writes as a feminist and deliberately engages with the voice of authority in a way that Garro does not, the residual authority that critics like Vega-Carney and Levins Morales find in her work is less compelling than in the Mexican writer's. In

Garro's novel Gregoria is a conventionally unreliable narrator who bears an authorized tale. In contrast, Ferré's Hermenegildo is quintessentially reliable: a powerful man whose job as notary is to certify the truth but whose story, though "authorized," is demonstrably false and challenged by the author herself, who empowers Gloria and Titina to burn it down. Furthermore, *Maldito amor* is a recent work, with little authority driven traditional criticism accruing to it. As such, it is relatively unencumbered by ready-made readings that predispose the reader to think about it one way or the other.

Ferré undermines residual authority by means of *Maldito amor's* multiple narrators and by bestowing the last word on Gloria, working together with Titina across class lines.[9] Like Garro's Gregoria, the exslave Titina is a believer in authority. It is not the most oppressed – the rural poor – who have the skill and knowledge to question upper-class authority but rather the working class, here in the figure of Gloria, who in order to survive and thrive (she is moving up the social and economic ladder) must be able to "read" the upper classes.

Maldito amor is, structurally, the wresting of the power of narration from the voice of authority, Don Hermenegildo, who alone narrates the first two chapters of the novella. The first of these is the beginning of his novelized, sentimental history of Guamaní, the town in which the action takes place. Ferré signals the notary's authorship orthographically, setting it inside quotation marks, which can function both to signal that the text is fictional (within the fiction) and that it is to be read ironically.

Hermenegildo loses control of the narrative little by little. Titina, loyal servant, believes her masters will take care of her and goes to the notary for help in making her claim to the small house she has been promised in return for her years of service. In the third chapter Titina tells her story to Hermenegildo, hoping he can intercede to help her make her claim on her cabin. Although her revelations begin to shake his confidence in the sugar plantation owners whose story he is composing, he recovers and works to undermine her in order to save his story. In subsequent chapters, Hermenegildo hears, one after the other, the stories of the members of the family Titina has worked for, and he continues to struggle to maintain his version of their life. It is the upwardly mobile Gloria who finally succeeds in unmasking the sentimentality and falsification of Hermenegildo's story and succeeds in wresting the narrative from him.

Only in Gloria's chapter does the narrative exclude Hermenegildo entirely, making her knowledge unavailable to his writing. Not he, but Titina, is Gloria's interlocutor in the final chapter. Gloria chides, goads, and harangues Titina, who until now has been all too loyal to her oppressors; Gloria insists finally that they collaborate in burning down the old plantation house. Hermenegildo is unlikely to escape the fire and will never return to the text to recover his novel:

> Allá debe de estar todavía, sentado junto al lecho de la difunta, inventando seguramente nuevos capítulos, nuevas maneras de tergiversar la historia que escuchó de los labios de los protagonistas mismos de este melodrama insigne. Y si se escapara, si lograra de alguna manera salvarse de los ríos de bencina azul que derramamos ahora sobre los tachos de bagazo reseco, sobre los montones de cañamiza sedienta que se aglomeran siempre alrededor de las casas de las haciendas, si logra hurtarle el cuerpo a la lluvia de pavesas de caña que se arremolina ya a nuestro alrededor como un presagio de infierno, nos quedará la satisfacción de saber que no podrá ya nunca escribir la apología de un hombre que él creía un líder y un prócer, y que estaba desde hacía tiempo tan corrupto. (Ferré, 75)

The novella ends with the conflagration: the fire next time, the end of discourse. Like Virginia Woolf in *Three Guineas*, Ferré's Gloria advocates nothing less than burning down the whole corrupt discursive and material structure on which class, race, and gender oppression rest.

The third text I look at with reference to residual authority is Luisa Valenzuela's "El lugar de su quietud," the final story in her collection *Aquí pasan cosas raras.* In this story and, as it turns out, in the collection as a whole, Valenzuela's narrator makes use of residual authority as camouflage. Here, then, residual authority is a narrative device, deliberately inscribed in the text by the author.

Most of the stories in *Aquí pasan cosas raras* are narrated as if by a disembodied voice. When the narrator submerges her own voice, the result is an erasure of gender that reinstates the generic narrative voice, which is inevitably read as the authoritative masculine narrator. The unmarked narrative authority of knowledgeable, objective masculinity is ascribed to her stories by default. In stories where the narrative voice shifts from singular to plural, or from masculine to feminine, the resulting indeterminacy once again encourages the reader to make sense of these narratives out of the store of culturally conditioned readings that rely on traditional forms of authority. Valenzuela's secretive writer who hopes someday to be able to write in the light of day and out of her own identity is mightily defended by her disguise, a mask in inverse: a peeling off rather than a laying on of features.

This reliance on the effect of residual authority in the reader notwithstanding, the authority most pressingly in question with regard to Valenzuela's collection of short stories is not residual; it is overtly imposed and ratified with violence. *Aquí pasan cosas raras* was published in 1975, a matter of months before the military coup of March 1976 that institutionalized state terror under the Proceso de Reorganización Nacional. Extratextual authority (the authorities), the threatening, unseen presence in the stories, makes it imperative that the narrator of these tales consciously disavow her identity. This narrative disguise, assumed as an act of self-preservation, ironically lends a credibility to the narrator's stories which is to a certain extent undermined when she reveals herself.

The flattened affect, reportorial tone, and absence of editorializing (the suppression of adjectives, for example) are penetrated at the end of the collection in "El lugar de su quietud," narrated and protagonized by a writer of stories with titles identical to those the reader has just read. In this final story, the writer reveals all her subterfuges and secrets, the most surprising of which is that she is a woman. As she unmasks, she is diminished, like the Wizard of Oz behind the curtain. These were not tales that were somehow destined to be told but rather contingent stories, written by a frightened woman not from the expansive panorama of Argentina but within a small, dark, imperiled space. On the other hand, the omniscient, disembodied voice gives way to the courage of the individual writer, the person composing the words, who, along with others like her, unobtrusively struggles to reclaim the language and write the collective story:

> Deben de haber empezado a narrar desde las épocas más remotas y hay que tener paciencia. Escribiendo sin descanso puede que algún día alcancen el presente y lo superen, en todos los sentidos del verbo superar: que lo dejen atrás, lo modifiquen y hasta con un poco de suerte lo mejoren. Es cuestión de lenguaje. (Valenzuela, 134)

Valenzuela's narrator is all but silenced during the time of writing, but by taking advantage of readerly expectations – the residual authority of the masculine voice that makes us assume that any voice not marked must be masculine – she is able to resist violence and political repression. Garro, from a stance of despair, contests any position of reliability even as she refuses traditional authority. Ferré engages authority and posits the political solution of cross-class coalition among women. Valenzuela subverts authority by invoking it actively, to inscribe resistance.

Notes

1. It should be noted that authority itself is a problematic issue in Latin American letters. Sara Castro-Klarén establishes the relationship between authority and canonicity in a way that calls for a re-evaluation of the two institutions. "In the history of Latin American letters, those who held to and upheld the 'established norms' have, throughout the last five hundred years, demanded

to know in the name of what authority did texts autographed by native born Americans such as the Inca Garcilaso, Sor Juana Inés de la Cruz, Ruiz de Alarcón, Sarmiento, Darío, Arguedas, Poniatowska or Ocampo, claim admittance into the rows of a canonical literary history" (p. 7).

2. Jean Franco in *Plotting Women: Gender and Representation in Mexico,* 129-138 (especially 134 and 137), and Sandra Boschetto, "Romancing the Stone."

3. Russ's solution, that feminist writers turn to science fiction, which announces from the outset its projection out of what Alcide Jofré terms "the current system of possibilities," does recognize the extent to which even that form is entangled in the old plots.

4. Juan Cariño believes that speech is dangerous, so every evening he goes out into the streets to gather up and safely dispose of the dangerous words that have accumulated in Ixtepec during the day. He may be mad, but he is quite right about the danger of words. The plot to support the Cristeros by inviting the general and his officers to a party is foiled by the conspirators' not keeping quiet about it in front of the servants, leading to the novel's tragic denouement. Garro undermines the truth-value of language altogether, by equating Juan Cariño's valid belief in the harmful power of words with, first, his dysfunctional belief in the materiality of words and, second, his conviction that he is the president of the Republic.

5. By Aurora Levins Morales and, implicitly, Nicolasa Mohr, as well as Carmen Vega-Carney. Nicolasa Mohr is highly critical of what she perceives as the inaccessible writing of island writers, and Levins Morales relies heavily on Mohr in her criticism of Ferré.

6. Vélez and Levins Morales's interchange brings up the question of intentionality. The critical assumption of authorial intention has been fairly well discredited, yet to talk about narrative strategy, as I am, is to assume intentionality and to presume that as readers we can figure out what that intention is. It makes no sense to discuss strategy without attaching it to the battle it is designed to win.

7. Margarita Fernández Olmos suggests, more optimistically, that testimonial writing is a collaborative effort that teaches humility to the collector of the oral story and provides a vehicle for the "gente sin historia."

8. The investment of new, more reliable, forms of authority, in testimony is one form of resistance to traditional authority. This

discussion opens up the question of the slip-sliding authority of traditionally respected and discredited discourses. I bring up testimony here, but gossip, anecdote, and memoir are others. These sometimes ephemeral discourses (especially the oral ones) disrupt the clean surface of hegemonic discourse, since they tell other stories in other ways. We need, in our oppositional readings, to pay attention, to these other discourses but not to overvalue them, replacing one form of authority with another.

How, for example, do we authorize the reading of literary gossip in order to bring it to bear on questions of how biography affects reading and writing processes? How do we make room for "what everybody knows" about Garro's marriage and subsequent relationship with Octavio Paz? Among the rituals of disempowerment and divestiture at play is the fall from literary grace Elena Garro suffered, according to literary gossip, at the hands of her famous ex-husband. But gossip is another form of discourse, and Paz is still powerful enough to make it sound foolish, even if it is as likely to be true as not. (There is, somewhere, a resonance between the conventional reading of Garro's text and the subsequent censorship of her work at the hands of a powerful exhusband.) How do I place my recollection of Luisa Valenzuela's public silence and private anger at the 1978 Congress of Interamerican Women Writers in Ottawa in the face of at least two Argentine writers who were apologizing for the military in response to young Canadian feminists' attacks on Argentina? What place does Valenzuela's 1990 oral recollection of her mother, María Luisa Levinson, have in my reading of her as a writer? How do we factor in Ferré's published version of her willful refusal of the trappings of the upper class, in her memoir about an all-night, postdivorce struggle with a typewriter that, fueled by many cups of coffee and several packs of cigarettes, produced her first story, "La muñeca menor," when we read her writing?

Another related question is Whom do we authorize as critics? It is undeniable that some of my ideas were derived, ultimately, from texts I have never read. Rather than dig those out, reinforcing their authority, what I really prefer to do is pay attention to their feminist readers: Bakhtin through Mae Henderson or Diana Vélez, Lacan through Luce Irigaray, Derrida through Gayatri Spivak.

It is no coincidence that these questions, and more important, these bits of information, are relegated to a footnote. I have not yet been able to figure out quite how to elevate them to the main body of this essay.

9. In fact, Laura, the widow of the plantation owner and ostensibly the most powerful figure in the family, is an author of the plan to redistribute the wealth of the sugar plantation, in her decision to will the plantation to Gloria and her son.

Works Cited

Alcide Jofré, Manuel. "Literatura, comunicación, y teoría literaria." *Revista Canadiense de Estudios Hispánicos* 13 (invierno 1989): 197-211.

Boschetto, Sandra. "Romancing the Stone." *Journal of the Midwest Modern Language Association* 22:2 (Fall 1989): 1-11.

Castro-Klarén, Sara. "By (T)reason of State: The Canon and Marginality in Latin American Literature." *Revista de Estudios Hispánicos* 23:2 (May 1989): 1-19.

Fernandez Olmos, Margarita. "Latin American Testimonial Narrative, or Women and the Art of Listening." *Revista Canadiense de Estudios Hispánicos* 13:2 (invierno 1989): 183-195.

Franco, Jean. *Plotting Women: Gender and Representation in Mexico* (New York: Columbia University Press, 1989).

Garro, Elena. *Los recuerdos del porvenir*. Mexico: Joaquín Mortiz y Lecturas Mexicanas, 1985. First ed. 1963.

Gilbert, Sandra M., and Susan Gubar. *The Madwoman in the Attic: The Woman Writer and the Nineteenth-Century Literary Imagination*. New Haven: Yale University Press, 1979.

Levins Morales, Aurora. "Between Two Worlds." *Women's Review of Books* 7:3 (December 1989): 1, 3.

———. Untitled response to Vélez. *Women's Review of Books* 7:5 (February 1990): 5.

Meese, Elizabeth, and Alice Parker, eds. *The Difference Within: Feminism and Critical Theory*. Philadelphia: John Benjamins, 1989.

Miller, Nancy K. "Emphasis Added: Plots and Plausibilities in Women's Fiction." *PMLA* 96:1 (January 1981): 36-48.

Mohr, Nicolasa. "Puerto Rican Writers in the U.S., Puerto Rican Writers in Puerto Rico: A Separation beyond Language." *The*

Américas Review 15:2 (1987). Reprinted in *Breaking Boundaries: Latina Writing and Critical Readings,* ed. Horno-Delagado, et al., 111-116. Amherst: University of Massachusetts Press, 1989.

Rich, Adrienne. "When We Dead Awaken: Writing as Re-Vision." *College English* 34:1 (October 1972). Reprinted in *On Lies, Secrets, and Silence: Selected Prose 1966-1978,* 33-49. New York: Norton, 1979.

Russ, Joanna. "What Can a Heroine Do: Or, Why Women Can't Write." *Images of Women in Fiction: Feminist Perspectives,* ed. Susan Koppelman Cornillon, 3-20. Bowling Green: Bowling Green University Popular Press, 1972.

Showalter, Elaine. "Feminist Criticism in the Wilderness." *Critical Inquiry* 8 (Winter 1981).

Vega-Carney, Carmen. Paper presented at the Fourth Annual Conference on Foreign Literature, Wichita State University, 1988.

Vélez, Diana. Untitled letter, *Women's Review of Books* 7:5 (February 1990): 5.

III

"Through All Things Modern": Second Thoughts on Testimonio

JOHN BEVERLEY

> This is why Indians are thought to be stupid. They can't think, they don't know anything, they say. But we have hidden our identity because we needed to resist, we wanted to protect what governments have wanted to take away from us. They have tried to take our things away and impose others on us, be it through religion, through dividing up the land, through schools, through books, through radio, through all things modern.
>
> – Rigoberta Menchú[1]

To explain the title and the quote: These are second thoughts both on the testimonio itself and on my own work on testimonio, represented by the article "The Margin at the Center: On *Testimonio* (Testimonial Narrative)."[2] As I noted there, by testimonio I understand a novel- or novella-length narrative told in the first person by a narrator who is also the real-life protagonist or witness of the events he or she recounts. In recent years it has become an important, perhaps the dominant, form of literary narrative in Latin America. The best-known example available in English translation is the text that the epigraph above comes from, *I. Regoberta Menchú,* the life story of a young Indian woman from the highlands of Guatemala, which, as she puts it in her presentation of the text, is intended to be "the reality of a whole people."[3]

I want to start with the fact of the February 1990 elections in Nicaragua, which reminds us of Jameson's redefinition of Lacan's category of the real as "that which hurts." A decade after the revolutionary high tide of 1979-1981, it is clear that the moment of optimism about the possibilities for rapid social transformation in Central America has passed. Whether this represents a new, postrevolutionary, stage in that region's history or simply a recession before the appearance of a new cycle of radicalization – perhaps also involving Mexico this time – is open to question. Testimonios like *I. Rigoberta Menchú,* or Omar Cabezas's *Fire from the Mountain* and Margaret Randall's *Sandino's Daughters* from Nicaragua, were very much part of the ideological imaginary of international solidarity with, or critical support for, the Central American revolutions. So the electoral defeat of the Sandinistas, while it is certainly not absolute – unlike Chile after the defeat of Allende, there is still quite a bit of room for maneuver and struggle – must force us in any case to reconsider the relation between testimonio, liberation struggles, solidarity work, and academic pedagogy. I want to center this reconsideration in particular around the question of the relation of testimonio to the academic field of literature. This will in turn connect with some questions about what it is that we do in the humanities generally, and particularly in connection with Latin American and third world literatures.

I ended my reflection on the testimonio in "The Margin at the Center" with the thought that

> literature, even where it is infused with a popular-democratic form and content, as in the case of *testimonio,* is not in itself a popular-

democratic cultural form, and (*pace* Gramsci) it is an open question as to whether it ever can be. How much of a favor do we
do *testimonio* by positing, as here, that it has become a new form
of literature or by making it an alternative reading to the canon
(one track of the new Stanford civilization requirement now includes *I. Rigoberta Menchú*)? Perhaps such moves preempt or
occlude a vision of an emergent popular-democratic culture that
is no longer based on the institutions of humanism and literature. (Beverley, 26)

I might have added "no longer based, that is, on the university,"
because I believe that literature and the university (in the historically specific form each takes during and after the Renaissance)
have been, appearances to the contrary, mutually dependent
on each other and as such deeply implicated in the processes
of state formation and colonial expansion that define early modern Europe. This legacy still marks literature and the university,
making their interaction in contemporary processes of decolonization and postcoloniality at the same time both necessary and
problematic.

Testimonios are in a sense made for people like us, in that
they allow us to participate as academics and yuppies, without
leaving our studies and classrooms, in the concreteness and rela-
tivity of actual social struggles ("we," "our," and "us" designate
here the readers – or potential readers – of this volume). To borrow a passage from Bakhtin's definition of prose art in his essay
"Discourse in the Novel" (with thanks to Barbara Harlow for bring-
ing it to my attention), testimonios are texts whose discourses
are "still warm from the struggle and hostility, as yet unresolved
and still fraught with hostile intentions and accents." But they
are (putting Derrida in parenthesis here) still also *just* texts and
not actual warm or not so warm bodies (victims of the death
squads, for example). I am not trying to guilt-trip people about
being academics and yuppies. I am both. Russell Jacoby's critique of the encapsulation of the academic left is misdirected;
the university is an absolutely crucial and central institution of
late capitalist society. I believe in Gramsci's slogan of a long march

through the institutions, and it follows that I think that our battle-
field is the classroom and conference hall, that the struggle over
the teaching and interpretation of literature has something to
do with the production of new forms of ideological hegemony.
As a concrete pedagogic issue, the use of testimonio has to do
with the possibility of interpellating our students (and all readers
are or were at one time students) in a relation of solidarity with
liberation movements and human rights struggles, both here in
the United States and abroad.

In the theoretical discussion on the form, much deconstructive zeal has been spent on the fact that a testimonio is a mediated narrative: as in *I. Rigoberta Menchú,* usually an oral narrative told by a speaker from a subaltern or "popular" social class
or group to an interlocutor who is an intellectual or professional
writer from the middle or upper class (and in many cases from
a different ethno-linguistic position), who then edits and tex-
tualizes the account, making it available as a printed book or
pamphlet to a similarly positioned national and international reading public. The possibilities for distortion and/or cooptation in
such a potentially dissonant social, economic, intellectual, ethnic, and linguistic context are many, as Gayatri Spivak has suggested in "Can the Subaltern Speak?" But the relationship of
direct narrator and interlocutor in the production of a testimonio
can also serve as both an allegorical figure for, and a concrete
means of, the union of a radicalized intelligentsia with a subaltern
social position. Moreover, it is a relationship in which neither
of the participants has to cancel its identity as such. Testimonios
have become, in certain sorts of conjunctures, a discursive space
where the possibilities of such an alliance can be negotiated on
both sides without too much angst about otherness or other-
ing. Spivak is correct that "contemporary invocations of 'libidi-
nal economy' and desire as the determining interest, combined
with the practical politics of the oppressed (under socialized capital) 'speaking for themselves,' restore the category of the sover-
eign subject within the theory that seems most to question it."[4]
But this is more a question – and not a simple one at that – of
the ideology of the consumers of testimonio rather than its pro-

ducers. Moreover, political struggle involves not only the critique of the forms of the dominant ideology but also the necessarily ideological production of new forms of identity. As Doris Sommer has noted, "to read women's testimonials, curiously, is to mitigate the tension between First World self and Third World other. I do not mean this as a license to deny the differences, but as a suggestion. . . . That distance can be read as a lesson in the condition of possibility for coalitional politics."[5]

I understand, of course, that "literature" is itself a matter of semiosis, of who defines what counts as such under what institutional circumstances. The political question is what is gained or lost by including or excluding under this name particular kinds of discursive practices. As in the Stanford civilization requirements, the pedagogic incorporation of testimonio in the academy has involved strategically a theoretical-critical struggle to define examples of the genre like *I. Rigoberta Menchú* not just as an ethnographic document or life history but as part of the canon of Great Works through which the humanist subject as such is formed in a modern, multicultural curriculum.[6] The authorizing operation of literary criticism, including "The Margin at the Center," in this regard has been to articulate testimonio as a form of contemporary literature that is particularly sensitive to the representation or expression of subalternity. Fredric Jameson gives it his imprimatur as an alternative to what he terms the "overripe subjectivity" of the *Bildungsroman;* Barbara Harlow makes it a key form of *Resistance Literature;* Cornell publishes Barbara Foley's book on "documentary fiction"– a category that subsumes the testimonio; Margaret Randall offers a "how-to" manual for would-be practitioners of the form; George Yúdice sees it as a third world form of a postmodernism of resistance; Juan Duchesne writes a doctoral dissertation at SUNY-Albany on Latin American guerrilla narratives; Gayatri Spivak and Elzbieta Sklodowska caution against a naive reception of the form . . .[7] Even to arrive at the situation we are now in, where it has become fashionable to deconstruct in de Manian fashion this or that testimonio,[8] still is to give it in effect a status as a literary text comparable to, say, Rousseau's *Confessions.*

This is fine and basically correct as far as I am concerned. There is no reason to suppose that Rousseau has anything more or less to tell us than Rigoberta Menchú or Esteban Montejo, the narrator of the *Autobiography of a Runaway Slave*. But we must also understand why testimonio comes into being outside, or at the margin, of the historically constituted institution of literature in modern western culture. At least part of its aesthetic effect – I mean this precisely in the Russian formalist sense of *ostranenie* or defamiliarization – is that it is *not* literary, not linguistically elaborated or authorial. We may note in this respect an ambivalence about the "artistic," as opposed to the "documentary," character of testimonio, and about the distinction between testimonio per se and the more elaborated "testimonial novel" (*novela-testimonio*" such as Miguel Barnet's (Capote's *In Cold Blood* would be an English-language equivalent).[9] Testimonio appears where the adequacy of existing literary forms and styles – even of the dominant language itself[10] – for the representation of the subaltern has entered into crisis. Even where the instrumentality of the testimonio is to reach in printed form a metropolitan reading public culturally and physically distant from the position and situation of its narrator, testimonio is not engendered out of the same humanist ideology of the literary that motivates its reception by this public or its incorporation into the humanities curriculum. And there are moments when testimonio actively *does not want to be considered as "literature."* Let me give two examples: one from a contemporary Salvadoran testimonio, the other from *I. Rigoberta Menchú*.

Ana Guadalupe Martínez's testimonio *Las cárceles clandestinas de El Salvador* (*The Secret Prisons of El Salvador*)[11] deals with her involvement in the Salvadoran guerrilla underground with the Ejército Revolucionario del Pueblo (Revolutionary Army of the People) and her capture, torture, and imprisonment by the army. She insists that her account is "the result of a collective and militant effort and *has no intellectual or literary pretensions;* it is a contribution to the ideological development and formation of cadres on the basis of concrete experience that should be discussed and analyzed by those who are consistently immersed in the making of the revolution." Her coprologuist, René Cruz, similarly notes: "There is considerable concrete experience which has been lost by not being processed and transmitted by militants and another large part has been deformed in its essence by being elaborated by leftist intellectual intermediaries who adjust what they are relating not in relation to revolutionary needs but *in relation to the needs of fiction and bourgeois revolutionary theorizing*" (Martínez, pp. 12–14; translation and italics mine).

The point about "no intellectual pretensions" is disingenuous, and more than a trace remains here of the intense sectarianism that has marked the Salvadoran revolutionary movement. The point about "leftist intellectual intermediaries" alludes to the most famous modern Salvadoran writer, Roque Dalton, who also worked in testimonial forms[12] and who, as it happens, was Martínez's adversary in an internal debate in the ERP in the mid-seventies over the direction of the armed struggle (a debate that led to his assassination by the leadership faction of the ERP that Martínez supported). Still, her point is worth taking. She wants to do something *other than* literature with her narrative; she feels what she wants to do would in some sense be compromised or betrayed by becoming literature, whereas Dalton, like Miguel Barnet, was concerned with the ideological and aesthetic problems of making testimonio a form of left-modernist literature.

I. Rigoberta Menchú begins with a strategic disavowal of both literature and the liberal concept of the authority of private experience: "My name is Rigoberta Menchú. I am twenty-three years old. This is my testimony. I didn't learn it from a book, and I didn't learn it alone" (Menchú, 1). The quote at the start of this essay belongs with a series of passages in the text where the narrator explicitly counterposes book learning to direct experience, or attacks the presence of no doubt well-intentioned school teachers in her village, arguing that they represent an agency of penetration and destruction of the highland Indian communities by the landowners and the Guatemalan state. Here are some other similar passages:

When children reach ten years old (in our village), that's the moment when their parents and the village leaders talk to them again. . . . It's also when they remind them that our ancestors were dishonored by the White Man, by colonization. But they don't tell them the way it's written down in books, because the majority of Indians can't read or write, and don't even know that they have their own texts. No, they learn it through oral recommendations, the way it has been handed down through the generations. (Menchú, 13)

I had a lot of ideas but I knew I couldn't express them all. I wanted to read or write Spanish. I told my father this, that I wanted to learn to read. Perhaps things were different if you could learn to read. My father said, "Who will teach you? You have to find out by yourself, because I can't help you. I know of no schools and I have no money for them anyway." I told him that if he talked to the priests, perhaps they'd give me a scholarship. But my father said he didn't agree with that idea because I was trying to leave the community, to go far away, and find out what was best for me. He said: "You'll forget about our common heritage." . . . My father was very suspicious of schools and all that sort of thing. He gave as an example the fact that many of my cousins had learned to read and write but they hadn't been of use to the community. They try to move away and feel different when they can read and write. (Menchú, 89)

Sometimes I'd hear how those teachers taught and what education was like in the villages. They said that the arrival of the Spaniards was a conquest, a victory, while we knew in practice that it was just the opposite. . . . This taught me that even though a person may learn to read and write, he should not accept the false education they give our people. Our people must not think as the authorities think. (Menchú, 169-170)

When teachers come into the villages, they bring with them the ideas of capitalism and getting on in life. They try and impose these ideas on us. I remember that in my village there were two teachers for a while and they began teaching the people, but the children told their parents everything they were being taught at school and the parents said: "We don't want our children to become like *ladinos* (in Guatemala a Spanish-speaking white or mestizo)." And they made the teachers leave. . . . For the Indian, it is better not to study than to become like *ladinos*. (Menchú, 205)

One aspect of the archeology of Menchú's position here involves the Spanish practice during the Conquest of segregating the children of the Indian aristocracy from their families in order to teach them literacy and Christian doctrine. Walter Mignolo has observed of this practice that it

> shows that literacy is not instilled without violence. The violence, however, is not located in the fact that the youngsters have been assembled and enclosed day and night. It comes, rather, from the interdiction of having conversations with their parents, particularly with their mothers. In a primary oral society, in which virtually all knowledge is transmitted by means of conversation, the preservation of oral contact was contradictory with the effort to teach how to read and write. Forbidding conversations with the mother meant, basically, depriving the children of the living culture imbedded in the language and preserved and transmitted in speech.[13]

But it is not that, coming from a predominantly oral culture, Rigoberta Menchú does not value literacy or formal education at all. Part of the oedipal struggle with her father recounted in her story involves precisely her desire, and eventually her success, as a teenager at learning first to memorize, then read, passages from the Bible in order to become a Catholic lay catechist (just as later she would learn Spanish and several other Indian languages because of the exigencies of her work as a peasant organizer, and she would lead a fight to have a school built in her community).[14] It is rather, as these passages suggest, that she does not accept literacy and book learning, or the narrative of cultural and linguistic modernization they entail, as either adequate or *normative* cultural modes. She is conscious,

among other things, of the holistic relation between the indi-
vidualization produced by the government schools and the attempts to impose on her community an agrarian reform based
on private ownership of parcels (as opposed to its pre-Columbian
tradition of communal ownership and sharing of resources). That
is why she remains a testimonial narrator rather than an "author"
– a subject position that in fact would, as in the case of Richard
Rodriguez's memoir *Hunger of Memory,* imply a self-imposed
separation from her community and culture of birth (and a loss
or change of name). As Doris Sommer has shown,[15] even in
the act of addressing us through the literary artifice of the testimonio – which is built on the convention of truth-telling and
openness – Menchú is also consciously withholding information
from us, on the grounds that it could be used against her and
her people by academically trained or advised counterinsurgency
specialists. She is aware, in other words, of something we may
have forgotten since the Vietnam War: the complicity of the university in cultural (and sometimes actual) genocide. The concluding words of her testimonio are "I'm still keeping secret what
I think no one should know. Not even anthropologists or intellectuals, no matter how many books they have, can find out all
our secrets" (Menchú, 247).

We could say that Menchú *uses* the testimonio as literature
without subscribing to a humanist ideology of the literary, or,
what amounts to the same thing, without abandoning her identity and role as an Indian activist to become a professional writer.
This may be one way of answering Spivak's question, "Can the
Subaltern Speak?" No, not as such (because "the subaltern is
the name of the place which is so displaced . . . that to have
it speak is like Godot arriving on a bus").[16] But the testimonial
narrator like Rigoberta Menchú is not the subaltern as such either,
rather she is something more like an "organic intellectual" of the
subaltern who speaks to the hegemony by means of a metonymy
of self in the name and in the place of it. (Sommer: "[Menchú's]
testimonial is an invitation to a tête à tête, not to a heart to
heart") [36-37]. Testimonio is located at the intersection of the
cultural forms of bourgeois humanism – like literature and the

printed book, engendered by the academy and colonialism and imperialism – and subaltern cultural forms. It is not an authentic expression of the subaltern (whatever that might be),[17] but it is not (or should not be) easily assimilable to, or collectible *as,* literature, either.

My work with Marc Zimmerman on the role of poetry in Central American revolutionary movements[18] showed that it was not just a reflection or expression of an already constituted ideology but, rather, a precondition for its elaboration as such; that something like the Sandinista revolution in Nicaragua depended in some significant ways on developments in modern Nicaraguan poetry initiated by the Granada Vanguardists in the 1930s under the influence of U.S. modernists like Stevens, Pound, and Eliot; that, in a strikingly postmodern way, literature was not only a means of revolutionary politics but also a model for it in Central America. Why this was so had to do not only with the content of individual texts (i.e., with something that might be revealed by a hermeneutic or deconstructive analysis) but also with the way literature itself was positioned as a social practice by processes of combined and uneven development in Central American history.

As the late Angel Rama argued, a "republic of letters" (*ciudad letrada*) and the consequent normative role of literature and of the writer are among the basic forms of institutional continuity between colonial and contemporary Latin America.[19] The availability of literary texts through the medium of the printed book to even a feminist and poststructuralist "ideal reader" is a historically and ethnically specific one, linked in Europe to the rise of the middle class, the commodification of literary production and distribution, and the corresponding growth of democratic forms of public education and a reading public, particularly in the nineteenth century. The mode of existence of literature in a caste-ridden, quasi-feudal society like colonial Latin American was in several respects quite different from this. To begin with, as Mignolo's comment illustrates, literature was itself a colonial import, with little or no continuity whatever with pre-Columbian discursive practices (where they existed, pre-Columbian texts were systematically destroyed). Most people in the colonies – perhaps 80 to 90 percent of the population – did not read at all, and many had no or only a rudimentary grasp of even spoken Spanish or Portuguese. In contrast to our contemporary concern with illiteracy (with its implicit equation of literacy, modernization, and democratization), however, this was regarded as a normal, even desirable, state of affairs. Access to written texts in Spanish or Latin was in itself a mark of distinction that separated colonizer from colonized, rulers from ruled, European from native.[20]

This was not just a question of functional literacy, however. The colonial fashion for the highly wrought and complex poetry represented by fashionable metropolitan models like Góngora involved the fetishization of writing as an aristocratic or sublime activity because it eluded through its difficulty the comprehension not only by the illiterate but also by those who might be functionally literate but were not university educated – sectors of the indigenous population to begin with, but also lower-class creoles and the *castas,* or mixed-bloods. What such a literature transmitted to its readers, the *letrados,* or men of letters (for they were almost always men), in the urban centers of the colonial viceroyalties was not only a sign of aristocratic worth – *honor* – and connection to a distant metropolitan center, but also a technique of power, an exercise or formal simulacrum of their ability to discern, organize, sublimate, and ultimately control productively.

This situation affected in part the literary text itself as a cultural artifact. In general, secular writing in the colonies was not intended for commercial publication and even less for a general reading public. There were printing establishments in the colonies, but – even at the end of the seventeenth century – a major project like the first anthology of the poetry of Sor Juana Inés de la Cruz required publication in Spain. It was common for literary texts to be available only in hand-lettered manuscript copies circulated privately to individual readers or special audiences (*tertulias*).

In its very form of circulation then but also in the cultivation of extreme forms of pedantry and linguistic complexity, Latin American colonial literature was not something intended for or available to everyone, certainly not for a socially amorphous public that could lay hold of it through the market in books. Literature (less anachronistically, *letras,* including, e.g., history, biography, sermons, letters, and, especially, the essay), in other words, not only had a central role in the self-representation of the upper and upper-middle strata of Latin American colonial society; *letras* was one of the social practices by which such strata constituted themselves as dominant. That is why for a neo-Machiavellian political theorist and moralist like the Jesuit Baltasar Gracián an "art of wit" (*arte de agudeza*) based on the study of literary conceits (*conceptos*) was a prerequisite for the formation of the baroque man of affairs. (In general, it was via the curricula established by Jesuit pedagogy at the end of the sixteenth and the beginning of the seventeenth century that the innovations in literature found their way into the hearts and minds of the colonial intelligentsia.)

This very acute sense of the power of literature – which involves both a recognition and an overvaluation of its cultural importance – accounts for the prohibition by the colonial authorities of both the publication and importation of novels: the novel was quite literally seen as a medium incompatible with the assumptions of colonial rule (although it could, with heavy censorship, be tolerated in Spain and Portugal). This anomaly, however, also made of literature a place where the ambitions and resentments of creole, mestizo, and in some cases indigenous or slave groups or agents could begin to take shape. The colonial intellectual was in the position of having to mediate in his or (much less frequently) her writing between an empirically vivid American reality and an increasingly absent and abstract European model of civilization represented by literature. As in the prohibition of the novel, problems of genre, style, decorum, neologism, and so on could easily become entangled and confused with political and social problems, and literature itself became a sign of the colony's connection to metropolitan centers in Spain and Portugal (themselves, it should be remembered, only dubiously and recently European) as well as a practical medium for the elaboration of an ultimately anticolonial sensibility among the creole upper and middle classes.

The later eighteenth century brought into this scene the sometimes clandestine influence of neoclassicism and Enlightenment literary models, Free Masonry, the Black Legend, Manchester School political economy, the French Revolution, and so on. But in a gesture of formal continuity with the colony, literature was also to be marked as a form of republican institutionality during the independence struggles of the nineteenth century. Latin American liberals – themselves formed pedagogically as *letrados* – saw the development of literature as a way to create a mentality appropriate for the consolidation under their authority of the newly independent republics. The new "national" literatures of Latin America therefore emerged in close connection both to state-formation and to the *letrados'* own formation and incorporation into the state as, simultaneously, an intelligentsia and an acutal or would-be ruling class. The literatures evolved with the process of social differentiation and status struggle of the members of this intelligentsia. They served to define their group and personal identity, their relationship to power and to other social classes or groups, their sense of the defects and possibilities of development of the new societies, and, in a sort of feed-back effect, their belief in the central role of literature and literary culture in assuring that development. But by reimposing, now under quasi-democratic and modernizing auspices, writing and literacy as standards of cultural performance, this liberal-romantic cult of literature put the predominantly oral practices of song and narrative of the indigenous population (a majority in some countries) and the mestizo peasantry and rural proletariat in a relation of subordination and domination, deepening the separation between a hegemonic Spanish language print-based culture and cultures and languages that had been made subaltern with the colonial institution of literature.[21]

The continued centrality of literature as a cultural form in Latin American society revealed in the popularity of, and critical hoopla about, Boom narrative involves something like a modernist (in the English-language sense of the term) revision of this ideology of the literary in its colonial and republican variants. In this revision, the development of new forms of literature is seen as intimately bound up with the question of the consolidation of the nation state and its economic and social modernization. In particular, high-culture literature is seen as an agency for a progressive process of "transculturation"– the term was coined by the Cuban ethnographer Fernando Ortiz to describe the interaction of European and African elements in the formation of Cuban culture – involving a sometimes agonic, sometimes beneficent, synthesis of European and non-European, high and low, urban and rural, intellectual and popular cultural forms. Angel Rama was the most explicit proponent of this concept on the left, relating it to the tasks of national liberation struggle in the sixties; but in one way or another it has tended to characterize Latin American literary criticism generally during the Boom and after (there is a neoconservative version of it in Octavio Paz, Emir Rodríquez Monegal, or Mario Vargas Llosa, for example). Directly or indirectly connected to this concept is the almost unchallenged assumption in Latin American literary history – its origins are in the work of Pedro Henríquez Ureña, the founder of modern Latin American literary criticism – that the writing of the colonial and independence periods represents a protonationalistic process of cultural mestizaje and differentiation. As Julio Ramos has noted, this assumption, which made literature and literary values the key signifiers of Latin American nationality for a national bourgeois intelligentsia, became institutionalized as part of the ideology of the humanities in the Spanish-American university system in the early twentieth century, precisely as a response to the perceived threat represented by proletarianization and U.S.-style mass culture.[22]

I do not want to place myself in the position of denying the sometimes progressive role of literature and the humanities in Latin American society: among other things, such a position would undermine the argument I tried to develop in the book on Central American revolutionary literature. At the same time, the aversion or ambivalence of the testimonio towards literature that we have noted here (and, in a related way, the failure of the poetry workshop experiment in the Nicaraguan revolution championed by Ernesto Cardenal) suggests not only that cultural democratization must involve a transformation of literature's dominant forms and character – most particularly a breakdown and renegotiation of the distinctions on which its status as a master discourse have rested – but also that literature itself (along with the concomitant standards and practice of "good writing") may in the process lose its centrality and authority as a cultural practice.

There is a critical moment in the introduction to *I. Rigoberta Menchú* where the interlocutor, the Venezuelan social scientist Elisabeth Burgos, debates with herself about what to correct in the transcription of the recordings of Menchú's conversations with her. Burgos decides to leave in, for example, repetitions and digressions that she considers characteristic of oral narrative; on the other hand, she wants "to correct the gender mistakes which inevitably occur when someone has just learned to speak a foreign language. It would have been artificial to leave them uncorrected and it would have made Rigoberta look 'picturesque,' which is the last thing I wanted" (Menchú, xx–xxi).

One might object here that the interlocutor is manipulating the material the informant provides to suit her own cosmopolitan, political, intellectual, and aesthetic predilections, if it were not for the fact that this is not something Menchú herself would have resisted or resented, since her point in telling her story to Burgos was precisely to make it available to reading publics that are defined by literature both in Guatemala and abroad. For what has happened between Menchú's speech and Burgos's preface is that Menchú's narrative has become both a "text" and "literary." There is perhaps no more mediated and editorially mutilated testimonial text in Latin American literature than the *Autobiography* of the Cuban exslave Juan Francisco Manzano, which was prepared in 1835 at the urging of the Cuban liberal Domingo Del Monte, corrected and edited by the overtly abolitionist novelist Anselmo Suarez y Romero, and subsequently abridged and translated for a metropolitan audience by the principal agent of British imperialism in Cuba, Richard Madden. Sylvia Molloy has compared the unedited version of Manzano's original, handwritten manuscript with the published versions in Spanish and English. She concludes that

> The *Autobiografía* as Manzano wrote it, with its run-on sentences, breathless paragraphs, dislocated syntax and idiosyncratic mis-spellings, vividly portrays that quandary – an anxiety of origins, ever renewed, – that provides the text with the stubborn, uncon-trolled energy that is possibly its major achievement. The writ-ing, *in itself,* is the best self-portrait we have of Manzano, his greatest contribution to literature; at the same time, it is what translators, editors and critics cannot tolerate. . . . [The] notion (shared by many) that there is a clear narrative imprisoned, as it were, in Manzano's *Autobiografía,* waiting for the hand of the cultivated editor to free it from the slag – this notion that the im-pure text must be replaced by a clean (white?) version of it to be readable – amounts to another, aggressive mutilation, that of denying the text readability in its own terms.[23]

Can we take this, mutatis mutandis, as an allegory of both the production of testimonio and its incorporation into the hu-manities? What was at stake in the Stanford debate about the core curriculum was the opposition of two different canons or reading lists – one traditional and Euro- and phallocentric, the other third worldist and feminist. But literature and the humani-ties as such – not to speak of Stanford's function in the forma-tion and reproduction of class power in the U.S. and global economy – were never put into question. They were rather the condition of possibility of struggle over the curriculum and the reading lists in the first place. I understand this position, and I pursue it in my own work of presenting and interpreting texts in the classroom (which has included teaching courses on Cen-tral American revolutionary literature at, among other places, Stanford).

But in dealing with the testimonio I have also begun to discover in myself a kind of posthumanist agnosticism about literature. I am not proposing that there is any more authentic or culturally

effective ground than the one we are on as producers and students of literature in the academy, and in any case ideologies
(even literary ones), like neuroses, defend themselves with very
powerful and effective systems of resistance: nothing you experience in an essay of this sort is going to make you reconsider
what you fundamentally believe. But in spite of Ernesto Laclau's
point, which I consider extremely important in other contexts,
that ideological signifiers do not have a necessary "class-
belonging," the problem of testimonio indicates that literature
cannot simply be appropriated by this or that social project. It
is deeply marked by its own historical and institutional entangle-
ments, its "tradition of service," so to speak. There may come
a time when we have a new community of texts we can call
literature; but not now. Among the many lessons testimonio has
to offer us is to suggest that it is no longer a question of "reading
against the grain," as in the various academic practices of textual deconstruction we are familiar with, but of beginning to read
against literature itself.

POSTSCRIPT:
TESTIMONIO AND POSTMODERNISM

I suggested in "The Margin at the Center" a complementarity
between Latin American testimonio and first world postmodernism, noting that

> The reception of testimonio . . . has something to do with a re-
> vulsion for fiction and the fictive as such, with its "postmodern"
> estrangement. Testimonio, if you want to look at it that way (and
> you certainly are not obliged to), could be seen as a form of post-
> modernist narrative closely related to established U.S. forms like
> drug or gay narratives, of which William Burroughs' *Junky* is
> perhaps the classic case, or Black, Chicano, and Puerto Rican
> autobiography (*The Autobiography of Malcolm X, Down These
> Mean Streets, The Autobiography of a Brown Buffalo*), John
> Rechy's work, and so on. (Beverley, 15, n. 9)

Some second thoughts are perhaps also in order on this score.
Clearly there is a problem in applying a term that is generally

conceived in relation to the narcissism and anomie of "post-Fordist" capitalist societies to those represented in much of Latin American and third world testimonio, which either have not gone through the stage of "modernity" (in the Weberian sense) yet, or display an "uneven" modernity (what society does not, however?). Clearly also there is a correspondence (sometimes quite direct, as in architecture) between cultural phenomena identified as postmodernist and the present sensibility and strategies of multinational capitalism, which gives some credence to the idea that postmodernism may be a form of cultural imperialism. There is the related danger that the production of a "postmodernist sublime" in relation to Latin America may involve the aesthetic fetishization, as in Didion's *Salvador,* of its social, cultural, and economic status quo (as "abject," chaotic, carnivalesque, etc.), thereby attenuating the urgency for radical social change and displacing it onto cultural dilettantism and quietism. As George Yúdice has noted, the flux of late capitalist commodity culture which is seen as liberating by postmodernist theorists like Baudrillard may represent in fact new forms of oppression and subalternity for third world peoples as it restructures and resemiotizes their cultures. In the same vein, there is Neil Larsen's useful warning that, even where there is a "promise of subversion" in postmodernism, this "seems no more and no less genuine than that long-ago discredited pledge of the modernist vanguard to, as it were, seize hold of capital's cultural and psychic mechanisms without firing a shot."[24]

However, I think there is also an important sense in which the forms of popular-democratic cultural resistance to imperialism represented by and in testimonio themselves rise up on a postmodern terrain.[25] The two interrelated problematics that are generally taken as defining postmodernism are the collapse of the distinction between elite and popular (or mass) cultures, sometimes expressed as the loss of aesthetic autonomy (Jameson); and the collapse of the "great narratives" of "western" progress and enlightenment – including both bourgeois and marxist historicisms – with which the specifically aesthetic project of modernism was associated. Similarly, the aesthetic and ideological significance of testimonio depends on its ability to function in the historically constituted space that separates elite and popular cultures in Latin America, and to generate postcolonial, non-Eurocentric narratives of individual and collective historical destiny. Where literature in Latin America has been (mainly) a vehicle for engendering an adult, white, male, patriarchal, "lettered" subject, testimonio allows the emergence – albeit mediated – of subaltern female, gay, indigenous, proletarian, etc., "oral" identities. In this sense it is coincident with postmodernism rather than its Other. It is true that part of what is designated as postmodernism is related to the rampant commodification and monopolization of even elite cultural production in late capitalist societies, which also affects peripheral social formations (the sort of Latin American national bourgeois publishing houses that might have published Borges as a young writer, for example, are being taken over or displaced by multinationals concerned with retailing translations of international best-sellers); at the same time, as Walter Benjamin understood, the loss of aura or desublimation of the art work that was portended by mechanical reproduction can also be a very radical form of cultural democratization. Like testimonio, metropolitan postmodernism has involved in cultural production and consumption broad lower middle class, working class and minority sectors of the population previously excluded in general form and by high culture forms like literature.

The critique of postmodernism by the Latin American left[26] tends to set up a dichotomy between complex, anti-representational, value-leveling, high-culture forms of literature of the sort represented by Borges or Boom narrative in general and simple, lineal, representational, value-affirming, "popular" narrative forms like the testimonio. That some of the force of that dichotomy has necessarily crept into my own thinking about testimonio I think is evident, but it needs also to be qualified. While testimonio implies a challenge and an alternative to modernist literary models based on a subversion or rejection of narratives of identity, it is not, as we have seen, a completely autonomous form deriving directly from subaltern culture. It is (usually) a written transcription and textualization of a spoken narrative. The nature of any piece of writing – for example, the perceived qualities of testimonial as opposed to Boom narrative – is determined intertextually by its place in an already constituted discourse system. (Among the models Rigoberta Menchú mobilizes in constructing her testimonio is certainly Biblical narrative, which as a Catholic lay catechist she knew intimately; there are clear traces of his readings of Boom novels as a university student in Cabezas's *Fire from the Mountain,* a text "spoken" into a tape-recorder; and so on.) Rather than a clear dichotomy between a purely oral popular culture of resistance and a purely colonial and/or neocolonial written high culture, Latin American culture has involved since the colonial period a series of "hybrid combinations of elite and subaltern forms."[27] In its very situation of enunciation, which separates radically the subject-positions of the emitter and the receiver, testimonio is a form of the dialectic of oppressor and oppressed, involved in, and constructed out of, its opposing terms: master/slave, literature/oral narrative and song, metropolitan/national, European/indigenous or mestizo, elite/popular, urban/rural, intellectual/manual work.

Testimonio is no more capable of transcending these oppositions than more purely "literary" forms of writing or narrative: that would require social and cultural transformations capable of initiating literacy campaigns and developing the educational and economic infrastructures necessary to create and sustain a mass reading public that has as a prior condition the victory of revolutionary movements in the first place. But testimonio does represent a new way of articulating these oppositions and thus of defining new paradigms for the relationship between the intelligentsia and popular classes. In this sense, it represents also a new sort of aesthetic agency in political struggles.

While testimonio has been in Latin America and elsewhere the "literary" (under erasure) form of both revolutionary activism and more limited defensive struggles for human rights and redemocratization, paradoxically and against the expectations of its original protagonists, it does not seem particularly well suited to become the primary narrative form of periods of postrevolutionary consolidation and struggle, as in Cuba in the 1970s and

1980s or Nicaragua after 1979, perhaps because its very dynamics depend on the conditions of dramatic social and cultural inequality that fuel the revolutionary impulse in the first place. One of the problems revealed by the electoral defeat of the Sandinistas is that the identification portended in testimonio between a radicalized intelligentsia – represented by the FSLN leadership and upper and middle cadre – and the popular sectors had to some extent broken down. Coincidentally, one had begun to note a problematization of the formula of testimonio itself in Nicaragua: testimonios continued to be produced, but, except for those dealing with the *contra* war, they lacked the urgency of the testimonios of the revolutionary period (and testimonio must above all be a story that *needs* to be told, that involves some pressing and immediate problem of communication). I conclude from this that, like postmodernism itself (and more particularly like its ancestor the picaresque novel), testimonio is a transitional cultural form appropriate to processes of rapid social and historical change, but also destined to give way to different forms of representation as these processes move forward (or, as in the case of Nicaragua today, backward) to other stages, and the human collectivities that are their agents come into the possession of new forms of power and knowledge.

Notes

With some minor editorial differences, this essay is reprinted from "Through All Things Modern: Second Thoughts on Testimonio," *boundary 2* 18:2, copyright 1992, Duke University Press. Reprinted with permission of the publisher.

1. Rigoberta Menchú, with Elisabeth Burgos, *I, Rigoberta Menchú: An Indian Woman in Guatemala,* trans. Ann Wright (London: Verso, 1984), 171.

2. John Beverley, "The Margin at the Center: On *Testimonio* (Testimonial Narrative)," *Modern Fiction Studies* 35/1 (1989): 11-28, a special issue on *Narratives of Colonial Resistance* edited by Timothy Brennan.

3. "My name is Rigoberta Menchú. I am twenty three years old. This is my testimony. I didn't learn it from a book, and I didn't learn it alone. I'd like to stress that it's not only *my* life, it's also the testimony of my people. It's hard for me to remember everything that's happened to me in my life since there have been many very bad times but, yes, moments of joy as well. The important thing is that what has happened to me has happened to many other people too: My story is the story of all poor Guatemalans. My personal experience is the reality of a whole people" (Menchú, 1).

4. Gayatri Spivak, "Can the Subaltern Speak?" in C. Nelson and L. Grossberg, eds., *Marxism and the Interpretation of Culture* (Urbana: University of Illinois Press, 1988), 278.

5. Doris Sommer, "Rigoberto's Secrets," *Voices of the Voiceless in Testimonial Literature,* special issue of *Latin American Perspectives 70,* 18/3 (1991), 48.

6. Thus, for example, Allen Carey-Webb, who teaches an undergraduate course on World Literature at the University of Oregon based entirely on testimonios, notes that *I. Rigoberta Menchú* "is one of the most moving books I have ever read. It is the kind of a book that I feel I must pass on, that I must urge fellow teachers to use in their classes. . . . My students were immediately sympathetic to Menchú's story and were anxious to know more, to involve themselves. They asked questions about culture and history, about their own position in the world, and about the purposes and methods of education. Many saw in the society of the Guatemalan Indian attractive features they found lacking in their own lives, strong family relationships, community solidarity, an intimate relationship with nature, commitment to others and to one's beliefs" ("Teaching Third World Auto-Biography: Testimonial Narrative in the Canon and Classroom," *Oregon English* [Fall, 1990]: 8).

7. See, respectively, Fredric Jameson, "Third World Literature in the Era of Multinational Capitalism," *Social Text* 15 (1986); his interview with Anders Stephanson, *Social Text* 17 (1987); Barbara Harlow, *Resistance Literature* (New York: Methuen, 1987); Barbara Foley, *Telling the Truth: The Theory and Practice of Documentary Fiction* (Ithaca: Cornell University Press, 1986); Margaret Randall, *Testimonios: A Guide to Oral History* (Toronto: Participatory Research Group, 1985); George Yúdice, "Marginality and the Ethics of Survival," in Andrew Ross, ed., *Universal Abandon: The Politics of Postmodernism* (Minneapolis: University of Minnesota Press,

1988); Yúdice, "Testimonio and Postmodernism," *Latin American Perspectives 70*, 18/3 (1991); Juan Duchesne, "Las narraciones guerrilleras: Configuración de un sujeto épico de nuevo tipo," in H. Vidal and R. Jara eds., *Testimonio y Literature* (Minneapolis: Ideologies and Literature, 1986); Spivak, "Can the Subaltern Speak?" and Elzbieta Sklodowska, "La forma testimonial y la novelística de Miguel Barnet," *Revista/Review Interamericana* 12/3 (1982).

8. See Roberto González Echevarría, *"Biografía de un cimarrón* and the Novel of the Cuba Revolution," in his *The Voice of the Masters: Writing and Authority in Modern Latin American Literature* (Austin: University of Texas Press, 1985).

9. An instance of this ambivalence may be found in the definition of testimonio in the contest rules of the prestigious literary prizes of Cuba's Casa de las Américas (it was the decision of Casa de las Américas in 1971 to offer a prize in this category that put testimonio on the canonical map of Latin American literature in the first place): "Testimonios must document some aspect of Latin American or Caribbean reality from a direct source. A direct source is understood as knowledge of the facts by their author and his or her compilation of narratives or evidence obtained from the individuals involved or qualified witnesses. In both cases reliable documentation, written or graphic, is indispensable. The form is at the author's discretion, *but literary quality is also indispensable"* (translation and italics mine). But is there a determination of "literary quality" which does not involve in turn an ideology of the literary? Against a modernist bias in favor of textual collage and/or editorial elaboration in the preparation of a testimonial text, one could argue that a direct, "unliterary" narrative might have both a higher ethical *and* aesthetic status.

10. See, for example, the remarks of the great Peruvian novelist José María Arguedas on the difficulty of reconciling in his own work an inherited Spanish-language model of "literariness" with the representation of the world of Quechua- or Aymara-speaking Andean peasants: "I wrote my first story in the most correct and 'literary' Spanish I could devise. I read the story to some of my writer friends in the capital, and they praised it. But I came to detest more and more those pages. No, what I wanted to describe – one could almost say denounce – wasn't like that at all, not the person, not the town, not the landscape. Under a false language a world appeared as invented, without marrow and without blood: a typically

'literary' world in which the word had consumed the work" ("La novela y el problema de la expresión literaria en el Perú," in *Obras completas* 2 [Lima: Editorial Horizonte, 1983], 196; translation mine). Arguedas's solution was to develop a novel, in Spanish, based stylistically and thematically on the tension between Spanish and Quechua. By contrast, there is the well-known example of the Kenyan writer Ngugi Wa Thiongo who in 1977, after publishing a series of successful anticolonial novels in English, decided to write his novels, plays, and stories exclusively in his tribal language Kikuyu. See his "The Language of African Literature," in *Decolonising the Mind: The Politics of Language in African Literature* (Portsmouth, NH: Heinemann, 1987).

11. Ana Guadalupe Martínez, *La cárceles clandestinas de El Salvador* (México: Casa El Salvador, 1979).

12. Cf. Roque Dalton's reconstruction of the life of one of the founders of the Salvadoran Communist party, *Miguel Mármol*, and his own autobiographical novel of the guerrilla underground, *Pobrecito poeta que era yo*.

13. Walter Mignolo, "Literacy and Colonization: The New World Experience," in R. Jara and N. Spadaccini eds., *1492-1992: Re/Discovering Colonial Writing*, Hispanic Issues 4 (Minneapolis: Prisma Institute, 1989), 67.

14. Mignolo similarly is careful to distinguish in the same essay the literacy of the colonial and neocolonial state from the contemporary literacy campaigns instituted for example by the Cuban and Nicaraguan revolutions based on the methods of Paolo Freire's "pedagogy of the oppressed," which he sees as a means of empowerment of the subaltern.

15. In Sommer, "Rigoberto's Secrets," noted above.

16. Gayatri Spivak, "On the Politics of the Subaltern," interview with Howard Winant in *Socialist Review* 90/3 (July-September 1990): 91. To anticipate the inevitable objections, see, e.g., Benita Parry, "Problems in Current Theories of Colonial Discourse," *Oxford Literary Review* 9/1-2 [1988]: the subaltern of course speaks quite a lot, but not *to* Gayatri Spivak, so to speak. It is not to trivialize Che Guevara's example to observe that his eerily prophetic sense – noted in the *Bolivian Diary* – of the blankness in the eyes of the peasants he encountered in the course of trying to establish a guerrilla *foco* in the Bolivian Andes might have been otherwise had he been able to speak their language, Aymara.

17. See on this point James Clifford, "On Collecting Art and Culture," in Russell Ferguson et al., eds. *Out There: Marginalization and Contemporary Culture* (Cambridge, Mass.: MIT Press, 1990).

18. John Beverley and Marc Zimmerman, *Literature and Politics in the Central American Revolutions* (Austin: University of Texas Press, 1990).

19. Angel Rama, *La ciudad letrada* (Hanover, NH: Ediciones del Norte, 1984).

20. China, the Indian subcontinent, and Islamic Africa had written literatures before colonialism and in this sense differ from Latin America, which experienced a much deeper degree of European colonization both culturally and demographically. But I would argue that, whatever their links to the past, modern literatures in the third world generally are also basically engendered by colonialism and imperialism.

21. See Rama, *La ciudad letrada;* and in particular Alejandro Losada, "La literatura urbana como praxis social en América Latina," *Ideologies and Literature* 1/4 (1977), reprinted in his *La literatura en la sociedad de América Latina* (Aarhus, Denmark: Romansk Institut Aarhus Universitet, 1981).

22. Julio Ramos, *Desencuentros de la modernidad en América latina: Literatura y política en el siglo XIX* (Mexico: Fondo de Cultura Económica, 1990).

23. Sylvia Molloy, "From Serf to Self: The Autobiography of Juan Francisco Manzano," *Modern Language Notes* 104 (1989): 417.

24. Yúdice, "Marginality and the Ethics of Survival"; Neil Larsen, *Modernism and Hegemony* (Minneapolis: University of Minnesota Press, 1990), xxxi.

25. I share Jameson's sense in the concluding remarks to his book on postmodernism that the concept, which has certainly been devoured by habitualization (and perhaps also by the current recession), is still worth using: "I occasionally get just as tired of the slogan "postmodern" as anyone else, but when I am tempted to regret my complicity with it, to deplore its misuses and its notoriety, and to conclude with some reluctance that it raises more questions than it solves, I find myself pausing to wonder whether any other concept can dramatize the issues in quite so effective and economical

a fashion" (*Postmodernism, or, The Cultural Logic of Late Capitalism* [Durham: Duke University Press, 1990], p. 410).

26. See, e.g., Yúdice's "Marginality and the Ethics of Survival," noted above.

27. See Nestor García Canclini, *Culturas híbridas: Estrategias para entrar y salir de la modernidad* (Mexico: Grijalbo, 1990).

Postmodernity and Postmodernism in Latin America: Carlos Fuentes's *Christopher Unborn*

RICARDO GUTIÉRREZ MOUAT

A PERIPHERAL POSTMODERNITY

The Latin American debate on postmodernism is recent and has to a large extent been informed by skepticism. To the suspicion that the postmodern question more properly pertains to the developed world of late capitalism is added the political apprehension that the debate itself legitimates economic and political changes that some still see as deleterious to the masses and as running counter to nationalist ideology:

> One tendency on the left is to view the "postmoderns" or the "postmos" as depoliticized rightwingers, while others distinguish between progressive and reactionary tendencies. For some people, postmodernism means simply the exhaustion of Marxism and the need for a new social and economic pact to achieve modernization. In contrast, for others it is a problem unique to post-industrial societies and has little to do with the underdevelopment of Latin America.[1]

It seems paradoxical to speak of the postmodern as a phase in which various players and discourses reevaluate and realign

themselves in search of new momentum to achieve modernization. But in fact this strange chronological reversal can move forward and be made linear if the question of modernization is
considered from the standpoint of the *peripheralized* cultures
and societies that make up Latin America. For them, the impulse and models for modernization have always come from
abroad, from the financial and technological metropolitan centers that successive elites in Latin America have tried to emulate
with uneven success. And they have always come late, not late
enough to have lost their aura of progress but not soon enough,
either, to prevent modernization from being first a fantasy or a
desire. Further, Latin American societies are still trying to become part of the modern world, regardless of the political ideology they officially subscribe to. Energetic calls for modernization were heard just as loudly in the Nicaragua of the Sandinistas
as in Pinochet's Chile, though the roads charted towards the
utopia of progress forked out in vastly different directions. No
observer in Latin America would speak today of a completed
project of social, economic, and political modernization anywhere
in the region – even if to complete such a project were theoreti-
cally possible. And while governments in Mexico and Argentina
struggle to modernize their economies through privatization
and increased exports, cultural pundits in Paris, New York, and
Frankfurt have begun to talk about postmodernity, thus raising
the stakes for societies eager to think of themselves as contemporary. The temporal gap that is created makes it possible to
speak of the postmodern in cultures that are still trying to reach
a properly modern stage.

At times the hope implicit in this debate seems to be that if
Latin America arrived at modernity too late, it can still catch up
to the postmodern while it is happening, a hope which at best
may be called nominalist. Yet to speak of the postmodern in
connection with Latin America is not entirely illegitimate as long
as the discussion – as Hugo Achugar cautions – does not become
"an automatic reflection of the metropolitan debates that occurred
in very different contexts": "The debate acquires relevance in
the context of our own culture and history only when it is viewed

against the background of the unequal and contradictory development of . . . Latin America."[2] And one should add that this debate is rendered necessary not because Lyotard and Habermas,
or deconstructionists and Marxists, have gone at it in Europe
but because the material conditions and social attitudes that un-
derlie it – consumerism, technocracy, state-of-the-art technology,
the culture of the image, etc. – have themselves carried over
into selected sectors of Latin American social and political life.
Implicit in Fredric Jameson's theory of the postmodern as the
cultural dominant of late multinational capitalism[3] is the global-
ization of this culture and its reproduction along the same information channels that promote the circulation of capital on a
worldwide scale. The Latin American economies can no more
prevent their integration into the capitalist world economy than
can the cultural sector of the superstructure remain static in the
face of the new information technology and the growing authority of the mass media and mass culture.

In order to grasp the notion of the postmodern, the noted
Chilean sociologist, José Joaquín Brunner, projects it against the
background of Latin America's unequal development and talks
noncontradictorily of a "sort of *avant la lettre* regional postmodernism that is nonetheless fully constitutive of our modernity."[4]
Brunner focuses critically on current modernizing blueprints that
fail to address the cultural heterogeneity of contemporary Latin
American societies in their call for a cultural rationality that would
mediate and naturalize the transfer of technology, behaviors, and
institutions from the center to the periphery. Social technicians,
he argues, are blind to the fact that no single cultural *ratio* is
viable in societies already characterized by a multiplicity of such
rationalities:

> The rationality of the market, for instance, is quite different
> from the rationality of politics, and both differ from techno-
> bureaucratic rationality. . . . Therefore, there are no "rational
> norms" outside their context: the laboratory, the competitive
> marketplace, the non-competitive marketplace, the state, politi-
> cal parties, etc. (214)

For Brunner, cultural heterogeneity is a direct result of the operations of the global market economy and has a twofold aspect:

> segmentation and segmented participation in that world market of messages and symbols, whose underlying grammar is U.S. hegemony over the "imaginary" of a great part of mankind. . . ; [and] differential participation according to *local reception codes,* comprising groups and individuals, in the ceaseless movement of transmission circuits that range from publicity to pedagogy (217-218; Brunner's emphasis)

Brunner makes the further points that what he terms cultural heterogeneity should not be confused with the ethnic or ethnographic kind (which, it is easy to see, is subsumed in the larger category of commodity production and distribution); and that this "postmodernism" that constitutes contemporary Latin American societies involves a plurality of "logics" that from a Eurocentric and Enlightenment perspective can be called modern: secularization, the increasing gains of formal rationality, bureaucratization, individuation, sense of futurity, self-identification in terms of economic and social class, and many others. Latin American social life thus appears to the cultural observer as postmodern *collage* or *pastiche,* as a paratactic collection of gadgets, images, motivations, and behaviors whose only common denominator is their external source:

> Our societies no longer appear as such but each one as a sector of the international market, especially in the cultural domain. Infinite local cultural exchanges remain and can even be said to form the fabric of our everyday life. . . . But through and above that fabric – Can we still call it national? – messages flow and institutions are articulated that are fully incorporated to a modernity whose heart is far from the heart of "our" culture. (217)

Thus it seems that Latin American cultures were already postmodern before the label was imported and affixed to them.

Jorge Edwards observed a decade ago the bizarre symbiosis in contemporary Chile between the forms of nineteenth-century political *caudillismo* (symbolized by Pinochet's military tunic and epaulets) and the gadgets of modern information technology surrounding the banking establishment: telex machines, computer banks, instant communications with Tokyo, Hong Kong, and New York, etc.[5] This temporal warp (that shares some affinities with Carpentier's script of magic realism) is the sign of the modern in Latin America and therefore of the postmodern. Both of these moments are but a prolonged instance of traditional societies' shifting their internal configuration to cope with their own demand for modernization and in the process creating fractures and contradictions that allow the effects of modernization to be read as a postmodern text, as bricolage, heteroglossia, and *pastiche*. To quote a Fuentes aphorism, in Mexico Quetzalcoatl coexists with Pepsi-Coatl.

Brunner's essay also engages the problem of nationalism, which is an ideologico-political reaction against the dissolution of society threatened by modernization, a reaction that in recent years has been superseded by a postmodern kind of political praxis. The argument is that in the 1960s the secularization of social life was promoted by modernization and stimulated an ideological inflation that favored revolutionary proposals for national liberation and social integration. Revolutionarism implied a messianic and fundamentalist political style that can be construed as a countersecular legitimation for authoritarian governments of varied ideological stripes. But the democratic recuperation of the 1980s in countries such as Argentina, Chile, and Uruguay has shown that secularism can also beneift the institutionalization of the most typically modern form of government by relieving politics of ethico-religious and affective compromises and thus "cooling" it. Brunner is referring here to a "disenchanted" notion of political praxis:

> This secularized politics echoes certain tendencies, themes, and attitudes of the postmodern movement . . . : there is in both a critique of the idea of the full subject, an abandonment of the *grand récits*, a conversion of time into an absolute present, a reduction of politics to an exchange of material and symbolic goods. (229)

The risk is that this decisively (post)modern and "de-dramatized" political style might exclude certain interests that cannot be exchanged in the political marketplace: "human rights, the sense of belonging, the desire for certainty, the need for transcendental referents" (230).

One of the most influential proponents of postmodern politics, Mario Vargas Llosa, is quite specific in assigning culture an affirmative role in the new order.[6] After calling for the dismantling of the patrimonial state in Latin America, Vargas Llosa pauses to underscore the point that such an overhaul does not mean the exoneration of the state from certain responsibilities, first and foremost the distribution of culture among all sectors of the population. Culture, he says, guarantees the survival of the critical spirit in civil society, but it is also a way

> in which a liberal state can neutralize one of the congenital dangers of modern capitalist society: a certain dehumanization of life, a materialism that isolates the individual, destroys the family, promotes selfishness, solitude, snobbism, cynicism, and other forms of spiritual emptiness. No modern industrial society has yet been able to meet this challenge head-on; in all of them a high standard of living and the massive availability of material progress have weakened that social solidarity which, paradoxically, is often very intense in primitive communities, and have generated the proliferation of madly irrational cults and rites whose only explanation seems to be the unconscious need somehow to replace that loss of faith to which apparently we are not able to resign ourselves.[7]

This view of the role of culture in a society dominated by the rationality of the market is idealist. It presupposes that the cultural sphere is somehow immune to the formal or instrumental rationality whose expansion through an ever-increasing number of cognitive, ethico-political, and aesthetic orders has characterized the advance of capitalism in the developed world. Jameson and others have often remarked on the spilling out of culture in the postmodern age from the autonomous institutional "container" where it was held at the height of modernism onto the general society, where it cavorts with other commodities:

> The dissolution of an autonomous sphere of culture is . . . to be imagined in terms of an explosion: a prodigious expansion of culture throughout the social realm, to the point at which everything in our social life – from economic value and state power to practices and to the very structure of the psyche itself – can be said to have become "cultural" in some original and as yet untheorized sense.[8]

This alternative view of postmodern culture, it must be added, also does away with the notion of a critical art so dear to Vargas Llosa. The conflation of artistic production and commodity production in general – as in the advertising industry which is the salient form of postmodern economic activity in some Latin American capitals – undermines the critical elan of artistic production by rewarding commercial uses of art. To be sure, this particular view of postmodernism, stressing its "consumerist hedonism and philistine anti-historicism, its wholesale abandonment of critique and commitment, its cynical erasure of truth, meaning and subjectivity, [and] its blank, reified technologism," is not the only one, as Terry Eagleton has remarked:

> From a radical viewpoint, the case for the defence of postmodernism might go roughly as follows. Post-modernism represents the latest iconoclastic upsurge of the avant garde, with its demotic confounding of hierarchies, its self-reflexive subversions of ideological closure, its populist debunking of intellectualism and elitism.[9]

But it is doubtful that this kind of avant garde revolutionarism is what Vargas Llosa understands by critical culture simply because critical culture is articulated within the context of the liberal state. Indeed, Vargas Llosa's conception of the subject who would benefit from the cultural largesse of the state is no other than the subject envisioned by liberal humanism: unique, autonomous, self-determining, self-identical. As Eagleton argues, this bourgeois subject is ideologically indispensable as a legitimating strategy for late capitalism but totally unfit for its workings:

> To turn the logic of the commodity against the imperatives of moral humanism – to pit the subject as a diffuse network of passing libidinal attachments against the strenuously self-directing agent which continues to represent the system's official ideal – is as unacceptable to the regulators of production as it is welcome to the stage managers of consumption.[10]

Consumerism cannot thrive on the bourgeois individual but needs him at the ideological level in order to facilitate its operations. Latin American advocates of modernization like Vargas Llosa thus want to have their cake and eat it too; they want free markets and pragmatic politics but are not willing to give up traditional values derived from a sense of community or from civil society, hoping that culture will mediate and absorb the contradiction.

More in line with the cultural and economic logic of postmodernism, Vargas Llosa asserts that to liquidate nationalism "is a *sine qua non* condition of our development and modernization." He excoriates economic and cultural nationalism as "one of the most stubborn aberrations of our history," and political nationalism as an artificial construction of national unity:

> At last we are learning that health does not lie in strengthening frontiers but in opening them wide in order to go out into the world to conquer markets for our products and so that technology and capital and the ideas of the world can enter and help our markets create the jobs that we so urgently need.[11]

While one must be careful to distinguish between cultural nationalism and national culture – problematic or irrelevant as this notion may have become in postmodern theory – it is remarkable that Vargas Llosa generally eludes the second of these issues in his paradigm for modernization, perhaps because the notion of a nationally undifferentiated, "universal" culture is ingrained in the concept of affirmative culture as defined by Marcuse:

As the purposeless and beautiful were internalized and, along with the qualities of binding universal validity and sublime beauty, made into the cultural values of the bourgeoisie, a realm of apparent unity and apparent freedom was constructed within culture in which the antagonistic relations of existence were supposed to be stabilized and pacified. Culture affirms and conceals the new conditions of social life.[12]

Surely, the critical potential that Marcuse attributes to affirmative culture comes closer to Vargas Llosa's view of the role of cultural production in a (post)modern society. For Marcuse, bourgeois idealism is not just an ideology that legitimates a set of material conditions and disguises social contradictions by inscribing the subject in an abstract equation according to which all are equal regardless of their economic status. Culture also preserves the traumatic traces of the institutionalization of the bourgeois order (and the liberal state) and keeps alive as well the best desires of people "amidst a bad reality":

By making suffering and sorrow into eternal, universal forces, great bourgeois art has continually shattered in the hearts of men the facile resignation of everyday life. By painting in the luminous colors of this world the beauty of men and things and transmundane happiness, it has planted real longing alongside poor consolation and false consecration in the soil of bourgeois life.[13]

Yet the achievement of the cultural ideal remains bound to a material transformation in a direction other than the increased economic competition implied in the development model favored by Vargas Llosa and other free-market advocates.

Ultimately, it is less important to decide the issue between the renewed dialectical materialism represented by Marcuse and the free-market policies and pragmatic politics espoused by a contemporary intellectual like Vargas Llosa, than it is to situate the latter's proposal in the context of a Latin American debate between modernizers and traditionalists. Vargas Llosa's modernizing discourse derives part of its interest from its attempt to synthesize points of view usually adopted by divergent factions and interest groups (sometimes belonging to the same discipline, namely, the social sciences). We have seen the problems inherent in the postulation of culture as a shock absorber for the insertion of an underdeveloped society into the world of late capitalism. Another palliative identified by Vargas Llosa to prevent the wholesale dissolution of such a society as it undergoes the stress of modernization is traditional religion:

> for the great majority religion seems to be, within our tradition, the soundest vehicle to restrain the instinct of death and destruction, to exercise solidarity, to respect certain ethic codes that might guarantee coexistence and order within the polity. . . .[14]

This is a rare moment in which Vargas Llosa specifically alludes to a component of national culture. Beyond the particulars of his text, however, looms a larger critique of modernization articulated by disaffected social scientists and Catholic intellectuals who argue for a "reenchantment" of life in the midst of the crisis of developmental schemes. Pedro Morandé, for instance, vindicates the notion of cultural synthesis as a critique not only of the various modernizing strategies implemented in Latin America since the end of the Second World War, but also of the social sciences themselves for neglecting to factor in the issue of culture, which for Morandé is coextensive with that of the social totality. According to this view, Latin American social scientists uncritically adopted paradigms elaborated in advanced capitalist societies and failed to acculturate them even when their external premises were thrown into question, for at this point what should have been a turn in the direction of cultural authenticity was preempted by the same ideological affiliations that divided world politics into antagonistic blocks. Nowhere – to press Morandé's argument to its conclusion – is the totality as evident in Latin America as in the cultural practices grounded on popular religion.[15] Clearly, Morandé's synthetic perspective is irrelevant to the kind of heterogeneous and differentiated social construct described by Brunner; but it nevertheless reflects the position of a powerful institution such as the Catholic church which in

Pinochet's Chile, at least, invested the symbolic capital accumulated in its determined stand against the human rights violations perpetrated by the regime in articulating a program of communicative rationality in direct opposition to the official cultural policy, whose aim was the privatization of the cultural sphere in accordance with the rationality of the market.[16]

To return one last time to Vargas Llosa's view of culture as a buffer zone between the practices of late capitalism and the traditional values of the liberal bourgeoisie (supplemented by the cohesive effect of popular religion), it is curious that the author of *Aunt Julia and the Scriptwriter* should have omitted any reference to mass culture, since access to mass culture may be considered the most common form of integration into modernity available to economically marginal sectors of the population. Common and frictionless, in the sense that this means of incorporation into what remains a segmented and differentiated – *refracted* – whole, mass culture bridges the gap between marginal cultures (popular and regional) and consumer culture, whose mode of production and circulation is now perceived to be hegemonic. Indeed, it is at this juncture that speaking of a Latin American postmodernity as a *structural* phenomenon begins to make sense. Brunner insists that the "explosion" of the culture industry in the 1960s marked a qualitatively different phase in the supply of massive cultural goods – previously entrusted to Church and School – because it fueled a complete redefinition and reorientation of everyday sociability:

> Here we run into the growth of a new "massive cultural market" which, in the case of television, unfolds itself in a brief span of time, extends its network nationally, penetrates into the home, and massively incorporates all groups and segments of society, including most significantly women, children and adolescents, senior citizens, provincial and small-town publics; and that, furthermore, connects with advertising, with certain bands of the educational spectrum, with the informative functions of the press, with the recording industry, with political staging and propaganda, etc.[17]

Brunner's emphasis on the rise of the cultural industry as a founding cultural moment cannot but recall Fredric Jameson's assertion that what all First World postmodernisms have in common is

> the effacement in them of the older (essentially high-modernist) frontier between high culture and so-called mass or commercial culture, and the emergence of new kinds of texts infused with the forms, categories and contents of that very Culture Industry so passionately denounced by all the ideologues of the modern . . . [18]

These new texts shaped by the culture industry began to appear in Latin America in the 1960s, even before the forms of the modern novel were fully exhausted. As early as 1971 José Donoso, author of the monumental *The Obscene Bird of Night*, published only in 1970, had sounded the death-knell of the "boom" by declaring: "The new generation finds the novel of the '60s excessively literary, and they devote themselves, like those in all avant-garde movements, to writing an 'anti-literature,' an 'anti-novel.'"[19] In this passage Donoso refers specifically to the adoption of film as narrative paradigm in the works of Manuel Puig, among others. He could have easily alluded to his younger compatriot Antonio Skármeta who, speaking for that new generation, states: "Those born around 1940 are the first in Latin America massively to confront the eloquence of the mass media,"[20] an encounter yielding a kind of literary minimalism self-consciously different from the aesthetic grandiosity of the modern novel. The general project of the modern novel – which Carlos Fuentes defined as the "critical synthesis of society"[21] – was the production of an autonomous and symbolic totality wherein all manner of contradictions would be subsumed, and that branched out into individual agendas ranging from Cortázar's quest for the absolute in *Hopscotch* to Carpentier's recreation of Latin American identity in the guise of magic realism. The postmodern successors to the Great Tradition, however, were admittedly more indebted to the forms of the culture industry – film, rock music, soap operas, advertising, television – and tried their hand at a more democratic and colloquial literature that nevertheless continued to hold the specificity of literary language in high esteem.

It is important to note, though, that despite the similarities in periodization schemes between literary developments, say, in the United States and in Latin America, there remains at least one important difference. Jameson, for example, portrays the American generation of the 1960s in terms analogous, if not identical, to Skármeta's characterization of its Latin American counterpart but also points out that the postmodernist turn is a reaction against the institutionalization of high-modernist culture and the defusion of its subversive potential.[22] In Latin America the absorption of modern fiction by cultural institutions – which is at best incipient – was inflected by the circulation of these texts among the general population through the mechanisms of the mass media, so that the stereotype of the canonical author coexists with the image of the author as media superstar, another instance of the overlapping of modernity and postmodernity in peripheral societies. In the Latin American time warp it is equally common to talk about the modern and postmodern phases of the same author as to identify different writers separately embodying the two cultural moments. This fast-forwarding in aesthetic continuity is the same kind of temporal distortion that allows us to speak, however tentatively, of postmodernity in relation to societies still striving to become modern.[23]

CHRISTOPHER UNBORN
AND CULTURAL IDENTITY

> "Was Laurence Sterne's *Tristram Shandy* proto-Modern or proto-Postmodern?"
>
> – John Barth

Christopher Unborn recapitulates in its content the key issues of the Latin American debate on the postmodern (social heterogeneity, nationalism, religious fundamentalism) but formally resists incorporation into the communicative mechanisms that make up postindustrial information society. Its polyphonic strategy seeks to grant all social languages equal access to the reader yet, contradictorily, the text's addressee is not the undifferentiated consumer of mass culture but the "Elector,"[24] a select reader willing and able to engage the author in a literary dialogue. This contradiction need not be projected against a populist/elitist axis but instead can serve to locate the novel in a site of transition between the modernist and postmodernist paradigms. Indeed, Fuentes's "Elector" is not substantially different from Cortázar's reader-accomplice in *Hopscotch* and, as such, harks back to the modernist paradigm.[25] Yet *Christopher Unborn* simultaneously deconstructs the notion of totality typical of the modern novel and thus claims a revised legitimacy less dependent on aesthetic synthesis and more on political heterodoxy.

The text is self-consciously heteroglossic:

> listen: here you can hear the político, the lover, the ideologue, the comic, the powerful, the weak, the child, the intellectual, the illiterate, the sensual, the vengeful, the charitable, the personage, but also history, society, language itself: the barbarous, the corrupt, the Gallic, the Anglic, the latic, the pochic, the unique, the provincial, and the Catholic. . . . (256)

Although in practice the question remains open as to whether all these languages have the same authority, or if, on the contrary, they are arranged in hierarchical fashion, the poetics of the text is a deconstructive response to the monologue of power fabricated and reproduced by ideologues in the mode of an overarching synthesis. Thus the ruling party's ideology allows the most contrary points of view to coexist within a common political framework:

> I am Catholic because I believe in the hierarchy and the sweet dogmas of my political church; but I am a revolutionary because I believe in its slogans and its most archaic proofs of legitimacy; I am conservative because without the PRI we head directly to communism; I am liberal because without the PRI we head directly to fascism; and I am a Catholic, revolutionary,

progressive, and reactionary millionaire all at the same time and for the same reasons: the PRI authorizes it. (246)

And when the modernization process spearheaded by the PRI sparks a fundamentalist revolt, the reigning ideology proves to be flexible enough to coopt the disaffected masses by reconciling the secular with the profane: "We've recaptured everything in order to achieve our heart's desire, National Unity. . . . I warn you, let us capture the world of the sacred before it captures us . . . : there is an Ayatollah in our Future" (236).

Don Homero Fagoaga is the character most closely identified with the harmonizing strategy of official discourse. An unconditional devotee of the party, his "national dialectic" is a multipurpose amalgam of ideological fragments:

> Mexicans we are because we are progressive because we are revolutionary because we are liberal because we are reformists because we are positivists because we are insurgents because we follow the Virgin of Guadalupe because we are Catholic because we are conservatives because we are Spaniards because we are Indians because we are mestizos. (153-154)

His body is as grotesque as his "ideology": "Uncle Homero got fatter and fatter. . . . The active dialectical organization of all opposites is immediately perceptible between his two cerebral hemispheres, as vast, conceivable [sic], as all the other paired fleshly parts of [his] abominable anatomy" (59). Homero is King Momus (cf. 435) and the carnival that he officiates in has more in common with a bloody and licentious popular revolt than with the (re)generative power of language and culture celebrated by the novel.

The narrative language, in fact, carnivalizes Homero's oratorical, rhetorical Spanish grounded on grammatical correctness and propriety. One of the character's roles is to serve as president of the Mexican Academy of Letters, a function that imposes on Homero the "nationalist task" to defend the Spanish language against the incursions of English. However, this new linguistic Cid ("Cid Lenguador") begins to be identified with the novel's cultural project precisely as guardian of a dying tongue once held in universal esteem. It is true that the monologic form of language upheld by Homero's *casticismo* is easily corrupted by power because it separates the "civilized" from the "barbarians" and because it excludes alternative linguistic formations for the sake of purity: "Language is always the companion of empire, and empire . . . is one monarch and one sword" (151), as the Spanish grammarian Nebrija is quoted as saying. But it is equally true that Fuentes's text is an explicit and implicit affirmation of Spanish as creative medium and as the national language of the Mexican nation: "Let the devil take us but let him take us in Spanish."[26] The contradiction is only apparent: a nationalist language differs from a national one. More to the point, *Christopher Unborn* is founded upon a "cannibalistic" notion of language:

> "Bathroom Campos!" giggled the drunken Buckley, inebriated with English and Spanish calambours, punnish the spinning spunning Spanish language! while Don Homero sighed in resignation, telling his niece and nephew that he in no way opposed the myriad puns they might create because he hoped that the Castilian language would digest them all and emerge triumphant from this test, that it would reach the beach of the twenty-first century alive, overcoming, digesting, excreting the Anglo-Saxon universe. . . . (175)

This subversion of linguistic and cultural hegemony, operated by transforming the identity of the hegemonic model into one more rooted in the vernacular, goes back in Latin American literature to Oswald de Andrade's 1928 "Manifiesto antropófago," and is a specific instance of what Angel Rama, following the Cuban anthropologist Fernando Ortiz, calls "transculturation."[27] It is the same process that in the text of *Christopher Unborn* is complemented by the reacculturation of certain literary classics of the Hispanic tradition, such as Quevedo and López Velarde. In a kind of avant-garde move – that is, in an attempt to desublimate culture by reintegrating it to everyday praxis – Fuentes endows his protagonist Angel with the external accoutrements of the Spanish and Mexican poets and peppers his discourse with fragments of their poetry.[28] By the same token, Angeles reads Plato (in Vasconcelos's venerated edition) as she makes love on the Acapulco beach and is showered – together with her lover – by Uncle Homero's excremental detritus:

> Mom, listen to me, no prohibition, no norm, life turned upside down, life in drag, wearing only a crown made of gold paper, let me be born laughing, Mommy, let me live my unborn novel, which is like a vast sacred parody, a scandalous liturgy, a eucharistic diablerie, a banquet, an Easter festival, the union of body and soul, head and ass, word and shit, ghost and fornication. . . . (385)

There is, however, another "poet" in the novel who practices a sort of carnivalesque *mésalliance* in reverse: Federico Robles Chacón, the technocratic creator of Mamadoc, of whose "singular synthesis" there is no "admirer more devout and impassioned" than Homero Fagoaga (60). Mamadoc, Mother and Doctor of all Mexicans, is assembled with the raw materials of mass culture and the techniques of cosmetology, and she represents a "subtle summa" of all the female stereotypes ingrained in Mexican machismo: Coatlihue, la Malinche, the Virgin of Guadalupe, Adelita, "the movie stars, the devouring women, the vampire women, the great rumba and exotic dancers of our immense adolescent dreams" (33), and "the supersecret Mothers all the gringas of our masturbatory dreams" (34). In a country where all that matters is "the symbolic legitimization of power" (30), this "Frankedenic" symbol of Mexican nationalism revalidates the utopia of modernization that has resulted in the apocalyptic Mexico of *Christopher Unborn*. The synthesis obtained in Mamadoc is monstrous because far from referring to some form of cultural truth, it disguises and disfigures the lasting face of Mexico, oriented to the past as much as to the future: "wipe off my makeup," (248) says the nation to Angel as he returns to his provincial roots.

This particular quotation is extracted from a passage that reprises Mary and Joseph's biblical trek to Bethlehem where the child Jesus (Christopher) is to be born. The pastiche is sustained by the previous allusion to the righteous destruction of sinful Acapulco (recalling the fate of Sodom and Gomorrah), the appearance of the Three Wise Kings in the streets of the city (Christopher was conceived on January 6, Epiphany), the massacre of the Innocents ordered by Ferdinand Marcos to forestall an impending challenge to his rule (from which Homero saves his Filipino valet Tomasito), and by the burro on which the "holy family" laboriously advances through the sierra.[29] The theme of the pastiche is the redemption of national life, for which both Angel and his "good" uncle Fernando Benítez have specific projects that the narrative submits to the readers' evaluation, even if the implicit author appears to arrogate to himself the authority to make the final decision. Benítez, the real-life author of *Viaje al centro de México,* attempts to synthesize "tradition and modernization, culture and democracy" (247). The good uncle is mostly concerned with the few surviving Indian cultures of Mexico, in whose fate he sees a prefiguration of the fate of all Mexicans:

> He says the Indians are all we have left; they are our ghosts . . . ; we owe loyalty to the world of the Indians, even if we disdain them, exploit them, because it's the loyalty we owe to death . . . we've become just as eccentric, just as fragile, just as condemned to extinction as they have. . . . (232)

His project is defeated by the useless violence of the Ayatollah Moreno's revolt, whereupon the would-be reformer withdraws to the sierra to commune with the last Huichole Indians. When the sacred moves, reasons the uncle, it is better to be at the origin and not in its final phase: "the sacred . . . is a celebration of origins. Here the only thing we're going to see is force disguised as religion" (426). Thus the rejection of the Ayatollah's "limitation apocalypse" puts the democratic Benítez on the road to a past whence the return to the future is uncharted.

Angel, on the other hand, is a self-described "conservative anarchist," a contradiction that generates many others as well as the need for its resolution: "He wanted to find the harmony of the contradiction that nibbled at the apple of his life: to be a modern Mexican conservative" (268). The desire to restore certain values (symbolized by the Mexican province and by López Velarde's poetry) grows out of the rejection of Mexico's present, of the "vast comedy of graft and mediocrity perpetrated in the name of Revolution and Progress" (117). Angel's ideal Mexico is a country "built to last," "a country identical to itself: hardworking, modest, productive, concerned in the first instance with feeding its people, a country opposed to gigantism and madness" (117). For this vision to be implemented the existing disorder must first be rectified, through terrorism if necessary. The destruction of Acapulco, however, only yields the contradictions inherent in the use of violence to attain political goals. In the end Angel gives up the hope for a dialectical synthesis and accepts the open-ended character of his and Mexico's predicament:

> death to the worst enemy of our . . . tradition: . . . the false revolutionaries, the modernizers, be they Russians, gringos, or just local upstarts. . . ; death to all their imitators, Mexican modernizers at-all-costs . . . : Angeles, Christopher, I don't want a world of progress which captures us between North and East and takes away from us the best of the West, but at the same time I don't want a pacific world which we will not deserve as long as we don't resolve what's going on inside here, . . . with all that which we are, good and bad, bad and good, but still unresolved. . . . (523)

The "pacific world" Angel refers to is Pacífica, the new utopia, the New World of the New World that the second Tomasito offers to the survivors of the Mexican shipwreck. This "technological paradise" is put forth as a synthesis of technology and communicative reason, of science and culture:

> In Pacífica we helped both the rapid advance of technology and the tragic awareness of life by taking seriously what a novel, a film, a symphony, a sculpture says: we decided . . . that there is no living present with a dead past, no acceptable future that does not allow exceptions to progress, and no technological progress that does not incorporate the warnings of art. (514)

Angel's and the novel's resounding answer to this almost mystical reconciliation of opposites and to all other totalizing discourses is "Kantinflas' categorical imperative: Mock de Summa!" (523). A deferred synthesis, an ongoing dialectic between identity and difference (confirmed by Heisenberg's often cited principle of indeterminacy) is the text's proposal for the representation of truth, and this is nowhere more evident than in Fuentes's view of Mexican culture as an interplay between historical identity (mediated and crystallized by the Mexican revolution) and the transformations of modernity:

> My parents have never been examples of Calvinist parsimony; no matter how postmodern, post-industrial, enlightened, conservative, Freudian, Marxist, or ecologist they declare or have declared themselves to be over the course of their brief and disturbed existences, Angel and Angeles are Catholic-Hispanic-baroque prodigals, spendthrifts, anachronisms. . . . (296)

The last epithet must be read dialectically: in the topsy-turvy, carnivalesque world of *Christopher Unborn* the postmodern is as chronologically misplaced in Mexico as Mexicans are in postmodernity, a reading that avoids any teleological implication of (post)modernity. The Bakhtinian carnival – that some may find too literary a reading of Mexican culture – allows the narrative discourse to present the grotesque aspect of the chronological mixture or warp (by deconstructing the authority of technocratic and political discourses) and, at the same time, to engage in a liberating praxis founded on an integrated notion of culture: "culture wresting control from ideology, ha! only culture would survive the ups and downs of politics, and culture was dancing, carnival, Saturnalia. . ." (174).[30]

The displacement of aesthetic synthesis to carnivalesque proliferation is ultimately connected to the political relegitimation of fiction that marked the exhaustion of modernism in Latin America.[31] Regional postmodernism, as characterized by Antonio Skármeta in the "manifesto" quoted earlier, involved a repoliticization of writing consistent with social changes such as

the democratization of education and with the ideological climate of the 1960s, the ideological "inflation" alluded to by Brunner
that in Mexico culminated with the student massacre of 1968.
The PRI's political crisis, Reagan's Contra war in Nicaragua, and
the economic debacle of the 1980s add urgency to a political
reading of contemporary Latin American history. *Christopher
Unborn,* however, is not a political intervention as much as an
act of resistance to political corruption and the manipulation of
the media. The text itself avows its "political impossibility" (133),
as if acknowledging the limitations imposed by its carnivalesque
form.[32] The novel's political strategy is adumbrated in Fuentes's
1969 program for a revolutionary modern literature:

> Our literature is truly revolutionary insofar as it denies the estab-
> lished order, the lexicon it might desire, and counteracts it with
> the language of the wake-up call for change, of renewal, of dis-
> order and humor. In sum, the language of ambiguity, of plural
> meanings, of the constellation of allusions: an open language.[33]

But in the modern novel the critical potential of language must
pass through the mediation of aesthetic form before it is released.
Fredric Jameson refers to this strategy as the utopian vocation
of high modernism and defines it as the attempt "to transform
the world by transforming its forms, space, or language."[34] When
aesthetic synthesis is renounced in favor of a destructuration of
form, then language is free to tangle with the discourses *hors
de texte.* This is the idea behind a recent theory of the politics
of postmodernism:

> In its political extension, postmodernism understands that politi-
> cal conflict is ultimately constituted in the structure of language
> (and in its uses – ideology, cultural codes, modes of intellectual
> production, etc.), rather than in overt forms of repression, in in-
> dividuals, or in the shape of historical events. . . .[35]

Christopher Unborn does not contradict this theory of political
engagement but does not fully endorse it either because it fails
to meet some of the other requirements inherent in the model,

notably the "pragmatic" tendency of postmodern fiction and its orientation toward "'private' rather than explicitly public sources of conflict."[36] Fuentes's text is "maximalist" as distinct from minimalist and speculative as opposed to pragmatic.

Fuentes's displaced postmodernism, finally, cannot be reduced to the antiaesthetic paradigm articulated by Hal Foster, for whom the idea "that art can now effect a world at once (inter)subjective, concrete and universal – a symbolic totality" is untenable.[37] *Christopher Unborn's* anti-Hegelian motto "Mock de Summa"[38] ranges the novel on the side of the antiaesthetic, but the narrator's insistence on intersubjective communication with the Reader – which is tantamount to the modeling of information potentially as boundless as the genetic chain – abruptly undermines this allegiance. By the same token, *Christopher Unborn* shares with postmodern theory:

> a desire to think in terms sensitive to difference (of others without opposition, of heterogeneity without hierarchy); a skepticism regarding autonomous "spheres" of culture or separate "fields" of experts; an imperative to go beyond formal filiations (of text to text) to trace social affiliations (the institutional "density" of the text in the world); in short, a will to grasp the present nexus of culture and politics.[39]

Yet Fuentes's text constitutes itself specifically as a literary object when it traces its genealogy and, therefore, implies the mediation of traditional literary institutions for its social functioning.

We must conclude that the postmodernism of *Christopher Unborn* is not dependent on the periodization schemes available in current postmodern theory, but that it is *synchronic* like carnivalesque discourse itself (which makes present any and all historical periods and brings together the antithetical times of birth and death) and like the putative postmodernity of Latin American culture. Eccentric like Sterne's book, Carlos Fuentes's *Tristram Shandy* engages the postmodern only from a syncretic perspective that informs it with cultural meaning.

Notes

1. Hugo Achugar, "Postmodernity and fin de siècle in Uruguay," *Studies in Twentieth Century Literature* (Winter 1990), 46.

2. Achugar, "Postmodernity," 47.

3. See Fredric Jameson, "Postmodernism, Or the Cultural Logic of Late Capitalism," *New Left Review* 146 (July-August 1984), 53-92.

4. José Joaquín Brunner, "Modernidad y posmodernismo en la cultura latinoamericana," in *Un espejo trizado* (Santiago: FLASCO, 1988), 216. All further page references to this essay will be given in parentheses in the body of my paper. The translations are mine.

5. Jorge Edwards, in "Mesa redonda: La experiencia de los novelistas," *Revista Iberoamericana* 116-117 (July-December 1981), 316.

6. "Affirmative culture," of course, is a notion associated with Marcuse. Here is how Marcuse defines the concept: "By affirmative culture is meant that culture of the bourgeois epoch which led in the course of its own development to the segregation from civilization of the mental and spiritual world as an independent realm of value that is also considered superior to civilization. Its decisive characteristic is the assertion of a universally obligatory, eternally better and more valuable world that must be unconditionally affirmed: a world essentially different from the factual world of the daily struggle for existence, yet realizable by every individual for himself 'from within,' without any transformation of the state of fact" ("The Affirmative Character of Culture," in *Negations: Essays in Critical Theory* [London: FAB, 1988], 95).

7. Mario Vargas Llosa, "El país que vendrá," *Vuelta* 14, 161 (April 1990), 44.

8. Jameson, "Postmodernism," 87. See also Terry Eagleton's remarks: "In a sardonic commentary on the avant-garde work, postmodernist culture will dissolve its own boundaries and become co-extensive with ordinary commodified life itself, whose ceaseless exchanges and mutations in any case recognize no formal frontiers which are not constantly transgressed" (*Against the Grain: Selected Essays* [London: Verso, 1988], 141).

9. Terry Eagleton, *The Ideology of the Aesthetic* (Oxford: Basil Blackwell, 1990), 373.

10. Ibid., 377.

11. Vargas Llosa, "El país que vendrá," 46.

12. Marcuse, "Affirmative Character of Culture," 95-96.

13. Ibid., 98-99.

14. Vargas Llosa, "El país que vendrá," 44. The relationship between modernization strategies and traditional religion is ironically glossed by Octavio Paz in an often quoted *boutade* to the effect that after decades of progressive ideologies, Mexicans only believe in the Virgin of Guadalupe and the national lottery.

15. See Pedro Morandé, *Cultura y modernización en América Latina* (Madrid: Ediciones Encuentro, 1987).

16. See José Joaquín Brunner, *Chile: Transformaciones culturales y modernidad* (Santiago: FLASCO, 1989), 166-173.

17. Brunner, *Chile,* 118. The translation is mine. Brunner is specifically discussing the explosion of the culture industry in Chile but his comments can be extended to other Latin American cultures as well, certainly including the Mexican.

18. Jameson, "Postmodernism," 14.

19. José Donoso, *The Boom in Spanish American Literature: A Personal History,* trans. Gregory Kolovakos (New York: Columbia University Press, 1977), 115.

20. Antonio Skármeta, "Al fin y al cabo, es su propia vida la cosa más cercana que el escritor tiene para echar mano," *Más allá del "boom": Literatura y mercado* (México: Marcha Editores, 1981), 273. The translation is mine. For other attempts to characterize Latin American postmodernism, see Roberto González Echevarría, "Severo Sarduy, the Boom, and the Post Boom," *Latin American Literary Review* 15, 29 (January-June 1987), 57-72; and Julio Ortega, "Postmodernism in Latin America," in *Postmodern Fiction in Europe and the Americas,* eds. Theo D'haen and Hans Bertens (Amsterdam: Rodopi, 1988), 193-208.

21. Carlos Fuentes, *La nueva novela hispanoamericana* (México: Joaquín Mortiz, 1969), 26.

22. "Historically, of course, [postmodernism] *did* begin as a reaction against the institutionalization of modernism in universities, museums and concert halls, against the canonization of a certain kind of architecture. This entrenchment is felt to be oppressive by

the generation that comes of age, roughly speaking, in the 60s and, not surprisingly, it then tries systematically to make a breathing space for itself by repudiating modernist values. In the literary context, values thus repudiated include complexity and ambiguity of language, irony, the concrete universal, and the construction of elaborate symbolic systems" (Anders Stephenson, "Regarding Postmodernism – A Conversation with Fredric Jameson," *Social Text* 17 [Fall 1987], 29).

23. Certain North American critics also find it useful to distinguish between (aesthetic) postmodernism and (cultural) postmodernity. See, for example, John Johnston, "Postmodern Theory/Postmodern Fiction," *Clio* 16, 2 (Winter 1987), 139-158.

24. In the English translation this appellative – a combination of "el lector" (the reader) and "elegir" (to elect or select) – is rendered as "Reader."

25. Julio Ortega attenuates the connection between the "Elector" and the modern novel: "Fuentes makes no concession to the audience; he is confident that the casual reader will soon lay down the book, and he summons the Electurer, the accomplice no longer active in the making of the text (the modernist ideal) but in the unrestricted verbalization of the world (because this novel is an inexhaustible conversation, at times a pleasant chat, at times manic, imprecatory, or witty" ("*Christopher Unborn:* Rage and Laughter," *Review of Contemporary Fiction* 8, 2 [Summer 1988], 287). There is no question that the demands placed on, and the freedom accorded to, the reader decrease in comparison to the work expected him/her by Cortázar, but there is still more than mere literary rhetoric in Fuentes's allusions to the "Elector" (such as the Shandyesque blank page in chapter 3 or the admonition to the reader in the final chapter to decide by him/herself whether it is worthwhile to be born in the Mexico of 1992). The select reader functions as the counterpart of the "minority, silenced author" and as the recipient of a narrative discourse that separates itself from the "reigning languages, which are, not those of the other, not those that belong to us, but those of the majority" (Carlos Fuentes, *Christopher Unborn,* trans. Alfred MacAdam and Carlos Fuentes [New York: Farrar, Strauss, Giroux, 1989], 256-257. All further citations of the novel refer to this edition and will be indicated in parentheses in the body of the text).

26. Carlos Fuentes, *Cristóbal Nonato* (Mexico: FCE, 1987), 110. The English translation omits the entire section at the end of chapter 2 that reflects on these linguistic questions.

27. A Spanish version of the manifesto may be found in Oswald de Andrade, *Obra escogida*, trans. Héctor Olea, ed. Haroldo de Campos (Caracas: Ayacucho, 1981). See also Angel Rama, *Transculturación narrativa en América Latina* (México: Siglo XXI, 1982). For a more radical reading of cultural cannibalism, see Roberto Fernández Retamar, *Calibán: Apuntes sobre la cultura en nuestra América* (México: Editorial Diógenes, 1971).

28. See above all pp. 120-121, where Angel engages in Dadaist terrorism against the Academy of Letters for fostering literary nationalism.

29. Pastiche as a form of allusion advances the case for the novel's postmodernism. Another example is the casting of the Oriental savior's arrival at the end of the novel in the form of a popular film (*Close Encounters of the Third Kind*). For a distinction between parody and pastiche as modernist and postmodernist modes respectively, see the chapter, "Capitalism, Modernism, and Postmodernism," in Terry Eagleton's *Against the Grain*. The source is Jameson, "Postmodernism." A syntactic trait of *Christopher Unborn* that also situates the text this side of modernism (because it "replicates" Brunner's notion of postmodern social heterogeneity) is parataxis.

30. Fuentes expands on this idea in an interview: "The illusion of progress is finished. On the other hand, the reality of culture was reborn and culture is what always saves Mexico in the end. The revolution may have failed in many ways – politically, economically, or socially – but culturally it didn't fail. It was the revelation that the country had a past, that the past was valid and represented a certain continuity that gave us an identity. In the disaster that is overtaking all of Latin America the only thing left standing is culture" (José María Marco, "Profecías y exorcismos, *Quimera* 68 [1987], 37).

31. Paraliterary form such as testimonial narratives have come to occupy a central place in literary studies in the last two decades. One may also think of Donoso and Cortázar, key figures of the modern novel who in the 1970s and 1980s attempted to graft the political to the aesthetic.

32. For a discussion of the political effectiveness of carnival, see

Peter Stallybrass and Allon White, *The Politics and Poetics of Transgression* (Ithaca: Cornell University Press, 1986), 6–26.

33. Fuentes, *La nueva novela*, 32. The translation is mine.

34. Fredric Jameson, "The Politics of Theory: Ideological Positions in the Postmodernism Debate," *New German Critique* 33 (Fall 1984), 61.

35. John Kucich, "Postmodern Politics: Don DeLillo and the Plight of the White Male Writer," *Michigan Quarterly Review* 27, 2 (Spring 1988), 329–330. The author adds: "Postmodern fiction, at least the kind that has aspired to political engagement, leans generally in this direction when it takes language as its subject not for formalist purposes, but in order to expose the politics embedded in language, and the ideological nature of the sign" (330).

36. Ibid., 331–332.

37. Hal Foster, "Postmodernism: A Preface," in *The Anti-Aesthetic: Essays on Postmodern Culture,* ed. Hal Foster (Washington: Bay Press, 1983), xv.

38. Fuentes continually opposes "los Helgels" to "los genes," ideology to aesthetics, reason to desire, and consistently takes the side of the body against the closure of the dialectic or its mystification in a transcendental synthesis.

39. Foster, "Postmodernism," xv.

IV

Archival Fictions:
García Márquez's Bolívar File[1]

ROBERTO GONZÁLEZ ECHEVARRÍA

Since the early 1950s, the Latin American novel has shown a preference for Latin American history as a source of plots and characters, and, within that preference, the colonial period has had a particular appeal. The reasons often given by the novelists themselves for this choice are varied, but the most common is that the clash of cultures provoked by the discovery and conquest created instances of what has been called "magical realism" that the authors could hardly resist. Novelists have also mentioned that the discovery of America was the first significant break in Western history since the advent of Christianity, a real watershed, or, as Abel Posse called it recently, a historical Big Bang, a beginning.[2] The classic statement on this is in the prologue to Alejo Carpentier's *The Kingdom of This World,* and the echoes in Gabriel García Márquez's Nobel prize acceptance speech, as well as in Mario Vargas Llosa's prologue to an anthology of colonial texts.[3] The colonial period offers other appealing facets. Many of the chroniclers of the discovery and conquest, from Columbus to Bernal, were men of action who participated, sometimes in leading roles, in the feats that they narrated. In them, novelists found a repository of rugged narrators who told

183

of astonishing adventures not derived from a literary tradition but that they had experienced in their own flesh. There is an air of originality in these accounts, intensified by the Spanish in which these chroniclers wrote, which was, as it were, freshly minted, not only because Spanish was then undergoing its last significant linguistic revolution, but also because it was in the process of incorporating many American words that would remain in the language until the present. As Carpentier said on several occasions, to write from the New World often meant to name things for the first time, like Adam in the Garden, and the chroniclers provided many examples of such acts of naming.[4]

These are all strong reasons for the novelists to explain their penchant for Latin American history. But it seems to me that the main cause that history appeals to Latin American novelists is that the historical texts are not literary. History drawn from original sources such as the *cronistas de Indias* can provide an understanding of Latin American culture that is at once truthful and legitimizing. Colonial texts have the allure of the beginning, a beginning that has not ceased being a beginning because the issues that it opened are still current in Latin America. To rewrite these texts is to narrate an urgent present as well as a surviving past. At the same time, the novel itself is legitimized as a bearer of authentic stories by its association with those texts that tell the first stories. In the most general sense, this turn, or return, to historical documents generates what I call "archival fictions," although not all such novels are set entirely or exclusively in the colonial period. I will devote most of my paper to a broad characterization of these novels and wind up with a reading of the latest of them, Gabriel García Márquez's *The General in His Labyrinth*.[5] This novel has moved away from the colonial period to take up the figure of the *Libertador* and a second historical Big Bang: the fragmentation of Latin America, right after independence, into the various countries it comprises today. My theory of archival fictions is based on a conception that I shall only be able to sketch here of the origins of the novel, situated in the Picaresque, the chronicles of the discovery and conquest, and Cervantes.

Having no fixed form of its own, the novel often assumes the shape of a given kind of document endowed with truth-bearing power by society at specific moments in time. The novel, or what is called the novel at various points in history, imitates such documents to reveal their conventionality, their subjection to strategies of textual engenderment similar to those governing literature. Through this counterfeit of legitimacy the novel makes its contradictory and veiled claim to literariness. In narratives that we call novelistic, the power to endow a text with the capacity to bear the truth is shown to lie outside the text; an exogenous agent bestows authority on a certain kind of document owing to the ideological power structure of the period, not to any inherent quality of the document or even of the outside agent. The novel, therefore, is part of the discursive totality of a given epoch and occupies a place opposite its ideologically authoritative core. Its conception is itself a story about an escape from authority, which is often its subplot. Needless to say, this flight to a form of freedom is a semblance of freedom predicated on textual mimetism that appears to be embedded in narrative itself, as if it were the irreducible story underlying all storytelling. This is perhaps why the law figures prominently in *La vida de Lazarillo de Tormes,* Cervantes's *Novelas ejemplares,* and the *crónicas de Indias.* The novel will retain from this origin its relation to punishment, the hoarding of knowledge, and the control of the state, which determines its mimetic penchant from then on. When the modern Latin American novel returns to that origin, it does so through the figure of the Archive, the legal repository of knowledge and power from which it sprung in the sixteenth century, whose institutional monuments were the state archives at Simancas and El Escorial.

The form assumed by the Picaresque was that of a *relación,* because this kind of letter, confession, or written report addressed to a figure of authority belonged to the huge imperial bureaucracy through which power was administered in Spain and its possessions. The early history of Latin America, as well as the first fictions of and about Latin America, are told in the rhetorical molds furnished by the notarial arts that determined the form of these texts. These *Cartas de relación* were not simply letters but also *charters* of the newly "discovered" territories. Both the writer and the territory were enfranchised through the power of this document which, like Lazarillo's text, is addressed to a higher authority. Hernán Cortés wrote his famous *cartas de relación* to Emperor Charles V. The pervasiveness of legal rhetoric in early American historiography can hardly be exaggerated. Officially appointed historians (with the title of *Cronista Mayor de Indias*) were issued instructions by the Crown and the Royal Council of the Indies to subsume these *relaciones* into their compendious works. These weighty tomes were the textual counterpart of Simancas and constitute, unwittingly, the earliest Latin American archival fictions. The best known, *Historia general de los hechos de los castellanos en las islas i tierra firme del mar Océano* (Madrid, 1601) was written by Antonio de Herrera y Tordesillas, a contemporary of Mateo Alemán and Cervantes.

Current archival fictions are historical novels, often set in the colonial period. Their archival quality comes from their being composed of documents of a legal or generally historical nature, which appear in the text in ways that do not conceal their provenance or kind. These are works with numerous explicit and implicit citations, where a process of culling or gathering knowledge is evident from the accumulation of texts marked, because of their origin, by their authenticity. A building, a room, a box, or some sort of enclosure contains these documents, as hypostases of the Archives. The way these texts are assembled, however, does not yield a coherent or complete story, nor does it ultimately furnish the sort of revelation that their pedigree promises. This assemblage of documents is often processed, copied, or guarded by an internal historian or archivist, who is in turn engaged in the production of a manuscript that may or may not be explicitly that of the novel we read, but that could be its prolegomenon or pretext. Although there are precursor archival fictions, such as Borges's story "Tlön, Uqbar, Orbis Tertius," the first full-blown archival fiction is Carpentier's *The Lost Steps* (1953); and the quintessential one, García Márquez's *One Hundred Years of Solitude*. With all due credit to Foucault, Derrida, and Bakhtin, I fancy to derive my approach from these novels. Other archival fictions are *Chronicle of a Death Foretold, Aura, Terra Nostra, I the Supreme, The Harp and the Shadow, Noticias del imperio, The House of Spirits, The Sea of Lentils,* and *La noche oscura del Niño Avilés.* Other significant Latin American novels share important features with these: *Three Trapped Tigers, Hallucinations,* and *Manuel's Manual* and *The Dogs of Paradise.* Archival fictions, in short, are novels about the origins of Latin American narrative discourse (both novelistic and historical) that also touch on the very origins of the novel.

Etymologically, "archive" has a suggestive genealogy that I hope supports the work that I make it perform here. Corominas writes: "Taken from late Latin *archivum,* and this from the Greek *archeion,* 'residence of the magistrates,' 'archive,' derived from *arkhē* 'command,' 'magistracy'."[6] The dictionary of the Spanish Academy reads: "From the Latin *archivum,* and this from the Greek . . . beginnings or origin. Building in which public or private documents are placed for safekeeping. 2. The sum total of these documents. 3. Figurative. A person to whom is entrusted a secret or very private knowledge and knows how to guard them." Power, secrecy, and law stand at the origin of the Archive; it was, in its most concrete form, the structure that actually housed the dispensers of the law and its readers, the magistrates; it was the building that encrypted the power to command. In philosophy, *arkhē* is the primordial stuff in the beginning, the first principle. In Anaximander and the earlier Greek philosophers it was a substance or primal element; with later philosophers, especially Aristotle, an actuating principle, a cause. All observable regularities were viewed as reflections of the *arkhē's* enduring presence in the cosmos.[7] So *arch,* as in *monarch,* denotes power, to rule, but also the beginning, that which is chief, eminent, greatest, principal; it denotes primitive, original. Through the *arkhē,* in addition, "Archive" is related to *arcane,* to *arcanum.* So "Archive" suggests not only that something is kept but also that that something is secret, encrypted, enclosed. It recalls *arca,* the old-fashioned Spanish word for chest, safe, or trunk, like the one in *Lazarillo de Tormes* and Carlos Fuentes's *Aura.*[8] *Arca,* according again to the Academy: "Box, commonly without a lining, which has a flat lid secured by several hinges on one side and one or more locks on the other. . . . Old Spanish, sepulcher, tomb." Power encrypts knowledge of the origin, the principles, kept in a building or enclosure that safeguards the law, the beginning of writing; it also kept the body after death, like a relic. It is no accident that the word *archivo,* according again to Corominas, appears to have entered Spanish in 1490, during the reign of the Catholic kings, two years before the discovery of America. It was in that period that modern archival practices began, organized by the new state created by Ferdinand and Isabella. A few years later, in 1539, a medieval castle at Simancas that had been used as a prison was turned into the state archive. The grandeur and mystery of the object, its prestige, is made a functional part in the foundation of the modern state and a key figure in the narratives therein generated.

Like the Archive, the modern Latin American novel hoards knowledge. Like the Archive's, this knowledge is of the origin, meaning that it is about the link of its own writing with the power that makes it possible, hence with the possibility of knowledge. In the beginning this power was the law, but later, other origins replaced it, though preserving the seal of the initial pact between power and writing. Modern novels retain those origins and the structure that made them possible. While the knowledge kept there is difficult to plumb, hence its secretiveness, it is common property, not private. It can be read, as it is indeed read. The very act of reading and sharing that knowledge assumes the form of ritual, of celebrating the common knowledge. Archives keep the secrets of the state; novels keep the secrets of culture, and the secret of those secrets.

In novels, the Archive is a modern myth based on an old form, a form of the beginning. The modern myth unveils the relationship between knowledge and power as contained in previous fictions about Latin America, the ideological construct that props up the legitimacy of power from the chronicles to the current novels. The Archive keeps, culls, retains, accumulates, classifies – like its institutional counterpart. Fictions are contained in an enclosure, a storehouse of narrative that is at the same time the origin of the novel. It is not by chance that Cervantes began to write the *Quixote* in jail, nor that the narrator-author of *The Story of Mayta* should seek the ultimate truth about his character in a prison. The Archive goes back to the origins of Latin American narrative because it returns to the language of the law, the language that the protagonist of *The Lost Steps* will find in the innermost recesses of the jungle, where a city (paradoxically) awaits him. That city, which the Adelantado has called Santa Mónica de los Venados, becomes Macondo, the story of which is the myth of the Archive, engendered in Melquíades's magical room.

Archival fictions reach back to the legal origins of the narrative to pry into the relationship between power and knowledge, or, better yet, into the empowerment of knowledge through language in the legalistic act of writing. This probe brings forth the violent, arbitrary nature of the act of empowerment and its link to punishment and incarceration. Empowerment is not knowledge; it is not, ultimately, discursive; at the core the Archive houses no secret, no word. Violence has no *arkhē*. Narrative, be it novelistic or historical, often veils the violence by thematizing the first escape from the strictures of hegemonic discourse, by fleeing the law, as in the Picaresque or, closer to us, in Miguel Barnet's *Autobiography of a Runaway Slave.* Archival fictions also deal with the accumulation of knowledge and how knowledge is organized as a concept of culture that grants political legitimacy. As storehouses of knowledge archival fictions are atavistic accumulations of the given. This is why they are nearly always historical and consist of a complex intertextual web that incorporates the chronicles of the discovery and conquest of America, other fictions, historical documents, and characters, songs, poetry, scientific reports, literary figures, and myths – in short, a grabbag of texts of cultural significance. The Archive, as is evident in Carpentier's *The Harp and the Shadow,* also stands for loss, for emptiness, frequently represented by old age and death. *The Harp and the Shadow* suggests that Columbus's bones, like the documents in the Archive, will be dispersed, will not constitute a body. Archival fictions are also crypts, like the Escorial itself in *Terra Nostra,* a figure of the very book we read, monumental repositories of death's debris, and documents lacking currency. If the Archive's secret is that it has no secret other than this dialectic of gain and loss, this secret of secrets is uncovered through a set of figures and stories that constitute a storehouse of topoi of Latin American fiction.

The "case" on which *Chronicle of a Death Foretold* is supposed to be based was culled from the legal brief drawn up many years before for the murder trial and gathered by the narrator from the flooded Palace of Justice of Riohacha. This remarkable passage in García Márquez's intense novella is one of the most meaningful appearances of the Archive in recent fiction. The passage recounts the narrator's search for the brief:

> Todo lo que sabemos de su carácter [the lawyer's] es aprendido en el sumario, que numerosas personas me ayudaron a buscar veinte años después en el Palacio de Justicia de Riohacha. No existía clasificación alguna de los archivos, y más de un siglo de expendientes estaban amontonados en el suelo del decrépito edificio colonial que fuera por dos días el cuartel general de Francis Drake. La planta baja se inundaba con el mar de leva, y los volúmenes descosidos flotaban en las oficinas desiertas. Yo mismo exploré muchas veces con las aguas hasta los tobillos aquel estanque de causas perdidas, y sólo una casualidad me permitió rescatar al cabo de cinco años de búsqueda unos 322 pliegos salteados de los más de 500 que debió tener el sumario.

> Everything that we know about his character has been learned from the brief, which several people helped me look for twenty years later in the Palace of Justice in Riohacha. There was no classification of files whatever, and more than a century of cases was piled up on the floor of the decrepit colonial building that had been Sir Francis Drake's headquarters for two days. The ground floor would be flooded by high tides, and the unbound volumes floated about the deserted offices. I searched many times with water up to my ankles in that lagoon of lost causes, and

after five years of rummaging around only chance let me rescue
some 322 pages filched from the more than 500 that the brief
must have contained.[9]

The dilapidated Palace of Justice, dating from colonial times,
obviously alludes to the constitutive presence of the law in that
founding period. The ruined palace stands for the presence of
the law as origin of the narrative, now hollowed out; it recalls the
stage-set Palace of Justice in the first page of *The Lost Steps,*
the Palacio de las Maravillas in *The Harp and the Shadow,* and,
of course, El Escorial in *Terra Nostra.* The construction of archives and the origins of the law are intricately connected, even
etymologically, as we have seen. But here is law as architecture,
as archtecture is a vestige. The detail that the Palace of Justice
became the headquarters of a dashing and lawless Francis Drake
suggests the reincarnation of the law as narrative fiction. But
there is more.

The volumes are unbound, unclassified, and float through
deserted offices because the power of the original Archive is sus-
pended. A ruined Palace of Justice, the Archive functions as
a sign, an allegory of the origin. Only the shell of the allegory
remains, an empty form from which other meanings emanate.
Descosidos does not really mean "unbound," in the sense that
the documents have never been bound. In fact, *descosidos* could
very well mean that these documents were once bound and have
now fallen apart, become unsewn. The Archive is like Borges's
study, but after that demolisher of fictions is through thrashing
the books. They only become volumes again when they are re-
assembled as novels, simulacra of the original Archive, by Carpentier, Fuentes, García Márquez, and others. The absence of
classification points to the importance of the unusual spaces between the documents. Here those gaps are filled with water. The
documents float as opposed to being grounded, to being connected solidly to matter – to the earth – a condition that would
provide them with a stable set of symbolic meanings, such as
in the *novela de la tierra.* ("Earth," *tierra,* is, of course, a metaphor for the congealed ideology informing the surface project

of telluric fiction.)[10] The fact that the offices are now deserted, that the *letrados* have disappeared, further diminishes the authority of these papers. The *letrados* have fled, leaving scattered traces of their foundational presence, as well as of their exit. They are a conspicuous and significant absence, like the ruined state of the Palace of Justice. The Palace of Justice is very much like the trash bin of Bogota's *audiencia* in Rodríguez Freyle's *El Carnero*, from which the author says he gathered his "casos."

One cannot fail to notice that it was chance that allowed the narrator – a figure of the author – to find the documents that he did recover. The author re-covers scattered documents. Hence, the story based on them and its ensuing arrangement is due to chance, not to any given rule or law. But chance could also be a reflection of fortune, the force that naturally rules the tragedy recounted in *Chronicle of a Death Foretold*. Chance abolishes precedence, is like the empty space at the core of the Archive. The story and the text that contains it duplicate each other on the sheen of the water that floods the Palace of Justice, turning its floor into a mirror, a reversed and illusory dome; an inverted law overarching, yet undermining, the constitution of the text. The watery image is the mirage of a roof that does not shelter, that only reflects. The floor, the ground, on the other hand, is here a watery mirror that cannot support anything.

The manuscript that the narrator seeks to assemble is a *sumario,* technically a "summary," but in any case a kind of adding up, of summing up, and merely 322 "pliegos *salteados*" (this important adjective was left out of the translation); that is to say, the pages were not consecutive, there were discontinuities between them. Actually, *sumario* conveys a sense of incompletion at the origin, since it is a gathering up of relevant documents leading to an eventual summation not yet accomplished.[11] The pages were slapped together to form the story, but then the story contains those gaps, the "saltos" that make the narrative a series of "pliegos salteados." Furthermore, the ideal number of pages, the round 500 that the brief is understood to have originally contained is now replaced by the very incomplete 322. But incomplete does not mean insignificant: 322 is also a number that appears to open an infinite repetition of twos, the sign of the initial repetition, the one that denies the originary power to one. And three, the opening, is full of mythic and tragic resonances. Furthermore, 322 also suggests a winding down, a diminution; not two-three, but three-two. The Archive in its modern version does not add up, literally and figuratively; it is not a *suma*, but a *resta*, an intermittent series of subtractions. Archival fictions reveal the constitutive blanks that shine between the documents in the watery flood of the Palace of Justice. In them, the Archive is something between a ruin and a relic.

The Palace of Justice at Riohacha reveals other features of the Archive. The Archive is at once capacious and incomplete. Capaciousness, which is related to safekeeping and the atavistic enclosure function of the Archive, reflect the totalizing force of the law. The law of laws would contain all. Melquíades's manuscript is said to encompass the entire history of the Buendía family. García Márquez's project recalls the history of *I the Supreme*, particularly Herrera y Tordesillas's. The Archive in *I the Supreme* presumably safeguards all of the nation's documents. The manuscript blown away by the hurricane in *Oppiano Licario* is a *summa*, the *Súmula nunca infusa de excepciones morfológicas*. The capacity of the Vatican Archive in *The Harp and the Shadow* needs not be belabored. Containing all knowledge, the Archive is therefore the repository of all power. Its cryptlike quality and its association with death are partly derived from this sense of completeness; the Archive is an image of the end of time. In *The Harp and the Shadow* Carpentier places a figure of the Archive in the afterlife, in a circle of Dante's *Inferno*. Capaciousness is sometimes reflected in the size of archival fictions, as in the case of the monumental *Terra nostra*, but size is not always the measure of totalization, as in the relatively brief *The Harp and the Shadow*. In some works, as in *One Hundred Years of Solitude*, capaciousness is achieved through the reduction of all of history to a mythlike story, or by centering, as in *The Harp and the Shadow*, on a mythic figure of the origin, like Columbus, who would contain all *ab ovo*. Columbus appears in this novel as the first Latin American narrator, revising his foundational texts on his deathbed. He is the most immediate precursor of García Márquez's Bolívar.

In addition to the unfinished or mutilated manuscripts, this fundamental discontinuity is often represented in archival fictions by old age and death. The proliferation of old, dying, or dead characters in current Latin American fiction is remarkable. I have alluded to several: Melquíades, Columbus, Manuel Montejo, and Consuelo. But there are many others, like Anselmo in *The Green House,* the dictator in *The Autumn of the Patriarch,* Dr. Francia in *I the Supreme,* Florentino Daza in *Love in the Time of Cholera,* the Señora in *Colibrí,* Cobra in the novel by that name, and Empress Carlota in Fernando del Paso's *Noticias del imperio.* These oracular figures are links with the past and repositories of knowledge, like living archives. But their memories are faulty. Senility curiously becomes a force for exuberant creativity and originality. Senility is a metaphor not only for the incompleteness of the Archive, but also for the gap at the core of the Archive. A whimsical creativity marks these characters' recollections, a creative elan born not as much of remembrance as of forgetfulness. Their age also approximates them to death, one of the founding tropes of archival fictions. Death stands for the gap of gaps, the mastergap of the Archive, both its opening and closing cipher. Consuelo's husband, author of the manuscript Felipe rewrites in Fuentes's *Aura,* is dead; so is Melquíades by the time his manuscript is read. Columbus, and Bolívar, are on the brink of death.

The lapse represented by death or by the faulty memory of old narrators signals, not an escape from the dominating discourse, but the opposite. The lapses and the Lapse stand for the gaps and cuts, the proscription of language, the origin of the law. Death is a trope for interdiction; and forgetfulness; for the creativity from within interdiction, which is the mark of the Archive. This explains both the deathlike countenance of Herbert Ashe and his posthumous production of the book. Archival fictions return to the gap at the core of the Archive because it is the very source of fiction. This installing of death and old age as founding tropes is a mythification of the Archive, the displacement of the language of method to the realm of myth and the sacred. Troping and mythifying the gap, death, and its appearance in archival fictions, is a metaphor for the negativity of limit. Hence the Archive is not a Bakhtinian carnival, but if it is, it takes place within the confines of Foucault's prison.

García Márquez's *The General in His Labyrinth* has a number of peculiar and telling twists that may very well mark a new beginning in Latin American historical novelistic writing. The most visible changes are that the novel is no longer set in the colonial period and the protagonist is the founding figure of Latin American independence. The work has other, more subtle, but no less telling, differences, though its affinity with previous archival fictions is clear, even in the Borgesian ring of the title. Bolívar's personal archives are lugged around in the novel as he travels home to Venezuela; he appears as a decrepit figure near death, and much is made of his frantic letter writing. (Bolívar is really only forty-seven when he dies, but he has been physically and mentally consumed.) The ten thousand letters he is said to have written not only play a prominent role in the novel but García Márquez has claimed that he spent two long years mired in "the quicksands of voluminous, contradictory, and often uncertain documentation."[12] By centering on Bolívar, García Márquez has gone to the core of the Archive, to that place where the secret of secrets would be lodged. Bolívar is not only the hero of independence, the Liberator, but the Redactor of the Charter, the Drafter of Constitutions, the figure in whom both writing and power coalesce. The most famous of those constitutions he wrote for Bolivia, the country named after him. But, as we know, he had a hand in the composition of several others, as well as countless proclamations that had the same charterlike intention. Bolívar is, in addition, the author of the most famous and influential letter in the modern history of Latin American writing, the Jamaica Letter of 6 September 1815, known sometimes as the *Carta Profética de Jamaica*. (This letter is one in a long line of important letters in Latin American history, from Columbus's letter to Luis de Santángel, Cortés's letters to Emperor Charles V, Aguirre's seditious letter to Philip II, to Martí's letter to Manuel Mercado on the eve of his death.) The *Carta* outlined Bolívar's political agenda for Latin America, most notably his desire to create a large league of Latin American nations, with its supra-capital in Panama.

García Márquez has dared to tamper with the source of much Latin American patriotic rhetoric. Latin American novels have often focused on historical figures, like Dr. Francia, Empress Carlota, Juan Manuel Rosas, and a host of dictators. But I cannot recall one that deals directly with one of the idols in the pantheon of Latin American republican iconography: Benito Juárez, José Martí, Simón Bolívar, San Martín. . . . García Márquez has certainly paid a price for his daring, having infuriated *bolivarianos* (Bolivarphiles) all over the continent, who have written enraged letters of their own, denouncing alleged historical mistakes in the novel and such transgressions as having the Liberator use foul language.[13] The author purports to have presented a truer Bolívar, closer to his Caribbean roots, including his African features, which had been progressively whitened out in busts, coins, and stamps, where he appears as a Roman senator. García Márquez has certainly played with the sacred. But the challenge of *The General in His Labyrinth* is more to Latin American historical narrative, including García Márquez's own.

Surely one of the most significant differences between *The General in His Labyrinth* and other archival fictions is the magnitude of the protagonist-hero. Columbus and Aguirre were foundational figures, but their actions were tarnished by controversy. Hence, in *The Harp and the Shadow* part of the novel takes the form of a trial, at which the canonization of the discoverer is debated and ultimately denied, both for his having brought slavery to the New World and for his somewhat licentious life. In *Daimón,* the mad Aguirre does make the first effort to create an independent state in what would become Latin America, but his indiscriminate violence against his followers, particularly his own daughter, marks him as a very troublesome hero. The same is true of Dr. Francia, in Roa Bastos's *I the Supreme.* No matter how much Francia's anti-imperialist stance can be admired today, his deadly grip on Paraguay and his irascibility bordered on lunacy, something Roa Bastos skillfully manipulates. Little need be said about the more clearly villainous dictators who appeared directly or indirectly in *The Autumn of the Patriarch, Reasons of State,* and other Latin American "dictator novels," all heirs to *Facundo,* which was itself the portrayal of a controversial foundational personage. Quiroga shared with all other such figures in the Latin American tradition a penchant for violence and willfulness, as well as his being a law unto himself. That is to say, such founders break the law to become the law, hence they can inhabit the formative recesses of the Archive. Perhaps the quintessential figure among all these, and the one, with Columbus, closest to García Márquez's Bolívar, is Fuentes's Philip II in *Terra nostra.* But Philip's dogmatism and ruthless persecution of "infidels" hardly qualifies him as a hero in the Latin American tradition. His niche in the Archive is marred by an aura of mystical dementia and necrophilia. Bolívar, on the other hand, is a modern hero, unsullied by such fanatical aspirations to transcendence and unstained by a propensity for indiscriminate violence. *His* niche in the Archive would reveal the rational secret of whatever it is that binds power and the law; the law of laws, a discourse of method. Curiously, in the Jamaica Letter, Bolívar calls his plans, using an oxymoron, "rational desires."[14]

In *The Harp and the Shadow,* Carpentier made Columbus the protagonist in order to rewrite what he considered to be the founding narrative of Latin America. Carpentier went as far back as was possible and endowed Columbus with the ambiguous glow of a founder. Historical fiction had in the Discoverer a controversial and contradictory beginning, where lust and the *Wille zur Macht* crystalized in texts that remain a vigorous presence in Latin American writing. To seal this unity, Carpentier made Columbus the lover of Queen Isabella of Castille. But at the same time the author discloses that Columbus's claim to the origin of the Archive is based on scattered documents, which, like his bones, have a doubtful legitimacy. (The Columbusphiles in Havana, Seville, and Santo Domingo all claim to have the authentic remains of the Discoverer). García Márquez has replaced the alluring figure of the Discoverer with that of the Liberator. But there is no question as to their connection. In *The General in His Labyrinth* Bolívar quotes from Columbus's *Diario* and in a sense is repeating the Discoverer's voyage, but backwards.[15] García Márquez's second origin is not independence per se, but the moment when the independence movement reaches its peak and the dismemberment of Latin America begins. It is the period when the *caudillos* appear. If Simancas and El Escorial were the implicit Archives in borgesian previous archival fictions, now the Archive would be placed in buildings like the one in Asunción, described by Roa Bastos in *I the Supreme,* or in the Palace of Justice at Riohacha. Bolívar is the hero of unity, of integration, and of freedom; his dream was to create a huge country, a Gran Colombia, as well as a league of Latin American nations, that would be prosperous, powerful, and ruled by his Enlightenment ideology. But no sooner had unity been achieved than local interests and regional differences pulled apart his elaborate political construct, which was precariously held together by the myriad documents that he generated and that García Márquez sedulously consulted, irritated by their tyranny.[16] *The General in his Labyrinth* narrates the dispersal of the Charter, the creation of the Archive by ripping apart the Document at the Origin. The novel's effect is to undermine the bonding of charters, writing, and political agendas, to dissolve the apparent union between the powerful, hero of origins, his textual production, and its endurance in history, except as fictional constructs. Colonel Aureliano Buendía has a vision of order as he faces the firing squad; General Bolívar has one of dissolution on his deathbed at San Pedro Alejandrino.

Bolívar's Archive in *The General in His Labyrinth* does not have, however, the mock monumental proportions of the one in Roa Bastos' Asunción, nor the historical patina of the Palace of Justice at Riohacha. It is not even a fixed Archive housed in a building, but a diminishing drove of mules, loaded with trunks containing all his papers, books, clothes, and memorabilia.[17] The subplot that tells the fate of these trunks leads to a fire in his mistress's house, years after the general's death. A story within that subplot involves a mysterious box that has been carried from place to place, which, when finally opened, turns out to contain nothing of interest after all (p. 211).

But the most significant difference of the Archive is the extremely literary cast of Bolívar's life, which is projected against a powerful narrative tradition, instead of feigning having its source in nonliterary documents. The *Odyssey*, the *Aeneid,* and, above all, the second part of *Don Quixote*, press heavily against the fictional enclosure of *The General in His Labyrinth*. If in Melquíades's room the founding books were the encyclopedia and *The Thousand and One Nights*, knowledge and fiction; here legal documents compete unfavorably against Homer, Virgil, Cervantes, and the emergence of a Latin American literary tradition about the General. The Homeric and Virgilian presences are evident in the structure of the plot. Like Ulysses and Aeneas, Bolívar is making his last voyage home, mostly by water, after a heroic life devoted to warfare. But the most telling presence is Cervantes: there is a Quixotic air to a Bolívar bent on creating an enormous country, against all odds, to match the utopian ideals he has absorbed from books. Like Don Quixote in the second part, Bolívar is confronted with literary works in which he appears, such as the book Manuela reads to him about life in Lima. And at one of the stops in the journey, a girl recites to him stanzas from Olmedo's "La victoria de Junín: Canto a Bolívar," a poem that the Ecuadoran wrote in consultation with the hero. But the Cervantean element is mostly felt in what could be called the retrogressive, or retrieval, element of the journey. Like Don Quixote in his final return home, Bolívar relives the experiences of his quest journey and meets characters who were part of it and who round off his adventures by their reappearance. It is as if Bolívar were already reading his life, as if this elaborate and protracted finale to the Liberator's life were essentially the creation of a reading of the quest journey, an end that would mark the beginning of reading. The quest journey, basically the whole of the Liberator's life before his decision to abandon Bogotá and relinquish power, is told as part of this redoubling. The quest cannot be told afresh, but always, already as part of the fiction from which the hero cannot escape. This

literary confinement of Bolívar's is conveyed from the very opening of the novel, in a scene that becomes recurrent: "José Palacios, su servidor más antiguo, lo encontró flotando en las aguas
depurativas de la bañera, desnudo y con los ojos abiertos, y
creyó que se había ahogado. Sabía que ése era uno de sus mu-
chos modos de meditar, pero el estado de éxtasis en que yacía
a la deriva parecía de alguien que ya no era de este mundo"
(p. 11: "José Palacios, his oldest servant, found him floating
naked with his eyes open in the purifying waters of his bath and
thought he had drowned. He knew this was one of the many
ways the General meditated, but the ecstasy in which he lay drift-
ing seemed that of a man no longer of this world"). Afloat like
a fetus or a drowned man, Bolívar is disconnected from the earth
and from temporality; he is groundless, cruising aimlessly, like
the documents in the Palace at Riohacha. In this sort of test-
tube or time capsule, the hero lacks all telos. He is like Cortázar's axoltl, a monster floating in a transparent enclosure, em-
barked in an infinite voyage. The redoubling nature of the journey
narrated in *The General in His Labyrinth* is also a journey without end: "un ir y venir hacia la nada" (p. 166; "their coming and
going to nowhere" [p. 161]; in the Spanish it reads, "toward noth-
ingness"). This is, clearly, the General's labyrinth. He cannot see
himself but in the reflection of Olmedo's ode, just as we cannot
see him but through the distorting lens of literature. The poem
that the General himself is said to be writing is in "octavas reales,"
the stanza of Renaissance epics used to sing about the heroes
of the conquest.[18]

This literary encirclement is significant in relation to Bolívar's
preoccupation with freedom, which in turn reflects the recurrent subplot in many novels involving an escape from the law.
Bolívar's journey is, after all, also a flight, only that, like much
else in the novel, it is a reverse flight; not an escape up river
to the jungle, like the journey of the protagonist in *The Lost Steps,*
but a voyage down river, to the sea. And instead of an escape
from power and authority, it is power and authority escaping,
abandoning its center. It is a rejection of the law before the law.
The General in His Labyrinth recounts not the accession to power,

or a struggle to retain power, but a renunciation of power. In this the novel is a radical departure from historical novels in Latin America, particularly those with a dictator or hero as some sort of protagonist. Dr. Francia goes mad in a mountain of legal documents; Bolívar, as he resigns and begins his last adventure, vows not to write another letter (a promise he does not keep, however). The pícaro writes to escape the law by mimicking its rhetoric, the hero escapes the law, which he has founded, by renouncing writing altogether. Besides, to whom would he be writing but to himself? He, being the absent authority to whom the legal document is addressed, removes with his departure both the point of departure and destination of the written. This is also the labyrinth from which the General tries to escape and a basic component of the literary enclosure in which he finds himself.

Where is freedom, in which direction is the escape to be successful? In an exchange with Sucre, the latter tells Bolívar that they have promoted independence so much that the new countries want to be free not only from Spain, but from each other too, hence the collapse of Bolívar's dream of integration:

> "Es una burla del destino," dijo el mariscal Sucre. "Tal parece como si hubiéramos sembrado tan hondo el ideal de la independencia, que estos pueblos están tratando ahora de independizarse los unos de los otros."
> El general reaccionó con una gran vivacidad.
> "No repita las canalladas del enemigo," dijo, "aun si son tan certeras como ésa." (p. 25)

> ———————

> "It's destiny's joke," said Field Marshall Sucre. "It seems we planted the ideal of independence so deep that now these countries are trying to win their independence from each other."
> The General's response was spirited.
> "Don't repeat the enemy's vile remarks," he said, "even when they are as accurate as that one." (p. 18)

This is a very telling exchange. The truth uttered by Sucre is a reflection of a slur by the enemy; what begins as a strategic lie winds up, in the mouth of the Marshall, inadvertently, as the truth. A truth that is guaranteed to be so by the General himself, no less, and which he wishes to suppress. It is as if the truth could only come as an echo of something intended as aggression and is spoken, like a script, by someone who would really wish to be saying the opposite and is not even its author. It is also noteworthy that the Marshall attributes all this to a joke played by fate. Behind the evil intention of the enemy lurks a larger source of truth that is incommensurate and expresses itself by indirection and humor. But what is even more significant is that the exchange should be about freedom, the overarching thrust of Bolívar's enterprise and what is ultimately at stake in all of the writing in the novel and in all novelistic writing. The gist of what Sucre says is that freedom has gone too far, that it has reached a point where no unity can be conceived save as coercion, where no order can be created except by betraying freedom. Bolívar's dream of integration would then be a return to a lack of freedom that it intended to abolish: repression in disguise, like the joke fate is playing upon them, and like the irony involved in having Sucre repeat the accusations first made by the enemy. Freedom thus appears as a master trope that can mean the opposite of what is intended. This, too, is the General's labyrinth, from which he appears unable to escape and is the reason for the melancholia that afflicts him in García Márquez's novel.

This melancholia also reflects the state of the Charter or charters that the General produces. Throughout the novel the General repeats disconsolately: "Nadie entendió nada" (p. 18: "Nobody understood anything"). This refers, of course, to his political project of binding together the Latin American nations that emerge from independence. But it is also in consonance with his secretary's refrain, "Lo que mi señor piensa, sólo mi señor lo sabe" (p. 181; "Only my master knows what my master is thinking" [p. 178]). There is hardly a correlation in the novel between Bolívar's inner thoughts and feelings and what he writes. Before his decline, his letter writing was so frenzied that "de allí surgió la leyenda nunca desmentida de que dictaba a varios amanuenses varias cartas distintas al mismo tiempo" (p. 226; "this was the origin of the legend, which has never been disproved, that he would dictate several letters to several different secretaries at the same time" [p. 225]). Taken literally this would have to mean that each utterance would appear differently in each letter, but that it originated as the same, given that it is impossible to say simultaneously different things. There would be a clear gap between dictation and writing, between original, oral expression, and its multiple written versions and perversions. But even figuratively it means that Bolívar is not a reliable source of authority for his writings, because to produce different letters at more or less the same time, he would have to be more a dictating machine than a self projecting reason and will through his writing. As he declines, the link between his self and his writings becomes even more tenuous. He depends on his nephew Fernando, his favorite secretary, to add spice to his writings ("era único para inventar recursos de folletín" [p. 65]; "he was unique in his ability to invent the kinds of devices used in serialized novels to keep the reader in suspense" [p. 59]). The avuncular, rather than paternal, relationship with the scribe, is indicative of the obliqueness of his authority. Toward the end, "Si tenía que escribir cartas se contentaba con instruir a Fernando, y no revisaba siquiera las pocas que debía rubricar" (p. 237; "If he had to write letters, he was satisfied with giving instructions to Fernando, and did not even look at the few he had to sign" [p. 237]). The Drafter of the Charter, the Redactor of the Constitution, the Author of the Prophetic Letter is but a shrinking figure on whose name texts are written.

The General in His Labyrinth ratifies the predominance of the Archive as symbol of the scriptural, legalistic, and bookish nature of Latin American literary and political culture. The Archive is not, of course, a celebration of that culture as something passive, but the place where narrative mulls over its own origin, and that of the culture within which it springs. *The General in His Labyrinth* further demonumentalizes the Archive by making it ambulatory and giving it a fundamentally literary character, and by portraying its central figure as a simulacrum of the source of power and writing. By focusing on the postindependence era, the novel opens a thematic line that, while clearly similar to novels concerned with the colonial period, deals with a more immediate Archive, a source of stories about power, writing, and the law that are closer to the beliefs that conform the ideology of most Latin Americans. *The General in His Labyrinth* situates the original coalescence of power and writing not in the *leyes de Indias* but in the constitutions of the republics, and links them explicitly to the theme of freedom. It is a freedom that, in all its Enlightenment abstraction appears in need of the opposite, the limitation of freedom. In the end, the Constitution, the Charter, must say No, otherwise it cannot be one. Narrative writes the contours of freedom, the clashes with the need for negativity. The novel absorbs those perimeters and repeats the story of escape, even if, in this case, it is the very figure of authority who escapes and shrivels out of existence.

The shattering of Bolívar's vision is significant at an immediate level as a commentary on today's dramatic political situation in Latin America. Bolívar even appears as a prophet whose admonitions have not been heeded, when he states that going into debt will lead the continent to ruin. But the shattering of that dream of unity also refers to the narrative itself, because, together with the physical ruin of the Liberator, the fragmentation of Gran Colombia carries, too, the fragmentation of any narrative project that purports to offer a global vision of Latin American culture and history. This is something that the Archive proclaimed before in other novels but that is made explicit here when seen in relation to the General's failed enterprise. Like the labyrinth in which the General is caught, archival fictions, and this one in particular, return us once and again to the beginning.

Notes

1. In the middle section of this paper, when I deal with archival fictions, I recast pages from my book, *Myth and Archive: A*

Theory of Latin American Narrative (Cambridge: Cambridge University Press, 1990). I would like to thank Georgina Dopico-Black for her help in improving not only the style but the substance of this paper.

2. Abel Posse, in a talk given at Yale on 2 February 1990. Posse is the author of *Daimón, Los perros del paraíso, La reina del Plata,* and *El viajero de Agartha.*

3. Alejo Carpentier, *El reino de este mundo* (Mexico: Edición y Distribución Iberoamericana de Publicaciones, 1949). There are several editions of the translation. For more details on the prologue, see my *Alejo Carpentier: The Pilgrim at Home* (Ithaca: Cornell University Press, 1977), pp. 97-154. There is a recent paperback, expanded edition of this book (Austin: University of Texas Press, 1990). See also my and Klaus Muller-Bergh's *Alejo Carpentier: Bibliographical Guide/Guía Bibliográfica* (Westport, Conn.: Greenwood Press, 1983). García Márquez's Nobel Speech was published in many places. I have used the version printed in *El Mundo* (San Juan de Puerto Rico), 12 December 1982, p. 21C. An English translation appears in *García Márquez: New Readings,* ed. Bernard Mc Guirk and Richard Cardwell (Cambridge: Cambridge University Press, 1987), pp. 207-211. Vargas Llosa's text appears in *La edad del oro,* ed. José Miguel Oviedo (Barcelona: Tusquets, 1987), pp. 11-27. I only use English titles in this paper for works that have been published in translation.

4. Alejo Carpentier, *Tientos y diferencias* (Mexico: Universidad Nacional Autónoma de México, 1964), p. 23. This topic appears repeatedly in Carpentier's essays and fiction.

5. Gabriel García Márquez, *El general en su laberinto* (Bogotá: Editorial Oveja Negra, 1989). Translations are from *The General in His Labyrinth,* trans. Edith Grossman (New York: Alfred A. Knopf, 1990).

6. Joan Corominas, *Breve diccionario etimológico de la lengua castellana* (Madrid: Gredos, 1961), p. 59.

7. *The Encyclopedia of Philosophy* (New York: Macmillan, 1967), vol. 1, p. 145.

8. I am referring to the box in chapter 2 of *Lazarillo* in which the priest hides the bread, and the trunk in *Aura* where Consuelo keeps the manuscripts left by her dead husband.

9. Gabriel García Márquez, *Crónica de una muerte anunciada* (Bogotá: Editorial La Oveja Negra, 1981), p. 129; *Chronicle*

of a Death Foretold, trans. Gregory Rabassa (New York: Knopf, 1983), pp. 98-99.

10. Carlos J. Alonso, *The Spanish American Regional Novel: Modernity and Autochthony* (Cambridge: Cambridge University Press, 1989).

11. The *Diccionario* of the Real Academia says: "for. [forense] Conjunto de actuaciones encaminadas a preparar el juicio criminal, haciendo constar la perpetración de los delitos con las circunstancias que puedan influir en su calificación, determinar la culpabilidad y prevenir el castigo de los delincuentes."

12. In the "Gratitudes" at the back of García Márquez, *El general en su laberinto,* p. 270; "My Thanks," *The General,* p. 272.

13. See, for example, *Diario de las Américas,* Sunday, 3 September 1989, p. 7B.

14. "Me atrevo aventurar algunas conjeturas que desde luego caracterizo de arbitrarias, dictadas por un deseo racional, y no por un raciocinio probable" (*Cartas del Libertador,* ed. Vicente Lecuna [New York: The Colonial Press, 1948], vol. 11, p. 45): "I shall venture some conjectures which, of course, are colored by my enthusiasm and dictated by rational desires rather than by reasoned calculations"; *Selected Writings of Bolívar,* ed. Vicente Lecuna, compiled by Harold A. Bierck, Jr., trans. Lewis Bertrand [New York: The Colonial Press, 1951], p. 110).

15. "'Como Andalucía en abril,' había dicho en otra época, recordando a Colón" (p. 178; "'Like Andalusia in April,' he had once said, remembering Columbus" [p. 174]). Earlier: "Cristóbal Colón había vivido un instante como ése. . ." (p. 137; "Christopher Columbus had lived a moment like this one. . ." [p. 132]). As Anthony Pagden has shown, Bolívar felt that he was beginning from scratch, that there was nothing in Latin America's past that he could use for his project. In this sense he is also like Columbus. See Pagden's *Spanish Imperialism and the Political Imagination: Studies in European and Spanish-American Social and Political Theory 1513-1830* (New Haven: Yale University Press, 1990), pp. 133-153.

16. In the "Agradecimientos" García Márquez thanks those who "me hicieron más fácil la temeridad literaria de contar una vida con una documentación tiránica, sin renunciar a los fueros desaforados de la novela" (p. 270; "made my literary audacity easier: I would recount a tyrannically documented life without renouncing the extravagant prerogatives of the novel" ["My Thanks," p. 272]).

17. "En sus siete mulas de carga, sin embargo, iban otras cajas con medallas y cubiertos de oro y cosas múltiples de cierto valor, diez baúles de papeles privados, dos de libros leídos y por lo menos cinco de ropa, y varias cajas con toda clase de cosas buenas y malas que nadie había tenido la paciencia de contar. Con todo, aquello no era ni la sombra del equipaje con que regresó de Lima tres años antes, investido con el triple poder de presidente de Bolivia y Colombia y dictador del Perú: una recua con setenta y dos baúles y más de cuatrocientas cajas con cosas innumerables cuyo valor no se estableció. En esa ocasión había dejado en Quito más de seiscientos libros que nunca trató de recuperar" (p. 38; "His seven pack mules, however, were carrying chests full of medals and gold tableware and numerous objects of a certain value, ten trunks of private papers, two of books he had read and at least five of clothing, and several chests; with all manner of good and bad things that no one had the patience to tally. All of this, however, was not even a shadow of the baggage he had brought with him on his return from Lima three years earlier, when he was invested with triple power as President of Bolivia and Colombia and Dictator of Perú: a drove of pack animals carrying seventy-two trunks and over four hundred chests with countless objects whose value had not been established. On that occasion he had left in Quito more than six hundred books, which he never attempted to recover" [p. 31]).

18. The poem is mentioned on p. 85. The General also "declamaba por las grietas de la voz sus estrofas preferidas de *La Araucana*" (p. 215; "through the cracks in his voice he declaimed his favorite stanzas from *La Araucana*" [p. 213]).

So-Called
Latin American Writing

LUISA VALENZUELA

This is a paper with a prologue and the prologue deals with carnival.

Compelled by my interest in masks but perhaps driven by an unconscious need to honor Bakhtin, less than a month ago I landed at twelve thousand feet in the Bolivian *altiplano* to watch the carnival in Oruro, with its *diabladas,* the devil dances. Little did I know then how useful this would be for a somewhat elliptical understanding of that other reality which constitutes our Latin American realm.

We all know that the time of carnival is the time of excesses, of transgressions and inversions. But the inversion of the inversion of the inversion? Oruro is perhaps the only place where this can be clearly detected.

The carnival parades are dazzling, one after the other the *comparsas* dance to honor the Virgin. Thousands of devils cavort for her along the streets of the mining town, donned with huge masks with horns, bulging eyes, and lizards and dragons sprouting from the forehead. Our Lady of the Mineshaft should be happy: this is the only time of the year she gets real attention. The rest of her days are spent in the reclusion of her sanctuary while the miners venerate the devil. Of course it is not the devil, not totally in any case, not such as the missionaries wanted it to be. He is Supay, the master of the underworld, he who has to be appeased to prevent landslides and cavings-in. So the miners make their everyday offerings to Supay, who looks very much like the Christian devil and has an effigy at the entrance of every mine. Supay gets the food, the drink, the invaluable *acullico* of chewed coca leaves. He also gets a cigarette a day. Things will be alright if he smokes it, but if he doesn't the miners will refuse to enter the shaft. Superstition! yell the *capataces* trying to force them in. Sheer laws of nature, concluded modern scientists: the unburned cigarette is proof enough that the tenor of oxygen is too low in the mine that day.

So the devil is a saviour. Or rather, what is all this Manichaeism about? They call the Supay "Tío," uncle, but philologists now say that because the Indians have no D, the lost word is "dío," *Dios* in their own pronunciacion.

The *collas* don't care about those niceties. In their dance dramas they even have a character who translates into Quechua the unspoken words of the mute Spaniards.

And the Virgin is not resentful to be venerated mainly in the topsy-turvy time of carnival. Her legends speak of her soft spot for thieves, and all the versions establish how the first icon of Our Lady of the Mineshaft (*Nuestra Señora del Socavón*) first appeared in the cave of a famous bandit who venerated her and whom she liked to protect. My feeling in this matter is quite reasonable: I surmise that miners consider themselves thieves, stealing the goods from the belly of mother earth, their venerated *Pachamama;* they need such a lenient protectress to feel safe while they dutifully dance as gorgeous, bejeweled devils.

No, I have not paraphrased, poorly, a short story by Armonia Somers, or an Asturias or an Augusto Céspedes novel. What really takes place in the Oruro carnival is not a run-of-the-mill Latin American novel, but it could well be symbolic of the intricacy of its pattern: Some kind of labyrinthine blueprint, where nothing is what it seems to be, where the game of inversions and reversions is fluent and constant but everything at the same time is there for a purpose.

In a sense, I would like you to feel as if in the Oruro carnival with the elements of this paper. I am trying to peer into a few ideas about writing south of the border and string them together, but I am well aware that the reversal of the said ideas might also be valid; even desirable, perhaps.

Doctor Faustroll, father of that glorious and somewhat neglected science of Pataphysics, used to sail from Paris to Paris by land on a vessel that was actually a sieve. As for us, writers and dwellers of a southern territory from which one never reaches Paris by land – decidedly not, even if some, sometimes, try to prove the contrary – we tend to believe notwithstanding in mythical navigations and are thus hooked to Pataphysics, that science of imaginary solutions.

Which does not make our reality that much different but deflects our point of view. We are and always have been navigators – first on dugout canoes, rafts, kayaks, *chalupas;* later on caravels, nãos, transatlantics, whatever – but the medium we navigate on is not water or even the "land" going from *P* to *P,* but language. Which of course also takes us from *P* to *P,* that is to say from one point to the other, through the most unsuspected shortcuts and associations.

We have heard the concept many times, but I like the way Clarice Lispector put it in *The Hour of the Star* (in translation by Giovanni Pontiero): "Why do I write? First of all because I have captured the spirit of the language and at times it is the form that constitutes the continent." In this watery continent where language is shaped and reborn, the catch is surprisingly rich. What nutritious stock, what pearls, what monsters, too!

It is mainly for the sighting of such monsters that we write, and it is because of them that we withhold writing during long and painful periods of time, in the struggle of trying to say what resists being said.

"No, it is not easy to write. It is as hard as breaking rocks. Sparks and splinters fly like shattered steel." This is Clarice Lispector, again, and I am following her in my talk because hers is the voice most unfairly hushed in the so-called boom of you know what.

I do not feel at ease speaking of Latin American literature even if I acknowledge its very distinctive flavor, and even if I am all for a Latin American integration that I think could help us out of economic chaos. You could blame me for having an arrogant Argentine perspective; I could excuse myself by saying that labels give me goose pimples: an extremely uncomfortable situation, being a gander . . .

Which reflects once more the avatars of language, for in my neck of the woods we would say it gives me "hen skin," and then there would be no problems except for cocks, who as we all know cannot bristle easily.

Once more I am a willing, joyful prey to language. Delectably ensnared in that which shapes us and conforms us. That's how we are and there's nothing to be done about it. It is constitutional, fortunately not regimented by any Constitution whatsoever. Let's see: there are Spanish-speaking countries and probably as many Constitutions, and, even better, as many or more approaches to the Spanish language and its by-products, making it sublime in all its proteic qualities.

This is not to say that the English language does not enjoy versatility, but perhaps we in Spanish focus less on the final results and more in the instances of transformations, in the alchemical transmogrifications of words. A fundamental part of my practice, and I don't know how to put it in theory. Perhaps I am even afraid to put it in theory and ruin the spontaneity, the surprise of the practice. But I know very well the joy and sometimes the perplexity and often the annoyance of starting a sentence heading towards a most foreseen destiny and suddenly somewhere in there one word pops up that acts as a shifter and shazam! in we dive into another current usually a strong one that will drag the character and perhaps even the whole story or novel to an uncertain destination. The connotative power of language.

This is just one instance of our writing, the other being the eye. The eye as the organ of vision, not the other, just signaled in the English language with one slim capital letter. That I of the first-person singular probably is the constant quest of so-called Latin American fiction to which I do not even allow an I (first-person singular) of its own. Because the other eye, the envisioning and sometimes visionary one, is there, and how! It is the eye of the tornado; the eye of the needle; the ay, ay, ay of many a lamentation. The eye of the *tuerto* (one-eyed man) who is king in the country of the blind, as the Spanish saying goes.

This is the point. In the sense that I find it irritating when this fiction we are here concerned with is described as "surrealistic," or surrealist of sorts. It is uttermost realistic, as we all know, but from another optic. Which could be semantic, for what we call reality usually goes beyond tangible and explicable limitations. Or philosophical or metaphysical or even pataphysical (the supplementary reality to the one we were taught to perceive). A world vision that writers from Latin America, inadvertently, share with Native Americans.

According to Jamake Highwater, the Indian elders advise:

You must learn to look at the world twice. First you must bring your eyes together in front of you so you can see each droplet of rain on the grass, so you can see the smoke rising from an anthill in the sunshine. Nothing should escape your notice. But you must also learn to look again, with your eyes at the very edge of what is visible. Now you must see dimly if you wish to see things that are dim-visions, mist and cloud people, animals which hurry past you in the dark. You must learn to look at the world twice if you wish to see all there is to see." (*Ritual of the Wind*, 1984, p. 73)

This wisdom seems to be cardinal to what we are given to call the Latin American novel, notwithstanding the fact that for very rare exceptions (Arguedas, let's say) our writers have very little in common with native thinking. Some drops of that blood, though, must have run through the veins of our very sophisticated Carpentier, pushing him to set the basis for the concept of the "real marvelous":

> . . . lo maravilloso comienza a serlo de manera inequívoca cuando surge de una inesperada alteración de la realidad (el milagro), de una revelación privilegiada de la realidad, de una iluminación inhabitual o singularmente favorecedora de las inadvertidas riquezas de la realidad, de una ampliación de las escalas y categorías de la realidad, percibidas con particular intensidad en virtud de una exaltación del espíritu que lo conduce a un modo de estado límite. (Prologue to *El Reino de este mundo*)

Carpentier also wrote, in *Problemática de la actual novela latinoamericana:*

> Pero nuestro continente es continente de huracanes (la primera palabra americana que pasó al idioma universal, agarrada por los naucheros del descubrimiento, es huracán), de ciclones, de terremotos, de maremotos, de inundaciones, que imponen un tremendo pulso, por su periodicidad, a una naturaleza muy poco domada, muy sometida, aún, a sus conmociones primeras.

The emphasis was placed on the grandiose dimensions of the landscape, a gigantism pervading the text.

All this is fine for our baroque, tropical writers, for García Márquez, his forefathers, and followers. But what about us austere River Plate people who travel along the line Macedonio-Borges-Cortázar even in spite of ourselves? We still can find our metaphor on a mirror held out by Carpentier. (For writers are always looking for a justification, a reason to exist, a metaphor that will explain this apparently useless labor of literature.)

Under this light Carpentier is not benevolent, but he is clarifying. I like to read his last novel as a testament, an avowal, a prank, a big hoax, perhaps, a lively, hearty recognition of all a writer pretends to be, is not, and finally is in spite of him- or herself.

The book is *The Harp and the Shadow*. The harp is the harp, the shadow is what is left of a person when all is said and done, or, better, when all is done and everything remains to be said and will never be uttered in the precise ear that is eager to hear.

Christopher Columbus is in jail, waiting for his confessor. He speaks, not to the confessor but to us, the nonlisteners. He tells of all his tricks, his lies, his stubborn shenanigans to get where he wanted to go without being too sure it would be there. How better to define a writer? Writers discover, but not absolutely, continents which in some way they already know are there, but they are not too sure they'll ever manage the trip and the trip is risky, "on the border of the abyss, like lighting a match near a gasoline tank," as Cortázar once put it.

Columbus doesn't lie to himself:

". . . cuando me asomo al laberinto de mi pasado en esta hora última, me asombro ante mi natural vocación de farsante, de animador de antruejos, de armador de ilusiones, a manera de los saltabancos que en Italia, de feria en feria – y venían a menudo a Savona – llevan sus comedias, pantomimas y mascaradas. Fui trujamán de retablo, al pasear de trono en trono mi Retablo de Maravillas.

In spite of that, he gets to know the real, terrifying dimension of his achievement:

Un día, frente a un cabo de la costa de Cuba al cual había llamado yo Alfa-Omega, dije que allí terminaba un mundo y empezaba otro: otro Algo, otra cosa, que yo mismo no acierto a vislumbrar y. . . Había rasgado el velo arcano para penetrar en una nueva realidad que rebasaba mi entendimiento porque hay descubrimientos tan enormes – y sin embargo posibles – que, por su misma inmensidad, aniquilan al mortal que a tanto se atrevió.

The writer, faced with her own obscure forces, with a knowledge like an impenetrable, putrid rainforest which she does not accept entirely, suddenly feels the danger of that knowledge, those passageways, but is forced to go ahead: the opposite would be despicable self-censorship.

Clarice Lispector delved deep into the contradictions and pain the writer is pulled by at all times. *The Hour of the Star* is the story of Macabea, of whom the author says:

> There are thousands of girls like this from the Northeast to be found in the slums of Rio, living in the bedsitters and toiling behind counters for all they are worth. They aren't even aware of the fact that they are superfluous and that nobody cares a damn about their existence. Few of them ever complain and as far as I know they never protest, for there is no one to listen. . .

Vogue magazine has a different opinion, dealing as it does with the finished product: "One of the great antiheroines of modern fiction. . . . The literary discovery of the decade."

What doesn't appear in the dust jacket, but along the terse 85 pages of the story is the everpresence of the writer, transvestite for the occasion, a man who is Clarice Lispector not in drag but masked in modesty, himself constantly complaining (And who listens? Do readers pay attention to the lateral manifestation of a trembling hand behind the scene?) about the choice of character. The force that pushes the writer to create the melancholic, hopeless Macabea is melancholy itself: the pain of something that is there and yet beyond reach.

In the authors' dedication, Lispector confesses: "What troubles my existence is writing." In the story proper the writer who is a man who is also the author of the dedication (alias Clarice Lispector), as she herself put it says:

It's going to be difficult to tell this story. Even though I have nothing to do with the girl, I shall have to write everything through her, trapped as I am by my own fears. The facts are sonorous but among the facts there is a murmuring. It is the murmuring that frightens me.

I love the last two sentences. "The facts are sonorous. . . ." Because the murmur, the rumor, is the one we care to find behind the written word. All that goes unsaid and yet is there. The no-place, the murmur, the rumble of something pouring beyond the writer's fear.

In this case, in many other such cases, identification might be the word to pinpoint the fear. In what corner of Lispector's soul did a wretched, nondescript girl sleep? She herself was a "nordestina," she felt a powerful nostalgia for her northeastern Brazil in the last year of her life, while writing *The Hour of the Star.*

Shortly before her death, Lispector found her "Lejana." She knew in the flesh what Cortázar intuited while writing "The Distances": an Other is there with us, lurking, perhaps ready to take over if we do not allow her some form of existence.

For writing is not an exorcism or a catharsis as much as it is an acknowledgment, a recognition. A moment of facing and often discovering for the first time (and it is freaking) not only the inner inhabitants but the obscure knowledge. A monster of loc Elliot Ness? appearing at the least expected instances of writing and disappearing the minute we try to capture it with a stroke of the signifier. The waters where the monster dwells, that ocean or marsh or swamp or torrential (overpowering) river called the unconscious by some can boast of a form of transparency.

T r a n s p a r e n c y.

A word vastly used and abused lately. Which is exactly as it should be, for no transparency worth its name is a vulgar see-through. It veils more than it shows, and what appears as underwater treasures is usually quite different from what was expected.

Probably this is why the Argentine government speaks of a

search for transparency in regard to the local economy, in one more involuntary homage to what we have agreed to call our Latin American literature.

The reference must be to Baudrillard's *La transparence du mal,* title of his new book, which he takes the trouble of explaining in an interview:

> The title is somewhat ambiguous and shouldn't be taken in its direct sense for, essentially, it is not that evil is transparent, meaning that we don't see through it. We can better say that evil appears now through ["se transparenta"] the dissemination of things; it is in all its nooks and crannies and in some way has turned into the transparency of things.

Writers knew this all along, dissemination or not. And what else was there to be done except to confront the murky terror of ambiguous clarity?

Terror, not error. There can be no lies, no mistakes, in real fiction. We leave them to fictional reality, the only one we have access to. And in this latter case I use the first-person plural meaning we human beings, not necessarily writers.

Hence the need to forget the old labels: neither magic realism nor the real marvelous, not even pataphysics or any form of suspension of disbelief. What writers in Latin America ultimately do is a kind of *literatura de denuncia.*

Martin Buber once said, "I write to understand." I think south of the border this is what all writers are aiming at, even if understanding is the most elusive of creatures. All traps are valid to catch a glimpse of it, traps that may be called the grotesque, the baroque, the absurd, and even "realism," but are just desperate attempts to reach some light.

"So long as I have questions to which there are no answers I shall go on writing," Clarice Lispector promised, oblivious of the one real big obliterating answer. But the questions endure for us who are still around, and newspapers confront us with the stuff the so-called Latin American literature is made of.

Contradictions and perversions and invasions and inversions and investments are a daily routine we are learning to live with at the expense of our lives. Fortunately, literature has taught us to detect the fallacies, the subtle and not so subtle manipulation of public discourse. But language being a double-edged weapon ("un arma de doble filo") they seem to be learning fast too, and as soon as writers sharpen one edge, our politicians in power use it against us and dull it. It is an everlasting struggle, and sometimes I am afraid we are giving them ideas, serving the tools of deception into their hands.

So, allow me to include a document I came upon in my search for ways to deactivate this most dangerous weapon, language. Somebody, who knows, might want to adhere to it.

Restructuralizations

We must get in touch with the world's men and women in order to establish once and for all the club's foundations and to draw up the statutes. The task could be simple if we came to an agreement, but we fear that the problem of the diversity of languages will complicate matters seriously; not to mention the problem of dialects. How I detest dialects! They confuse everything, making third-class citizens feel self-important, masters of their speech; they arouse subversion. I don't even want to think of what will happen in Africa where those who scarcely live kilometers apart cannot even understand each other. Or in Guatemala where up to thirty-three different languages and dialects are spoken. Not that it matters to us whether or not they understand each other; actually, mutual understanding could be detrimental to the club's rules, but it is essential that there should be an absolute consensus among us, and Blacks and Latin Americans are crucial to our work. Almost an apostolate, as I always point out, and I say almost because I wouldn't want to scare away new candidates. Better say, recruits. Language is a delicate matter: we must tune our instrument to perfection and allow no room for even a shred of doubt, not the slightest drop of ambiguity or uncertainty.

Everyone shall know everything and in this way I will be free of responsibilities.

The club does not aspire to anything but knowledge, the club is (would be) a non-profit association. Universal, eternal, all-encompassing, just as our statutes will affirm. Naturally, eternity will not be a preliminary condition for the club, it will be the cause; rather, it will be the end we aspire to. One must speak accurately, we will never become weary in repeating it, one must give words their true value, their importance. We will have word calibrators but first we will have chosen the club's unifying language. The Club, as we will call this ex-planet Earth from now on. Such an ambiguous name, Earth, with unhealthy implications which we will erase with one stroke of the quill, yes, done with the quills of a feather duster which is most appropriate in these circumstances.

And the day will come when the entire Universe will be the Club and there will no longer be any more verse, in the double meaning of poetry and deception (one and the same). Herein lies the problem of the double-entendre: it lends itself to confusion without offering us the least possibility of enrichment. We do not grow with the double-entendre, we find ourselves crushed beneath its enormous weight, and because of this, I tell thee and I repeat: we shall abolish the double-entendre by decree. Nothing of which is said shall have a meaning other than the brilliant, denotative meaning. And because of this, I tell thee: there will be no more haziness, nor slips of the tongue, nor malicious intentions, nor hidden meanings. I tell thee and repeat, no one will be able to want that which is the opposite of what he is claiming, there will be no more contradictory messages. *Interpretation* will be a theme of the past; we will preserve its museum and while passing through the long galleries of couches, the vast, inaccessible libraries, the false diagrams of the mind, the club's members (which will soon be all the people of this planet) will have a convincing impression of what that horror had been.

No one will say white if they mean to say black, no one saying bad shall make reference to good. No one will use the false negative which is an assent.

Naturally, diplomacy will be abolished with this simple resolution, and politics also. Those vile arts. Art itself will be abolished, for it has been and was the worst of all disgraces. The word art will be abolished in all languages until the club's unifying language makes language obsolete and along with them, that word that embodies confusion.

And not to mention the so-called artists. They would deserve all our contempt if it were not for the fact that they too are human beings and, consequently, potential club members, distinguished colleagues. There will be special rehabilitation camps for them, at a considerable distance from the rehabilitation camps for politicians.

We will maintain peace by reinforcing certainty. In unifying the language we will have unity of meaning, of ideals, there will be no way of designating presuppositions nor starting conflicts. There shall be no allusion and there will be no metaphors.

Every club member, every inhabitant of this planet Club, shall be designated by myself, personally, and registered in the members book.

And from now on we shall call bread, bread, and wine, wine, as it always should have been. There will be no more misunderstandings, bread will not be my body nor will wine be my blood; the sexes will be clearly defined, as well as the individual attributions.

You will no longer have to call me God. Not even president of the Club. I will retire in the country, although to retire will no longer be the word, nor will the word country be the word.

(*Restructuralizations* translated by Cynthia Ventura)

Contributors

JOHN BEVERLEY, Professor of Spanish at the University of Pittsburgh, has most recently published *Del Lazarillo al sandinismo: Estudios sobre la función ideológica de la literatura española e hispanoamericana* and, with Marc Zimmerman, *Literature and Politics in the Central American Revolutions*. A new book, *Against Literature,* is forthcoming from University of Minnesota Press.

FERNANDO CORONIL, a native Venezuelan, received his Ph.D. from the University of Chicago. He currently holds joint appointments in History and Anthropology at the University of Michigan. In the Working Paper series of Notre Dame's Kellogg Institute for International Studies, he has published *The Magical State: History and Illusion in the Appearance of Venezuelan Democracy.* He has a book in progress on state formation as a cultural and political project in Latin America.

ROBERTO GONZÁLEZ ECHEVARRÍA, a Cuban, is Bass Professor of Spanish and Professor of Comparative Literatures at Yale University. His book-length works include *Alejo Carpen-*

tier: The Pilgrim at Home, The Voice of the Masters: Writing and Authority in Modern Latin American Literature, and *Myth and Archive: A Theory of Latin American Narrative.*

RICARDO GUTIÉRREZ MOUAT, is Professor of Spanish at Emory University and the author of *José Donoso: impostura e impostación* and *El espacio de la crítica.*

FREDRIC JAMESON is presently Professor of French and Comparative Literature at Duke University. His work in literary theory encompasses such well-known titles as *The Prison-House of Language, Marxism and Form,* and *The Political Unconscious: Narrative as a Socially Symbolic Act.*

AMY KAMINSKY is Associate Professor in the Department of Women's Studies at the University of Minnesota. She is the author of *Reading the Body Politic: Latin American Women Writers and Feminist Criticism* and is editor of *Flores del Agua / Waterlilies,* a bilingual anthology of Spanish women writers before the twentieth century (forthcoming from University of Minnesota Press).

MARY LOUISE PRATT is Professor of Spanish and Comparative Literature at Stanford University. Fundamental essays have appeared in such collections as *Writing Culture* and *The Linguistics of Writing.* She is the author of *Toward a Speech-Act Theory of Literary Discourse.* Her *Imperial Eyes: Studies in Travel Writing and Transculturation* was published in 1992 by Routledge, and she is also co-author of *Women, Culture, and Politics in Latin America.*

LUISA VALENZUELA, from Argentina, is one of Latin America's leading voices in fiction. She has been writer-in-residence at Columbia University and at the Center for Latin American Relations. Several of her novels and short-story collections have appeared in English translation: *Strange Things Happen Here,* *The Lizard's Tail,* and *Other Weapons. Black Novel with Argentines* is forthcoming from Simon and Schuster.

Editors

STEVEN M. BELL received his Ph.D. from the University of Kansas and now teaches Latin American literature at the University of Arkansas. He has published many articles and essays, especially in the areas of Mexican literature, Latin American fiction, and critical theory.

ALBERT H. LE MAY received his Ph.D. from Indiana University. He is Associate Professional Specialist at the Kellogg Institutes for International Studies and Concurrent Associate Professor of English at the University of Notre Dame. He has published essays and reviews as well as fiction.

LEONARD ORR received his Ph.D. from Ohio State University. He is Assistant Professor of English at Washington State University. He has published a number of books, including, most recently, *A Dictionary of Critical Theory* and *Problems and Poetics of the Nonaristotelian Novel*.